MARX'S *CAPITAL* TODAY

Marx's 'Capital' Today

by Tom Kemp

NEW PARK PUBLICATIONS

Published by New Park Publications Ltd.,
21b Old Town, Clapham, London SW4 0JT

Copyright © New Park Publications Ltd
1982

Set up, Printed and Bound
by Trade Union Labour

Distributed in the United States by:
Labour Publications Inc.,
GPO 1876 NY
New York 10001

ISBN 0 86151 027 5

Printed in Great Britain by
Astmoor Litho Ltd (TU)
21-22 Arkwright Road, Astmoor, Runcorn, Cheshire

Contents

Preface	1
1 Introduction to Marx's political economy	5
2 Commodity fetishism in Marx's 'Capital'	15
3 In defence of the theory of value	29
4 Marx on the labour-process	43
5 Marx's theory of capital accumulation: an introduction	57
6 Marx on the formation of an average rate of profit	70
7 Marx on the declining rate of profit	87
8 Marx and the theory of capitalist crisis	99
9 Marx and the theory of rent	115
10 Revisionism and the crisis	128
11 The unknown *Capital*: Marx's second volume (I)	142
12 The unknown *Capital*: Marx's second volume (II)	158
13 The unknown *Capital*: Marx's second volume (III)	167
14 Mandel or Marx?	182
Index	197

Das Kapital.

Kritik der politischen Oekonomie.

Von

Karl Marx.

Erster Band.

Buch I: Der Produktionsprocess des Kapitals.

Das Recht der Uebersetzung wird vorbehalten.

Hamburg
Verlag von Otto Meissner.
1867.
New-York: L. W. Schmidt. 24 Barclay-Street.

The first edition of Volume I of Marx's 'Capital', published in 1867

Preface

The articles brought together in this book were written for publication in *Labour Review*, theoretical journal of the Workers Revolutionary Party, in the course of 1978-79. They grow out of, and were intended to contribute towards, the educational work of the Party which has always paid great attention to economic questions. During the boom years of the 1950s and 1960s the publications of its predecessor organisations steadfastly upheld Marxist theory in a struggle against all those revisionists and reformists who claimed that capitalism had changed and that unemployment and crises were no longer conceivable. It insisted that capitalism is a regime of crisis and that the boom, however prolonged, had not changed its essence and was, indeed, below the surface, preparing a crisis of even greater dimensions than that of the 1930s. Events have clearly vindicated this position and underlined the importance of a return to basic principles in order to prepare the working class for the taking of power.

Since this was not planned as a book the reader will not find a systematic, textbook-like treatment of Marxist political economy. The intention was to draw attention to certain aspects of Marx's *Capital* (including its fourth volume, published as *Theories of Surplus Value*) and encourage fresh study in the light of the crisis and the attacks being made on the working class, its living standards and organisation. These works are more than ever necessary today, not only for the working class to understand its position as an exploited class, but because they show that it has in its hands the power to do away with a mode of production which increasingly threatens mankind with catastrophe and is today the deadly enemy of all progress and social advance.

In putting these articles into book form only the minimum amount of editorial work has been done. No attempt has been made to re-think and re-write them as a whole and to eliminate weaknesses or fill gaps. They were written, so to speak, in response to the questions of the hour and usually to meet a deadline set by the need to produce *Labour Review* regularly. There is no intention of presenting some new 'reading' of *Capital*, tailored to the needs of economists. No excuse is made for quoting or paraphrasing Marx on many occasions; commentators have rarely improved upon Marx's own words. Moreover, the reader is then able to see that the alleged 'difficulty' of Marx's writing is only intended to create a barrier in his mind. It cannot be denied that it requires a mental struggle to grasp points of theory to which Marx devoted a lifetime of sustained intellectual effort. Every reader, however experienced, has to return time and time again to the texts in the light of practice.

These articles sought to incorporate what was new and positive in works such as those of Rosdolsky and Rubin which had recently been made available to English-speaking readers. Implicitly they oppose those self-styled Marxists — some of whom have made big names for themselves — who treat with negligence or even contempt Marx's critique of bourgeois political economy as opposed to the more brilliant and 'humanist' Marx of the other writings. Marx was always convinced that the work on *Capital* was the most important of his life and he acted on that conviction. He had been drawn to the writings of the political economists when he found that his investigations into the state could not be continued without a thorough investigation of the economic foundations of society, thus developing the materialist conception of history. He discovered, too, that the old mechanical materialism was itself of no use as a method in this enquiry. He thus turned to the dialectics of Hegel, standing that state-worshipper on his head and making dialectical materialism the methodology for 'laying bare the laws of motion' of the capitalist mode of production. Emphasis has been laid on Marx's debt to Hegel and to the dialectical quality of his thought as revealed in *Capital* and readers may note a growing appreciation of this from chapter to chapter.

In the course of writing these articles a number of attacks on Marx's method and revisionist works appeared — they now turned

PREFACE

up in the book catalogues with unfailing regularity from month to month. It was thus necessary to turn to polemics against some of these attacks and to uphold the revolutionary content of Marx's *Capital*. It was necessary to insist that the unfolding of the crisis not only acted as an enormous vindication of Marxism but made the study of *Capital* more urgent. Of course, there are no instant recipes to be found; Marx did not write a cook-book. His analysis has to be mastered, applied and developed, tested in practice and further improved and extended — but without discarding the essence or abandoning the dialectical method as the revisionists like Mandel do. It is always fatal to turn Marx into some superior kind of economist with better answers and more fruitful ideas than anybody else.

In this connection, too, the integral connection of the different parts of Marx's analysis has to be stressed. Bits and pieces cannot be broken off and treated as things in themselves. To abandon the law of value is to destroy the whole edifice of Marx's thought. It is indispensable, for example, to the understanding of the tendency for the rate of profit to decline. Those who want to abandon Marx do so by destroying the dialectical heart of his work.

In short, this book is intended as a guide and introduction to the study of Marx's *Capital* as part of the struggle for revolutionary theory. It is dedicated to the memory of Bob Shaw, Jack Gale and George Myers who played a leading part in that struggle.

T.K.

Chapter 1
Introduction to Marx's political economy

It is only in recent years that English-speaking readers not familiar with German have had access to the full range of Marx's writings on political economy. The first British 'Marxists' of the Social Democratic Federation lived off the first volume of *Capital* as did most of their successors right down until after World War II. Failing to understand Marx's method, and having only part of the theory, it was not surprising that they were not able to launch an effective attack on the dominance of bourgeois economics or even educate the labour movement. These weaknesses were compounded by the general theoretical sterility of the Stalin period during which, for a long time, the bureaucracy was unable even to agree on the production of a textbook of political economy. Those which did appear were thin and dogmatic, again concentrating mainly on Volume I and making no contribution to theoretical thought. Most of the writing by British and American economists claiming to be Marxist, notably Maurice Dobb, Paul Sweezy and R.L. Meek, was done wholly or partly under Stalinist auspices. Many students had to depend on their books for knowledge of Marx's untranslated writings and what filtered through was partial and distorted, reflecting the pressures both of Stalinism and the predominant Keynesian thinking of the academic milieu. There was no attempt, anyhow, to deal fundamentally with Marx's method.

For many years, even decades, relatively few Marxists in Britain had read the second and third volumes of *Capital*. It is now possible to do this with the assistance of the full range of Marx's writings available in English. Published in Chicago by Charles Kerr over seventy years ago they had become rare and were scarcely to be found outside libraries. This gap was rectified by the publication of Volume II in 1957 (at the height of the crisis following the 20th Congress of the Communist Party of the Soviet Union) and Volume III in 1960 by the Foreign Languages Publishing House in Moscow for reasons of its own. However, other pressing issues raised by the ferment following 1956 overshadowed their appearance. While no doubt many availed themselves of the opportunity to acquire these volumes at a reasonable price, in most cases they probably remained on the shelves, unread.

These deficiencies are far from having been removed today despite, or perhaps because of, an enormous increase in the number of books and articles on political economy purportedly written from a Marxist standpoint, or at least taking Marx seriously as a political economist. We have to be as wary and critical of these new interpreters of Marx as of Dobb and Sweezy in the past. Some of this literature has to be taken seriously and requires serious rebuttal if only because of the influence which it exercises, at least in intellectual circles.

It is now possible to do this with the assistance of the full range of Marx's writings available in English. The *Theories of Surplus Value*, of which only extracts were previously available, was translated and published, again for reasons of its own, by the Foreign Languages Publishing House in Moscow between 1969 and 1973. *A Contribution to a Critique of Political Economy* (first published in English in 1904) was newly translated and published in 1970.[1] A much more significant event, however, was the appearance in 1973 of the long awaited English translation of what has become known as the *Grundrisse*, Marx's notebooks written in 1857-58, otherwise referred to as *Foundations of a Critique of Political Economy (Rough Draft)*.[2] These work books, in which the development of Marx's thought is, as it were, on the surface instead of being worked into the substance of the text, cast an entirely new light on the whole of Marx's work on political economy and are indispensable for understanding his method, dialectical thought. Also to be noted are Marx's last comments on political economy before his death, *Marginal Notes on Wagner*.[3]

It cannot be said as yet that the availability of these translations, especially the *Grundrisse*, has so far generated as much new work in political economy as could have been hoped for. Taking into account what the various revisionist schools have produced, it probably does not equal in volume the outpouring which followed the publication of Marx's manuscripts of 1844, the *Economic and Philosophical Manuscripts*. Many commentators took the opportunity to extol 'the Young Marx', champion of 'socialist humanism', against the Marx of maturity whose political conclusions they opted not to accept. Equally one-sided was the Althusser school growing out of the Stalinist party in France; it drew a sharp dividing line between the early writings and the time when Marx was supposed to have become truly 'Marxist'. Both these trends have provided rich fields for academic sociologists and revisionists to wallow in. In an esoteric language remote from the working class they create their own 'problematics' and act as yet another barrier to the grasping of the revolutionary dialectic of Marx's thought. Perhaps it is because the kind of ambiguity possible from a reading of *Economic and Philosophical Manuscripts* cannot be supported from the *Grundrisse*, with its uncompromising dialectical (Hegelian) method, that although these same circles have paid lip-service to its value they have been less able to turn it to their own purposes. What is clear is that a study of the *Grundrisse* must be an integral part of the whole, if uncompleted, edifice of Marx's critique of political economy in *Capital* Volumes I to II and the *Theories of Surplus Value*.

Of considerable value in this connection is the massive study of the *Grundrisse* by Roman Rosdolsky, *The Making of Marx's 'Capital'*, now also available in English (if at a staggering price).[4] Rosdolsky reviews large parts of Marx's work in the light of the *Grundrisse* and examines some of the main controversies about Marx's economic theories as well as providing a guide and interpretation to the notebooks as a whole. The major virtue of his study is that it deals in depth and in a systematic manner with Marx's *method*, for without a grasp of the method it is not possible to understand what Marx was trying to do, far less develop and apply his analysis to the crisis-ridden capitalism of the epoch of imperialism. He emphasises the close link-up between the formation of *Capital* and the Hegelian dialectic, especially the *Logic*, and connects the study of Marx's work with Lenin's *Philosophical Notebooks*.[5] It is notable that although the Stalinists were forced to publish both this work and the *Grundrisse* they did so reluctantly and belatedly, rather as an act of false piety, since both are a condemnation of their own position, social and philosophical.

It is proposed in these articles to pick out some of the points made by Rosdolsky and also to look at a quite different enterprise, a presumptuous attempt to revise and 'bring up to date' some major aspects of Marx's teaching. We refer to the recently-published *Marx's 'Capital' and Capitalism Today*,[6] the first volume of which, written by Messrs. Cutler, Hindess, Hirst and Hussain, claims to be 'a radical departure from all previous interpretations of Marx's *Capital*' and to provide 'a comprehensive re-appraisal of the Marxist theory of capitalist economies'. It is, therefore, nothing if not ambitious, not to say pretentious, as will be seen. There is, however, a world of difference between Rosdolsky's book and theirs, despite the similarity in the titles. The most significant difference is that our sociologist improvers of Marx are unable to apply (or understand?) the method of Marx and thus slide back into the crudest empiricism of bourgeois economics from which they want also to be distinguished. One is reminded of a point Marx made in a letter to Engels (June 27, 1867) who had pointed out some objections which the economists of those days were likely to make to his theory of value. This concerned the fact that some unsolved problems in the first volume of *Capital* would only be taken up in the third book.

> Here it will be shown whence *the way of thinking* of the philistine and the vulgar economist derives, namely from the fact that only the immediate form in which relationships appear is always reflected in their brain, and not in their *inner connections*. If the latter were the case, moreover, what would be the need for science at all?
>
> If I were to *silence* all such objections *in advance*, I should ruin the whole dialectical method of development. On the contrary, this method has the advantage of continually *setting traps* for those fellows which provoke them to untimely demonstrations of their asininity.[7]

One of the tasks of Marxists today is to spring such traps, as we shall try to do when we come, in due course, to the work of Messrs. Cutler & Co.

By way of introduction let us consider the light Rosdolsky sheds on Marx's method by his study of the *Grundrisse*. He stresses that categories of central importance for Marx and constantly used by him in *Capital* stemmed directly from Hegel's *Logic*.

If Hegel's influence on Marx's *Capital* can be seen explicitly only in a few footnotes, the *Rough Draft* must be designated as a massive reference to Hegel, particularly to his *Logic* — irrespective of how radically and materialistically Hegel was inverted! The publication of the *Grundrisse* means that academic critics of Marx will no longer be able to write without first having studied his method and its relation to Hegel.[8]

This clearly echoes Lenin's conclusion in *Philosophical Notebooks*, although Lenin was for obvious reasons unaware of the existence of the *Grundrisse:*

It is impossible completely to understand Marx's *Capital, and especially its first chapter, without having thoroughly studied and understood the whole* of Hegel's *Logic*. Consequently, half a century later none of the Marxists understood Marx!![9]

(Lenin is referring to the theoreticians of the Second International who, as Trotsky once put it, 'lived on the interest from *Capital*', but it applies also to their successors.)

As an example of the misunderstanding of Marx's relationship to Hegel we may cite a contribution to a recent anthology entitled *The Economics of Marx* likely to have a fairly wide circulation and thus to misinform many people interested in Marxism.[10] In a centenary article on *Capital* Thomas Sowell investigates one of 'the current myths about Marx, belief in a pervasive Hegelian influence'.[11] He comes up with a verdict of not guilty, or almost, reducing the supposed influence to the use of certain 'phrasings and conceptualisings', notably a particular use of 'contradiction'. Misinterpreting what Marx wrote in the Preface to *Capital* he makes out that the Hegelian style of its presentation arose simply out of a desire to do justice to a thinker who the German public was treating like a 'dead dog'. He does, however, attribute the discussion of 'value' to an undefined Hegelian influence. An essay by the late Ronald Meek in the same anthology supposedly on 'Karl Marx's Economic Method' sums it up as an intricate form of 'modelbuilding'.[12] Again, while mentioning Marx's early schooling in Hegelian studies it does not occur to him to examine the methodology of *Capital* in the light of the Hegelian dialectical method. He prefers to see Marx operating with a kit of tools and techniques picked up from the Classical political economists or devised by himself.

In the Preface to *Capital* Marx did point out that: 'My dialectic method is not only different from the Hegelian but is its direct opposite.' But he explained quite clearly what this meant:

> To Hegel, the life-process of the human brain, i.e., the process of thinking, which under the name of 'the Idea', he even transforms into an independent subject, is the demi-urgos of the real world, and the real world is only the external, phenomenal form of 'the Idea'. With me on the contrary, the ideal is nothing else than the material world reflected by the human mind, and transformed into forms of thought.

In other words Marx declares himself an uncompromising materialist in opposition to Hegel's idealism. As he goes on to say:

> The mystification which dialectic suffers in Hegel's hands, by no means prevents him from being the first to present its general form of working in a comprehensive and conscious manner. With him it is standing on its head. It must be turned right side up again, if you would discover the rational kernel within the mystical shell.

Those who criticise Marx's use, and development, of the Hegelian dialectic — or, more usually in the case even of some self-styled 'Marxists' — ignore it altogether, have not understood the method of *Capital* and in their hands the *Grundrisse* is unlikely to fare any better. The point is that the dialectic is not something imposed on matter but is a reflection of the self-movement of the objective world. As␠enin puts it:

> *Dialectics* is the teaching which shows how *Opposites* can be and how they happen to be (how they become) identical, under what conditions they are identical, becoming transformed into one another — why the human mind should grasp these opposites not as dead, rigid, but as living, conditional, mobile. En lisant Hegel.[13]

How to grasp the complexity of the reciprocally inter-acting phenomena which made up the capitalist mode of production and its contradictions, by penetration from appearance to essence, and revealing the motive force of their self-movement — for this Marx had to go back to Hegel 'and turn him right side up again'. All that is to be found in *Capital*, from its very starting point in the *commodity* because, as Lenin saw: 'In this very simple phenomenon (in this "cell" of bourgeois society) analysis reveals *all* the contradictions (or the germs of *all* the contradictions) of modern society'.[14] In the purchase and sale of the commodity there is unity and division and, necessarily, money; as for crisis 'its possibility lies solely in the separation of sale from purchase'. Again, Marx writes: '*Crisis* is nothing but the forcible assertion of the unity of phases of the production process which have become independent of each other.'[15]

This example is given by way of showing the dialectical (Hegelian) nature of Marx's analysis and does not preclude further discussion of the point or mean that the twofold character of the commodity (use-value and exchange value) or of labour (abstract and concrete) have been overlooked. On the contrary, it is precisely these attributes of the commodity which contain 'the germs of crisis'. However, Marx did not decide to begin with the commodity straight away. The difference between the opening of *A Contribution to the Critique of Political Economy* ('The wealth of bourgeois society, at first sight, presents itself as an immense accumulation of commodities, its unit being a single commodity') and *Capital*, Volume I ('The wealth of those societies in which the capitalist mode of production prevails, presents itself as "immense accumulation of commodities", its unit being a single commodity') on the one hand and that of the *Rough Draft* is striking. Here Marx opens much more conventionally (by the standards of classical political economy) with 'Material production'. 'Individuals producing in society — hence socially determined individual production — is, of course, the point of departure.'[16]

Why the change? The *Grundrisse* itself is really an explanation. Marx's original opening and the whole chapter which follows may appear to be logical. Actually it begins with too general an object of cognition, production as a whole, and thus not with what was *specific* to the capitalist mode of production, the key to the social relations of this mode of production but *not* of its predecessors. It took much work in historical material and in detailed critique of the writings of the political economists before Marx made the breakthrough to 'the cell form' and therefore was in a position to begin the exposition of the 'laws of motion' in *Capital* itself. In fact, it is the weakness of Rosdolsky's book that he passes over this point, perhaps regarding it as too obvious.

In his striving for a point to begin Marx rejects the necessity to begin with the real and concrete when he turns to discuss the method of political economy, in the Introduction written in the summer of 1857. Despite the brilliance of Marx's insights and the many points it deals with, some of which were to be expanded in

Capital, the *commodity* is not mentioned. In fact, it is not clear how (or when) Marx made the leap to the commodity. The further advance from the *Critique*, where it is still tied to production, to Chapter One of *Capital* has also to be explained. Despite weaknesses in Nicolaus's Foreword to the *Grundrisse*, what he says on this point seems to be acceptable, speaking of the commodity as the starting point:

> It is a beginning which is at once concrete, material, almost tangible, as well as historically specific (to capitalist production); and it contains within it (is the unity of) a key antithesis (use value *v.* exchange value) whose development involves all the other contradictions of this mode of production. Unlike Hegel's *Logic*, and unlike Marx's own initial attempts earlier, this beginning begins not with a pure, indeterminate, eternal and universal abstraction, but with a compound, determinate, delimited and concrete whole — 'a concentration of many determinations, hence unity of the diverse' (p.101). In a word, this 'impure' beginning with which the *Grundrisse* ends is superior as *dialectics* to the previous starts, because it *contains* contradiction from the outset, in embryo; whereas the 'pure' (indeterminate, eternal, absolute and universal) beginning starts, falsely, by *excluding* an opposite (else it would not be pure!) and hence has to pull its antithesis in by the hairs, out of 'nothing', by magic, which procedure then becomes the bad precedent for all subsequent developments and transformations. Only a materialist beginning, that is a beginning with the concrete, the determinate, and hence (as Hegel himself maintained) the contradictory in-itself, can therefore be a truly dialectical beginning, and can alone realise the powers latent in the method which Hegel both perfected and mystified.[17]

It was only at the end of these capacious notebooks (over 800 pages) that Marx arrived at the beginning he was finally to adopt! Headed 'Value' and noting that it was to be brought forward, he then decides the matter: 'The first category in which bourgeois wealth presents itself is that of the *commodity*. The commodity itself appears as unity of two aspects.'[18] He then goes on to distinguish *use value* from *exchange value*. 'Although directly united in the commodity,' Marx insists, 'use and exchange value just as directly split apart' (i.e. they are opposites in unity). This is the essence of the dialectical superiority of this method of exposition over that of the first notebook.

Only through this wrestling with the whole subject matter which was to make up his critique of political economy did Marx finally and decisively break with, overcome, the forms of thinking of bourgeois economics to which *Capital* stands in complete opposition. Without this it would have been impossible to drive the point further home as he did in what became the famous attack on 'the Trinitarian formula' — still at the heart of bourgeois economics — with which Volume III of *Capital* concludes. As Marx put it, even the best of the classical economists 'remain more or less in the grasp of the world of illusion which their criticism had dissolved, as cannot be otherwise from a bourgeois standpoint, and thus they all fall more or less into inconsistencies, half-truths and unsolved contradictions'.[19] The claim that the 'factors of production' — capital, land and labour — each have their contribution, as interest (profit), rent and wages, according to their 'marginal product', remains the basis of orthodox economics. Losing itself in appearances in 'this enchanted and perverted world', they make capital the dominant category, concealing the real source of value and surplus value. 'Capital thus becomes a very mystic being since all labour's social productive forces appear to be due to capital itself,' says Marx. In this economic trinity 'we have the complete mystification of the capitalist mode of production, the conversion of social relations into things, the direct coalescence of the material production relations with their historical and social determination . . .' 'This formula simultaneously corresponds to the interests of the ruling classes by proclaiming the physical necessity and eternal justification of their sources of revenue and elevating them into a dogma.'[20]

As Rosdolsky aptly puts it: 'Marx was the first to succeed in finally overcoming the forms of thinking of bourgeois economics: and it is due to him that we possess the proof that the more the capitalist mode of production develops, the more the social relations of production confront mankind as external, dominating and alien power.'[21] However, as we shall see, not all self-styled 'Marxists' have overcome the 'forms of thinking of bourgeois economics': this is, indeed, one of the most important matters to be investigated. As the crisis sharpens, the division becomes clearer and revisionism in its different forms becomes at once more virulent and more dangerous. The safeguard against this is to be found in the study, and grasping, of Marx's method as worked out in the *Grundrisse* and applied in *Capital*.

Notes

[1] Progress Publishers (Moscow), edited with an introduction by Maurice Dobb.

[2] Penguin Books, translated with a Foreword by Martin Nicolaus. The German edition was first published in Moscow in 1939-1941. According to Rosdolsky, *op.cit.*, below, few copies found their way out of the Soviet Union. A new German edition appeared in 1953, twenty years before the full English translation, though extracts had appeared earlier suggesting, however, that its significance for Marx's *method* had not been appreciated.

[3] English translation in *Value: Studies by Karl Marx* (New Park, 1976). This important volume also contains three other items previously unobtainable in English: Chapter One, Volume I of the First Edition of Capital; The Form of Value, an appendix to the First Edition, subsequently dropped; and an unpublished 'chapter' of *Capital*, 'Results of the Immediate Process of Production'. The translation and notes are by Albert Dragstedt. These writings are significant for a study of Marx's method.

[4] Published by Pluto Press (1977) at £18 in a translation by Pete Burgess. Little is known about Rosdolsky. According to revisionist Ernest Mandel, he helped to found the Communist Party in the Western Ukraine and later the Trotskyist movement. His claim that Rosdolsky was close to him theoretically is hardly born out by the methodological gap between Rosdolsky's work and Mandel's doctoral thesis *Late Capitalism* (New Left Books, 1975).

[5] V.I. Lenin, *Collected Works*, Vol.38 (FLPH, Moscow, 1961).

[6] Published by Routledge & Kegan Paul (1977). Paper, £3.25.

[7] *On Capital*, by Frederick Engels, p.120 in the Marxist-Leninist Library edition published by Lawrence & Wishart.

[8] Rosdolsky, *op.cit.*, p.xiii.

[9] *Collected Works*, Vol.38, p.180.

[10] Published by Penguin Books (1976) and edited by M.C. Howard and J.E. King.

[11] 'Marx's *Capital* after One Hundred Years', pp.49-76 in this volume.

[12] 'Karl Marx's Economic Method' (sic), *ibid.*, pp. 114-128. Meek broke away to the right after leaving the Communist Party in 1957. Amongst his oeuvres is a laudatory article on Stalin's *Economic Problems of Socialism*.

[13] *Collected Works*, Vol.38, p.109. This remains a closed book to Meek & Co.

[14] 'On the Question of Dialectics', *Collected Works*, Vol.38, pp.360-361. In the *Philosophical Notebooks* Lenin observes: 'Just as the simple form of value, the individual act of exchange of one given commodity for another, already includes in an undeveloped form *all* the main contradictions of capitalism — so the simplest *generalisation*, the first and simplest formation of *notions* (judgements, Syllogisms, etc.) already denotes man's ever deeper cognition of the world. Here is where one should look for the true meaning, significance and role of Hegel's *Logic*. This NB.'

[15] *Theories of Surplus Value*, Part Two, pp.508, 509.

[16] *Grundrisse*, p.83.

[17] Foreword to the *Grundrisse*, p.38.

[18] *Grundrisse*, p.881.

[19] *Capital*, Vol.III, Ch XLVIII, p.809.

[20] *ibid.*, p.806, 809, 810; the whole chapter should be studied.

[21] Rosdolsky, *op.cit.*, p.439.

Chapter 2

Commodity fetishism in Marx's 'Capital'

All too little attention has been paid to Marx's treatment of commodity fetishism by self-styled Marxist writers on political economy. It has too often been dealt with in passing, or in a perfunctory manner, as though it did not play an integral part in his analysis of the capitalist mode of production and the whole critique of political economy. As we may expect, the revisionist pundit and temporary Cambridge professor, Ernest Mandel, is no exception. In a 70-page introduction to a new edition of *Capital*, packed with errors, it takes up just one obscure sentence in a section purporting to deal with Marx's theory of money traced, by the learned professor, to a 'significant flaw in the Ricardian system'.[1] On the other hand, other revisionists, notably the Frankfurt School,* seeing this as one of Marx's 'theories', abstract it from the analysis of capitalist property relations as a whole and subsequently appear to have decided that it has no application to what they call 'late capitalism'.[2]

Another view, that commodity fetishism in some way represents a left-over from Marx's 'utopian' pre-1844 days, is hardly borne out by the role it occupies in *Capital*. It may be true, of course, that the germ of 'fetishism', as Marx uses the term, came out of the struggles between the 'Young Hegelians' and that it owes a great deal to Feuerbach. Marx did not use it in the first edition of *Capital*, though the concept was there, but only in the second and

---

* A group of German academics who built their reputations on obscure writings purporting to go beyond Marx. The school became fashionable in the 1960s; its best known representatives are Marcuse and Adorno.

third editions (used for the English translation by Moore and Aveling). Then a separate section, 'The Fetishism of Commodities and the Secret Thereof', concluded Chapter One. The concept, though not the term, can be traced back to the 1844 Manuscripts and it figures at various points in the *Grundrisse*. Likewise, in *The Critique of Political Economy*, the idea is there expressed in words similar to those later to be found in *Capital* but without mention of 'fetishism'.

Although it is true that Marx had very little to say about why he re-arranged the first chapter of *Capital* to give prominence to commodity fetishism, it would be fair to say that it is worked into the texture of *Capital* and is essential to it. The concept reappears significantly in Volume III of *Capital* and in *Theories of Surplus Value*.

One Marxist whose work has lately been rescued from oblivion did attach special importance to commodity fetishism and it will be useful to begin by drawing attention to his contribution. I.I. Rubin wrote his *Essays on Marx's Theory of Value* in the 1920s, but he later became a victim of Stalinism and his books were forgotten.[3] The first part of his book discusses commodity fetishism in some detail, insisting that 'The theory of fetishism is, *per se*, the basis of Marx's entire economic system, and in particular of his theory of value.'[4] His ground for saying so is that it provides a general theory of production relations of the commodity-capitalist economy. It thus serves to distinguish Marx's critique of political economy from bourgeois economics, based as it is, not upon surface phenomena, but upon an analysis of the unity and conflict between productive forces and production relations. It is only thus that Marx is able to reveal that what seem to be 'natural' relations which take the form of things are relations between people in the process of production. In particular, 'commodity fetishism' is peculiar to the capitalist mode of production and will disappear with it. It is also one of its main ideological supports, and thus stripping it away to reveal the naked reality of capitalist relations of production to the exploited class contributes essentially to the preparation for their revolutionary overthrow.

Before taking up Rubin's discussion in greater detail let us examine more fully what Marx actually wrote. The first thing to note is that it came after the vital and basic discussion on the nature of the commodity, the twofold nature of the labour embodied in commodities and forms of value culminating in the money form. Its appearance at this point was evidently very deliberate and intended to drive home the preceding analysis embodying basic discoveries by Marx concerning value and its forms. This need for emphasis and further elaboration seem to explain the re-writing of Chapter I to extend the treatment of commodity fetishism.[5] We must imagine Marx wrestling with the concept of the commodity itself and seeking those forms of expression which would most accurately express the dialectical nature of his thought.[6] (Readers might care to examine and compare the various attempts to render Marx's German texts into English.) 'A commodity appears, at first sight, a very trivial thing, and easily understood' begins the Moore-Aveling translation. 'Its analysis shows that it is, in reality, a very queer thing, abounding in metaphysical subtleties and theological niceties.'[7] This mysterious quality arose not from its use-value, which expresses the fact that man turns materials present in nature into useful things, but from its exchange value: when, in fact, the product of labour becomes a commodity and assumes a particular social form. That is to say when, as commodities, different forms of human labour become exchangeable for each other in the shape of equal values.

As Marx puts it:

> A commodity is a mysterious thing, simply because in it the social character of men's labour appears to them as an objective character stamped upon the product of that labour; because the relation of the producers to the sum total of their own labour is presented to them as a social relation, existing not between themselves, but between the products of their labour. This is the reason why the products of labour become commodities, social things whose qualities are at the same time perceptible and unperceptible to the senses.

In this way, 'a definite social relation between men . . . assumes, in their eyes, the fantastic form of a relation between things'. And Marx goes on to say that fetishism 'attaches itself to the products of labour, as soon as they are produced as commodities . . .'; it arises 'in the peculiar social character of the labour that produces them'.[8]

Thus commodity fetishism is not something incidental but is integral to all commodity production. In the structure of *Capital* it provides the bridge between the analysis of the commodity and the process of circulation bound up with the use of money. It is in the act of exchange that the social character of each producer's labour shows itself, equalising as it does the most varied forms of labour. But the producers themselves are not aware of this. The fact that different forms of labour are brought into relation with each other as values is not apparent on the surface but is knowledge obtained through science. In appearance the social character of labour, Marx points out, appears to us to be an objective character of the products themselves; bourgeois economics remains at this level of appearance, preoccupying itself with market prices and taking for granted the social relations of production (i.e. that some men personify capital through their ownership of the means of production while others have nothing to sell but their labour power). Market relations between commodities also conceal the operation of the law of value. 'The determination of the magnitude of value by labour-time,' Marx writes, 'is therefore a secret, hidden under the apparent fluctuations in the relative value of commodities.'[9]

This 'secret' is closely bound up with the necessity for money as the universal equivalent of commodities already established by Marx earlier in Chapter I. 'It is, however, just this ultimate money form of the world of commodities that actually conceals, instead of disclosing, the social character of private labour, and the social relations between the individual producers.'[10] In fact, the commodity producer is connected to all other members of society subject to the capitalist mode of production (the world market) in a complex system of division of labour, and is thus subject to the laws of the market. All these relationships are based on purchase and sale: it is only by alienating (selling) the product of their own labour that commodity-producers can buy commodities to satisfy their needs (i.e. products of labour) constantly passing into and out of the money form until extinguished in consumption. Thus, to consume at all it is necessary to have money, and money can only be obtained by selling something for which there is a (social) demand.

Where commodity production has passed into the capitalist mode of production proper, labour-power itself becomes a commodity while the means of production take the form of capital with the ability to squeeze out surplus value from those forced to sell this commodity in order to exist (i.e. to appear on the market as purchasers). This raises fetishism to a further, higher level, but in fact Marx is able to make the main points about it assuming only relations between commodity-producers; even then 'the social character of labour appears to us to be an objective character of the products themselves'.[11] It is in Volume III that Marx takes up more precisely the situation which arises when capitalists and wage-labourers confront each other in the light of the theory of fetishism.

Marx explains that he uses the term 'fetishism' by analogy with religion — 'the mist-enveloped regions of the religious world. In that world the productions of the human brain appear as independent beings endowed with life, and entering into relations both with one another and with the human race.'[12] Having created the fetish himself, man then worships it and obeys it; it becomes something independent of himself. Objects are treated as divinities just as, especially under capitalism, money assumes a divine power over society. Thus also the worker exists 'to satisfy the needs of development on the part of the labourer. *As in religion, man is governed by the products of his own brain, so in capitalistic production he is governed by the products of his own hand.*'[13] (Emphasis added.) The parallel with religion is also made in the 'Chapter on Money' in the *Grundrisse*:

> The cult of money has its asceticism, its self-denial, its self-sacrifice — economy and frugality, contempt for mundane, temporal and fleeting pleasures. Hence the connection between English Puritanism, or also Dutch Protestantism, and money making.[14]

As we have noted, commodity fetishism in its developed form is specific to the capitalist mode of production. 'The whole mystery of commodities,' writes Marx, 'all the magic and necromancy that surrounds the products of labour as long as they take the form of commodities, vanishes, therefore, so soon as we come to other forms of production.'[15] To drive the point home Marx then considers other forms of production: Robinson Crusoe on his island (a situation much beloved of classical political economists), the European middle ages (i.e. feudalism) and 'a community of free individuals, carrying on their work with the means of production in common' (socialism).[16] In these examples commodity fetishism does not exist.

Once on his island, Robinson, 'like a true-born Briton' keeps a set of books. He allocates his labour-time between the different types of work in order to satisfy his wants from the means at his disposal; his relation between his labour and things is simple and clear.

Under feudalism, personal dependence was the determinant of the social relations of production, services and payments being made to the ruling class. The bulk of the labour was carried on by the serfs (i.e. unfree people) obliged to provide compulsory labour services for their lords. Social relations between the products of labour: 'Every serf knows that what he expends in the service of his lord, is a definite quantity of his own personal labour-power.' Likewise, in a self-sufficient peasant household the different kinds of labour would be allocated to the various members in accordance with age, sex, etc. Under these conditions:

> The labour-power of each individual, by its very nature, operates . . . merely as a definite portion of the whole labour-power of the family, and, therefore, the measure of the expenditure of individual labour-power by its duration, appears here by its very nature as a social character of labour.[17]

Still more interesting is the brief sketch that Marx gives of a socialist society 'in which the labour-power of all different individuals is consciously applied as the combined labour-power of the community'. Here the total product is a social product, divided between the provision of fresh means of production and consumption. Instead of commodity production, production would be social, labour being apportioned 'in accordance with a definite social plan (which) maintains the proper proportion between the different kinds of work to be done and the various wants of the community'. The labour time furnished might be the basis of each individual's share in consumption (Marx assumes this 'merely for the sake of a parallel with the production of commodities'). Then 'the social relations of the individual producers, with regard both to their labour and to its products, are in this case perfectly simple and intelligible, and that with regard not only to production but also to distribution'.[18] Marx does not have to say that in such a society labour-power would no longer be a commodity and therefore there would be no wages. It is, Marx shows, only under a planned economy that the mystical veil (of commodity fetishism) is torn off, but this also requires a certain development of the productive forces, a control over nature through the understanding of

COMMODITY FETISHISM

its laws. Earlier forms of society, though not subject to commodity fetishism, or keeping it in a subordinate place, were, however, subject to other forms of mysticism, notably religion. Or, to put it in another way, commodity fetishism resembles religion in that it cloaks actual relations in a mystical form (it is here, no doubt, that the influence of Feuerbach's criticism of religion is echoed, though, of course, Marx himself had gone beyond it already in 1844). In passing, as it were, he notes that the Protestant forms of religion, more individualistic than the Catholic, were more suitable for bourgeois society based on the production of commodities.

As long as labour is represented by the value of its product and labour time by the magnitude of that product, argues Marx, the process of production has the mastery over man, instead of being controlled by him. In other words, the operation of the law of value, specific to capitalist society, inevitably involves the subjection of men to things and economic activity is controlled by the blind laws of the market. The selling of labour-power (the furnishing of the human activity of muscle and brain) as a commodity is an index of this: its embodiment in things as exchange value which then dominate men leads inevitably to fetishism. While this may be clear in the early stages of commodity production, when it appears in societies in which other forms of production relations predominate, 'when we come to more concrete forms, even this appearance of simplicity vanishes'.[19] For example, the merchant or trader, and particularly the usurer (who lends money at interest) meet with hostility in feudal society. The State, as well as the Church, tried to control or prevent such operations as free market dealing, speculation and money-lending.

As capital develops it overthrows all such legal or moral barriers to its self-expansion and subjects all aspects of social life to the laws of the market. At the same time, the practical domination of men by things becomes less evident; in fact the appearance is of exchanges between equals in which everyone gets their deserts. It is taken for granted that in the course of these exchanges some men appear as owners of the means of production while the majority have nothing to sell but their labour power. Only the dialectical method developed by Marx could penetrate beneath these appearances and reveal the true nature of production relations in commodity capitalist society. This separation between the means of production and the direct producer, the worker, made up the social relation characteristic of capital giving it the power to extract surplus-value from value-creating labour behind the back of the worker. That is to say, because the worker sells his labour-power at (or about) its value the procedure by which he is exploited takes place behind his back. This is summed up nowhere better by Marx himself than in Chapter LI of *Capital*, Volume III, 'Distribution relations and Production Relations'.

Under the capitalist mode of production products are produced as commodities and most labour is wage-labour. Members of society are related to each other as 'personifications' of the different factors of production, meaning that these relations take the form of relations between things. What governs the operation of the system as a whole is the law of value. As Marx expresses it: 'Only as an inner law, vis-a-vis the individual agents, as a blind law of Nature, does the law of value exert its influence here and maintain the social equilibrium of production amidst its accidental fluctuations.'

And Marx adds, 'already implicit in the commodity, and even more so in the commodity as a product of capital, is the materialisation of the social features of production and the personification of the material foundations of production, which characterise the entire capitalist mode of production'.[20]

Thus the capitalist appears on the scene not through any special qualities he may possess but exclusively as the owner of capital, which he 'personifies' in the process of production. His position as a capitalist determines in large measure what he can or cannot do. He is compelled to make a profit, i.e. to extract surplus value from the workers he employs, on pain of extinction as a capitalist. His relations with his workers are determined by this overwhelming necessity. The workers likewise relate to their employer strictly as owners of the commodity labour-power, an exchange value to them which they must sell in order to exist, but a use value to the capitalist which he needs to purchase in order to extract surplus value and accumulate capital. Thus, as Rubin puts it, '*people* enter direct production relations exclusively as commodity owners, as owners of *things*. On the other hand, *things*, as a result, acquire particular social characteristics, a particular social form.'[21]

Where the means of production take the form of capital, and machine production develops, fetishism is carried a stage further.

Labour itself assumes a more generalised and less specific form and the means of production instead of being used by the worker are the instrument for the extraction of surplus value from him. As Marx puts it:

> The means of production are at once changed into means for the absorption of the labour of others. *It is now no longer the labourer that employs the means of production, but the means of production that employ the labourer.* Instead of being consumed by him as material elements of his productive activity, they consume him as the ferment necessary to their own life-process, and the life-process of capital consists only in its movement as value constantly expanding, constantly multiplying itself. [Emphasis added.][22]

Only through the dialectical method of thought was Marx able to break through the surface appearances of the capitalist mode of production in which bourgeois economists remained entrapped and reveal how things (i.e. products of labour) took on the form of persons, and relations between persons, social relations, took on the form of things. This is particularly so in the case of capital itself. 'Capital is not a thing,' wrote Marx, 'but rather a definite social relation, belonging to a definite historical formation of society, which is manifested in a thing and lends this thing its specific social character.'[23] Only extensive studies, many of them recorded in the *Grundrisse*, enabled Marx to arrive at such penetrating conclusions of seminal importance. Nevertheless it is important to relate such conclusions to the whole of Marx's work and not seize upon it as an open sesame as the revisionist sociologists of the Frankfurt School and similar tendencies have done. Otherwise the distortion is just as great as it is with the bourgeois economists themselves, prisoners of the commodity fetishism they are unable to recognise.

It may seem from the comparative paucity of references to fetishism, and to commodity fetishism in particular, apart from the section of the first chapter of *Capital*, Volume I, that Marx did not develop the concept. This would be wrong, for although he may not use the term itself the concept is certainly woven into the whole critique of political economy for which it was quite indispensable. It is the great virtue of Rubin's book to have demonstrated this and readers can be left to pursue the study for themselves.

No doubt influenced by Rubin, Rosdolsky also recognises this, emphasising that commodity fetishism is closely tied up with the formation of money.[24] We might say, more accurately, that it begins there: without money there can be no commodity and thus no development of the capitalist mode of production. In that sense fetishism is inseparable from money ('the objective bond of society') so that Rosdolsky rightly traces the concept back to Marx's discussion of money in his early writings, the *Economic and Philosophical Manuscripts* of 1844. A further working out of the concept can be traced out in the sections of the *Grundrisse* dealing with money. Yet Marx did not begin *Capital* with money; to get to money he had to begin with the commodity. Until that was done money still remained something of a mystery and its enormous social power (vividly depicted in the *Economic and Philosophical Manuscripts*) could not be scientifically explained. It cannot be emphasised enough that in deciding to analyse the commodity to begin with Marx made an enormous stride forward compared with what he had previously achieved and that it was the outcome (not the starting point) of a dialectical process in his thought bringing it into correspondence with matter itself.

There is one particular explicit reference to fetishism in another of Marx's writings which deserves more attention than it has received. This comes in the 'Addenda' to *Theories of Surplus Value* Volume III and it illustrates in particular the relevance of the concept to the era of monopoly capitalism and finance capital. It shows that it applies not only to relations between commodity producers but even more to the everyday operations of the business world of the present day. This is the question of interest-bearing capital.

These Addenda, headed 'Revenue and its Sources. Vulgar Political Economy', made up Notebook XV of the material which went into *Theories of Surplus Value* written in 1862-1863 and concerned with merchant capital and the movement of money. Some of the work contained in this notebook went into the unfinished Third Volume of *Capital*. It begins as follows:

> The form of revenue and the sources of revenue are the *most fetishistic* expression of the relations of capitalist production. It is their form of existence as it appears on the surface, divorced from the hidden connections and intermediate connecting links. Thus the *land* becomes the source of *rent*, *capital* the source of *profit* and *labour* the source of *wages*.

COMMODITY FETISHISM

The distorted form in which the real inversion is expressed is naturally reproduced in the views of the agents of this mode of production. It is a kind of fiction without fantasy, a religion of the vulgar.

After taking a knock at the vulgar economists for their apologetic treatment of these categories, Marx goes on: 'However, of all these forms, the most complete fetish is *interest-bearing capital*'.[25]

Later Marx describes interest-bearing capital as:

> ... capital in its finished form — as such representing the unity of the production process and the circulation process and therefore yields a definite profit in a definite period of time ... (it) is the consummate *automatic fetish*, the self-expanding value, the money-making money, and in this form it no longer bears any trace of its origin. The social relation is consummated as a relation of things (money, commodities) to themselves ... It is clear that capital, as the mysterious and automatically generating source of interest finds its consummation in capital and interest. It is therefore especially in this form that capital is imagined. It is capital *par excellence*.[26]

The owner of money, without taking any part in the production process or buying and selling commodities, is able, by lending it at interest, to draw on part of the surplus value created by labour at the same time as his principal is preserved. Money is thus 'rented out as a value-creating thing' and we have the 'complete *objectification inversion* and *derangement* of capital — in which, however, the inner nature of capitalist production appears in its most palpable form — is capital which yields "compound interest".[27] It appears as a Moloch demanding the whole world as a sacrifice belonging to it of right, whose legitimate demands, arising from its very nature, are however never met and are always frustrated by a mysterious fate.'[28]

The whole of capitalist production is today based, as we know, upon a mountain of debt (credit) and the Moloch-like demands of interest-bearing capital are represented by the banks and financial institutions interlocked with and frequently dominating the whole of capitalist production. Compared to this what Marx was aware of in Victorian England was a mere embryonic form of interest-bearing capital; but its subsequent development bears out what Marx was already able to designate as 'capital *par excellence*', finance capital as later Marxists were to call it following Hilferding.[29] The industrial capitalist is nowadays no longer able to function without resort to the banks and the money market and a substantial part of the surplus value extracted from the working class passes over to the owners of interest-bearing capital. Yet this fact is concealed; nothing seems more natural than that the lender of a sum of money should draw interest on the loan and its source is nowhere to be seen. Mere ownership of money capital therefore qualifies for its part of surplus value and interest is only a special name for that part.

Loan capital in the form of big banks, vast multinational corporations, becomes the main instrument of surplus-value extraction as Marx foresaw.[30]

> Thus it is *interest,* not profit, which appears to be the *creation of value* arising from capital as such and therefore from the mere ownership of capital; consequently it is regarded as the specific revenue created by capital. This is also the form in which it is conceived by the vulgar economists [even today!]. In this form all intermediate links are obliterated, and the fetishistic feature of capital, as also the concept of the *capital-fetish* is complete. This form arises necessarily, because the juridical aspect of property is separate from its economic aspect and one part of the profit under the name of interest accrues to *capital* which is completely separated from the production process, or to the *owner of this capital*.[31]

In fact, interest-bearing capital has legally a privileged position as, for example, in the bankruptcy of a firm, we can add.

It should be noted that Marx insists that interest-bearing capital must not be singled out as the villain of the piece, as some petty-bourgeois 'socialists' and subsequently fascist and other right-wing demagogues have done. Those sections of the bourgeoisie in thrall to debt would dearly love to find some way of having capitalist property relations without the grip of the banker, but this is an illusory desire. The credit system is an integral part of capitalism and will only be superseded when capitalism is itself superseded by a socialist planned economy, simply because, as Marx has shown, interest-bearing capital (credit) is the most consummate form of capital. The separation out of interest-bearing capital, its separation from commercial capital and industrial capital — and its development since Marx's time in the form of finance-capital — was a necessary product of capitalist development.[32]

Interest-bearing capital is an inseparable part of capital as such, not some kind of parasitic growth which could be removed leaving a healthier host. It expresses the contradictions inherent in the commodity-money relationship when money becomes capital. It represents the fact that mere ownership of capital, apart from the playing of any role in the production process, gives the right to appropriate the labour of other people. Of course, it is a matter of indifference to the worker whether the surplus value he produces goes to one or another group of capitalists. In fact the more centralised capital becomes in the hands of a few big corporations and banks the easier it will be to take it over and organise socialised production. And it becomes more obvious that those who appropriate the product of his labour themselves make no contribution to production but speculate on the stock market, juggle prices, speculate in necessary commodities and the other activities reported on the city page. Without supplying any use-values a horde of parasites, constantly at each others' throats, are enabled to live well at the expense of the working class.

We began with the fetishism of commodities, which Marx first worked out in connection with the simpler forms of commodity production and exchange. But we find that the concept of fetishism is very essential to Marx's whole task of laying bare the laws of motion of the capitalist mode of production. It is directly relevant to an understanding of the nature of present-day capitalism and thus it becomes a valuable tool which must be developed in order to deal with the various revisions of Marxism current today and in preparing the working class for dealing with its deadly enemy.

Notes

[1] Introduction to *Capital* Volume I, Pelican Marx Library edition, 1976, p.74. For a quite different treatment readers should be referred to Cliff Slaughter's *Marxism and the Class Struggle*, New Park Publications, 1975, Chapter VI.

[2] Thus an anthology devoted to the Frankfurt School, *Critical Sociology* edited by Paul Connerton, Penguin, 1976, saw fit to include Marx's section on commodity fetishism as one of the influences on the School. From the same stable, in the same year, came *The Economics of Marx*, edited by M.C. Howard and J.E. King with the very same extract from *Capital* albeit in a different translation! The editors' comment on the subject (pp.15-17) shows little understanding: it is just another one of Marx's 'theories'.

[3] I.I. Rubin, *Essays on Marx's Theory of Value*, English translation by Milos Samardzija and Freddy Perlman, Black and Red, Detroit, 1972. Perlman also contributes an introductory essay on Commodity Fetishism.

[4] Rubin, *op.cit.*, p.5.

[5] For an English translation of the first German edition see *Value: Studies by Karl Marx*, edited by Albert Dragstedt, New Park Publications, 1976.

[6] *Op.cit.*, Dragstedt's comments, p.306.

[7] *Capital*, Volume I, Progress Publishers, Moscow 1974, p.76.

[8] *ibid.*, pp.42-43; see also *Value* . . . p.34, and compare other translations of these passages, e.g. the Fowkes Translation, Penguin Books, 1976.

[9] *Capital*, p.80.

[10] *ibid.*, p.80.

[11] *ibid.*, p.79.

[12] *Capital*, Volume I, p.77.

[13] *Capital*, Volume I, p.582.

[14] *Grundrisse*, p.232.

[15] *ibid.*, pp.80-81.

[16] *ibid.*, pp.82-83.

[17] *ibid.*, p.82.

[18] *ibid.*, p.83.

[19] *ibid.*, p.86.

[20] *Capital*, Volume III, FLPH, Moscow, 1959, p.858. (Compare Volume I, p.80, '. . . in the midst of all the accidental and ever-fluctuating exchange relations between the products, the labour socially necessary for their production forcibly asserts itself like an overriding law of nature.').

[21] *op.cit.*, p.22. See the first part of Rubin's work for a detailed discussion of these points, especially Chapter Three.

[22] *Capital*, Volume III, pp.293-294.

[23] *Capital*, Volume III, p.794.

[24] R.Rosdolsky, *The Making of Marx's 'Capital'*, Pluto Press, 1977, pp.123-129.

[25] *Theories of Surplus Value*, Part Three, Progress Publishers, Moscow 1971.

[26] *ibid.*, p.453.

[27] *Theories of Surplus Value*, Part Three, pp.454-455.

[28] *ibid.*, p.456.

[29] Hilferding's book *Finance Capital*, used by Lenin in writing *Imperialism*, has yet to be translated into English.

[30] Though we could more properly speak of institutions like unit trusts as the most fetishistic forms of capital, particularly liable to fraud on that account, as for example the famous Bernie Cornfeld get-rich-quick scheme, IOS, which found gullible investors all over the world. However, the multinationals and big banks are the real power centres of modern capitalism.

[31] *Theories of Surplus Value*, Part Three, p.462.

[32] See also Marx's points about 'fictitious capital', *Capital*, Volume III, pp.454 seq., also very relevant to today's monetary crisis.

Chapter 3

In defence of the Theory of Value

There is nothing new about attacks on Marx's theory of value; in fact, since it is at the centre of his theoretical work it has always been a principal target for critics. The only point in taking up one of the most recent of these attacks, therefore, is to discuss the methodology of the theory which such critics ignore, misunderstand or wilfully distort. It should be understood that such criticisms are never socially neutral. In the present case we have a full-scale and pretentious attack on *Capital* by a number of academics claiming to set Marx right by rejecting a series of his most basic concepts, value being only one of the victims.[1] Intellectuals of this sort have now become something of a commonplace. They are divorced from the class struggle and the working class, separate theory from practice, and, in a private language bordering at times on gibberish, set out to destroy the meaning of Marxism. There are various such tendencies, representing different revisionist schools or operating as 'free-lances', as seems to be the case with Messrs Cutler, Hindess, Hirst and Hussain. Like the others they take great pride in demolishing to their own satisfaction, and no doubt that of those they hope will be impressed by their 'brilliance', the most essential parts of Marxist theory. Not only is it a case of pygmies against a giant, but, by creating a theoretical vacuum they are unable to fill, they open the way for it to be filled from the only possible source — from the ruling ideas in our society, the ideas of the ruling class. To suppose that there is an in-between only reveals the more clearly their class position, in the petty-bourgeoisie. Meanwhile, they typically accept no *political* responsibility for the consequences of their own theories and provide themselves in advance with implausible alibis.

The errors of Messrs Cutler and Co. already extend over several volumes. Their attack on *Capital* already fills a volume of over 300 pages and another is promised to complete the job. Dealing with every point they raise would require even more space and no attempt will be made to do that. Instead their attack on the theory of value is selected for attention, both because it comes first and because it is the key to what follows. After all, a major part of Marx's work was done on the theory of value and to reject it leads inevitably to the revision of Marxism as a whole.

While the political economists, notably Ricardo, had seen labour as the substance of value they had not been able to penetrate to the essence of the question. Marx was able to do this precisely by showing the contradictory nature of the commodity in which value was embodied, that it had to be both a use value and an exchange value. Further, that its value could only be expressed in relation to other commodities and then manifest itself in exchange value. Marx began with the simplest form of exchange, in which no new value was created and there was no profit. Even in this simplest form he was able to reveal the contradictions in the commodity and show that relations between men took the form of a relation between things. This perversion was immensely magnified as commodity production developed and particularly as labour-power itself became a commodity in the capitalist mode of production. Marx's thought moves all the time from appearance to essence and back to appearance. Value is not something visible on the surface but manifests itself in different *forms* in the course of exchange. It is particularly the distinction between the substance of value and forms of value which critics like the present ones are unable to deal with. The value of a thing could only be expressed in something else, never in itself, hence the necessity for the leap to the money form. At the same time, Marx resolved the contradiction in the labour theory of value inherent in classical political economy by marking off abstract, value-producing labour from concrete labour which produces use-values. As Rubin points out: 'Marx approaches human society by starting with things, and going through labour. He starts with things which are visible and moves to phenomena which have to be revealed by means of scientific analysis.'[2]

Opponents of Marx's theory of value employ a quite different method themselves and impute a similar method to Marx. Thus the authors now under consideration accuse Marx of setting off with the presupposition of exchange as the equalisation of labour time in order that he could then claim that profit arose from the exploitation of wage-labour. Instead they reject any relationship between labour time and value, and, since the value-creating power of (abstract) labour is abandoned, so are the concepts of exploitation and surplus value. Their theory of profit is that it is the result of many factors, and thus that these factors as well as labour produce value. In other words they end with a theory of value and profits which is still more eclectic than that of modern bourgeois economics. As they admit: 'Having argued that the distribution (circulation) of the product does not correspond to the contributions of the agents, that "exploitation" is incalculable and that surplus value is not the source of profit, one has passed a long way from *Capital*.'[3] At least it can be admitted that some of the authors' statements are valid.

Behind a good deal of learned and mystifying terminology we can glean that they more or less arbitrarily reject parts of Marx's analysis and make no attempt to deal with his methodology. They as good as say that there is no point in quoting what Marx himself wrote; they are the only ones able to do that, when it suits them. Their standpoint, they claim, is outside that of the contest between Marxist and bourgeois economic theory, or, as they put it, 'Our critique does not start from a place within that terrain but questions the space of contest itself.'[4] Whatever that means, it enables them to shift their position as they please, always to snipe at Marx and without obliging them to state explicitly where they stand, though that is not difficult to discover.

Let us take up the crucial question of the value creating power of labour. Here we have the famous contradiction between Volume I and Volume III of *Capital*. In the former Marx assumes that commodities tend to exchange at their values. Only by making some simplifying assumptions was he able to show how labour was the source of value and how surplus value was appropriated by the owners of the means of production. In Volume III, however, account was taken of the different organic compositions of capital in the various industries or firms in the same industry. Marx showed that competition tended to bring about an average rate of profit on the total capital employed so that commodities tended to exchange at their prices of production rather than their values. Far from being an attempt to correct a mistake as some critics have supposed, the relevant passages of Volume III were written at the same time if not before Volume I.[5] Indeed, the problem of the average rate of profit had been solved in the *Grundrisse*, written before either. The transformation of values into prices of production and the formation of the average rate of profit have, in any case, nothing in them which runs contrary to the value-creating power of labour; quite the opposite, they pre-suppose it.

What Cutler and Co. claim is that Marx elaborated the theory of value on the basis of simple commodity production and that it does not apply under capitalism. What they fail to see is that the working out of the law of value is not visible on the surface, as appearance, and does in fact reach its fullest expression only when labour-power has become a commodity and commodity production imposes itself on the whole of society. They refuse to examine the nature of the commodity and its contradictions; hence they pass very rapidly over Chapter I of *Capital*, the key to the whole of Marx's subsequent analysis, as do all superficial critics. As already mentioned, the fact that Marx is able to begin with the simplest form of exchange, with the commodity, was the great strength of his method, able, as it was, to resolve problems of increasing complexity posed by empirical facts. Thus, 'in the midst of all the accidental and ever-fluctuating exchange-relations between the products, the labour time socially necessary for their production forcibly asserts itself like an over-riding law of nature. The law of gravity thus asserts itself when a house falls about our ears. The determination of the magnitude of value by labour time is therefore a secret, hidden under the apparent fluctuations in the relative values of commodities.'[6]

Continuing his enquiry in a dialectical way, Marx traced the derivation of money from commodity exchange and of capital from money, the very categories of the capitalist mode of production. New value could only arise if there was a commodity whose use-value, in the course of consumption, had precisely this quality. 'In order to be able to extract value from the consumption of a commodity, our friend, Moneybags,' writes Marx in a pivotal passage, 'must be so lucky as to find, within the sphere of circulation, in the market, a commodity, whose use-value possesses the peculiar property of being a source of value, whose actual consumption, therefore, is itself an embodiment of labour, and consequently, a creation of value. The possessor of money does find on the market such a special commodity in a capacity for labour or labour-power.'[7] Such plain speaking is too crude for our sophisticated sociologists. Because 'exchanges in capitalism are not the equation of labour time', as they put it, they reject this basic point of Marx's analysis, joining the whole tribe of bourgeois economists.

Like the clever people they are they make some grandiose errors in their efforts to be smart. Having lighted upon Marx's *Critique of the Gotha Programme*, written in 1875 as a commentary on the new programme of the German Workers' Party (forerunner of the Social Democratic Party), they try to pose some passages in it against *Capital*. According to them, '*Capital* cannot accept this reference to another text, to the *Critique*.'[8] This is to make Marx out to have been a fool and an inconsistent one at that. At the very time that he penned the critique he was working on the proofs of the French translation of *Capital* and he did so from the standpoint that in drawing up the programme his supporters had made indefensible concessions to the Lassallians with whom they had unified.

This was particularly so in the acceptance in the Programme of vague phrases about the so-called right of the workers to the 'whole product of their labour'. Marx showed that deductions would have to be made to replace means of production used up, to enable production to be increased and to constitute a reserve fund. In his references to the distribution of the product under capitalism Marx did not do anything so fatuous as to suggest that it corresponded to the 'labour contribution of the agents', to use Cutler and Co's terminology. Nor did Marx suppose that this was so in *Capital*: they deliberately insinuate that he thought that what applied to simple commodity production also applied to the developed capitalist mode of production. To try to use the *Critique* against the concept of surplus value and exploitation is a complete fraud.

Equally arbitrary is the rejection of the value-creating power of labour, from which they can then deduce: 'There is no reason to ascribe profit to an origin in labour, as the product of "unpaid" labour.'[9] Of course, if value is created by something other than, or as well as, labour, Marx's theory of surplus value and exploitation would fall to the ground. But Cutler has not proved this. Instead of following the dialectical development of Marx's thought from appearance to essence and from essence to appearance, they operate with the categories of formal logic. They try to catch Marx out with a contradiction between two texts. Because products do not exchange at their values, they are saying, then the labour theory of value cannot be true and something other than labour must create value in the capitalist mode of production.

Opponents of the labour theory of value always reject the connection between the simple commodity production assumed by Marx in Chapter I and the developed capitalist mode of production. As Rosdolsky puts it: 'Of course, bourgeois economics has to sever the connection between the mode of appropriation of the simple commodity economy and that of capitalist production — it is unable to grasp their mutual relation as a "unity of opposites". In the first place it does not possess the tool of the dialectical method, and in the second it has no theoretical understanding of either the simple commodity economy, or the capitalist mode of production itself, as having a merely relative, historical character.'[10] As he had previously noted, the same lack of comprehension applies to the law of value 'which on the one hand no longer seems to apply to the capitalist mode of production, but on the other hand requires this mode of production in order to attain its full validity'.[11] Cutler and Co. consider what appears on the surface of the capitalist mode of production to be the true reality. For them value is no more than 'a theoretical category (a form existing in abstraction) but not as an abstraction from reality. Like the other concepts in *Capital* it is part of an abstract process of reasoning which appropriates reality in thought.'[12] The value-creating power of labour is seen as an assumption, valid for simple commodity production but not for the capitalist mode of production.

As Marx repeated several times, if the truth could be obtained from surface appearance there would be no need for science. If the operation of the law of value in the capitalist mode of production was immediately obvious there would have been no need for *Capital*. If commodities actually exchanged at their values, and not at their prices of production, there would have been no need for the third volume of *Capital*. We now know enough about how Marx worked over his theory and the dialectical movement of his thought to state that there was no question of correcting an error, as critics supposed from the very beginning. Thus Engels quotes Loria, one of the first of these critics, as follows:

> No economist with any trace of rationality had ever concerned himself or will ever want to concern himself with a value which commodities do not sell for *and never can sell for* . . . In asserting that the value for which commodities *never* sell is proportional to the labour they contain, what has he (Marx) done, if not repeated in an inverted form the thesis of the orthodox economists, that the value which commodities really sell for is *never* proportional to the labour expended on them . . .
>
> At the very beginning of the book, Marx says, exchange can equate two commodities only by virtue of a similar and equally large element contained in them, namely the equal amount of labour therein contained. And now he most solemnly repudiates himself by asserting that commodities exchange with each other in a totally different ratio than that of the amount of labour contained in them.
>
> Was there ever such an utter *reductio ad absurdum*, such complete theoretical bankruptcy? Was ever, I ask, scientific suicide committed with greater pomp and more solemnity?[13]

Writing in 1895, Loria only says more bluntly and succinctly what Cutler and Co. say today in their own pretentious style. Like other economists who reject the labour theory of value, he identifies 'value' with 'price' and thus is unable to distinguish the real determinants of capitalist development from the day-to-day fluctuations of the market place. Like the other critics cited by Engels, they did not 'make sufficient allowance for the fact that we are dealing here not only with a purely logical process, but with a historical process and its explanatory reflection in thought, the logical pursuance of its inner connections'.[14] This could only be brought out by scientific inquiry and the dialectical method. In his own explanation of the matter Marx writes:

> In theory it is assumed that the laws of capitalist production operate in their pure form. In reality there exists only an approximation; but the approximation is the *greater*, the more developed the capitalist mode of production and the less it is adulterated and amalgamated with survivals of former economic conditions.
>
> The whole difficulty arises from the fact that commodities are not exchanged simply as *commodities*, but as *products of capitals*, which claim participation in the total amount of surplus-value proportional to their magnitude, or equal if they are of equal magnitude. And this claim

is to be satisfied by the total price for commodities produced by a given capital in a certain space of time. This total price is, however, only the sum of the prices of the individual commodities produced by this capital.[15]

Rosdolsky is fully justified in concluding that:

In order to understand the prices of production, which appear on the surface, we must go back to the hidden cause, value. And those who do not agree to this must confine themselves to mere empiricism, and therefore, abandon any attempt to give a real explanation of the capitalist economy.[16]

Cutler and Co. want to abandon the theory of value and thus everything that flows from it. Let us return briefly to Marx's position. An excellent summary is to be found in Volume II of *Capital* in Chapter XIX, section 5, headed 'Recapitulation'. There he rejects the view, stemming from Adam Smith, that the value of commodities resolves itself into the revenues of the three factors of production, wages, profit and rent.

Capitalist production [writes Marx] is based on the fact that the productive labourer sells his own labour power, as his commodity, to the capitalist, in whose hands it then functions merely as an element in his productive capital. This transaction, which pertains to circulation — the sale and purchase of labour power — not only inaugurates the process of production, but also determines implicitly its specific character. The production of a use value, and even that of a commodity, is here only a means of producing absolute and relative surplus value for the capitalist.[17]

He goes on:

The appropriation of surplus value — a value in excess of the equivalent of the value advanced by the capitalist — although inaugurated by the purchase and sale of labour power, is an act performed within the process of production itself, and forms an essential element of it.

The whole process of capitalist production 'rests on a distribution of the *elements* of production which preceded and presupposed the distribution of *social products*, namely on the separation of labour power as a commodity of the labourer from the means of production as the property of non-labourers'. Labour power produces new value for which there is no equivalent, surplus value. 'The substance of value,' continues Marx, 'is and remains

THEORY OF VALUE

nothing but expended labour power — labour independent of the specific useful character of this labour — and the production of value is nothing but the process of this expenditure.'[18] (Hence the importance, of course, of the concept of *abstract labour*; it is not one specific kind of labour which produces value, but labour in general).

Under capitalism the entire value of the commodity belongs to the capitalist, including that part, surplus value, which he has not paid for. One portion of the value (constant capital) is but the value of the means of production expended in the production of the commodity and re-appearing in a new form. One part is the money laid out in wages (variable capital), while surplus value represents the unpaid portion of the past expenditure of labour power. It was the appropriation of surplus value which was 'the compelling motive that induced our capitalist [Moneybags of Volume I] to engage at all in the manufacture of commodities'.[19]

Now anyone who wants to contest Marx's analysis has to discover some other value-creating factor in the production process or abandon the search for an objective basis for value determination altogether and return to marginal utility economics. Messrs Cutler and Co., always going one better than Marx himself, have discovered an alternative source in *Capital* itself. Their brilliant discovery is that machinery creates value and they have quotations to 'prove' it. Quotation number one is as follows:

> After making allowance, both in the case of the machine and the tool, for their average daily cost, that is for the value they transmit to the product by their average daily wear and tear . . . they each do their work gratuitously, just like the forces furnished by nature without the help of man. The greater the productive power of machinery compared with that of the tool, the greater is the extent of the gratuitous service compared with that of the tool. In Modern Industry man succeeded for the first time in making the product of his past labour work on a large scale gratuitously, like the forces of nature.[20]

They add:

> For Marx this difference of machine cost and machine capacity means that the product cannot be ascribed to labour as an origin: human labour is no longer the primary determinant of the transformation of raw materials into a product. The productive power of a machine is determined by its technical characteristics and not by the labour that

was needed to make it (that labour determines its value). The value embodied in the machine (its cost to its productive consumer) is transmitted piece-meal to the products it creates during its normal working life; the mass of those products is not determined by that labour.[21]

But there is a great difference between Marx's insight into the role of science and technology under capitalism and the claim that 'human labour is no longer the primary determinant of the transformation of raw materials into a product'. Marx never said that, nor did he mean it. Indeed he had already shown that the cost-reducing benefits of co-operation and division of labour through their effects on the productivity of labour were also appropriated gratuitously by the owners of the means of production. What they leave out is that capital is a social relation. It is capital which sets the labourer to work; 'it is now no longer the labourer that employs the means of production but the means of production that employ the labourer'. In its machinery system, writes Marx, 'Modern Industry has a productive organism that is purely objective, in which the labourer becomes a mere appendage to an already existing material condition of production.' Notwithstanding this, Marx is categorical that 'the machinery, while always entering as a whole into the labour-process, enters into the value-begetting process only by bits. *It never adds more value than it loses* by wear and tear.'[22]

Marx is always clear about the distinction between the technical conditions of production, which presuppose a definite level of organisation and technology whose results are thus available, as it were, gratuitously, and the need for labour to activate the value-creating process in the manner already discussed. As he puts it in a footnote:

> Science, generally speaking, costs the capitalist nothing, a fact that by no means hinders him from exploiting it. The science of others is as much annexed by capital as the labour of others.[23]

It is therefore quite illegitimate to blur over the distinction between the technical conditions of production and the value-creating process which requires human labour-power as the ferment. But wait, Cutler and Co. have another quotation ready, this time a familiar one from *Grundrisse* to justify their claim that 'the labourer and labour-time become insignificant in relation to the

THEORY OF VALUE

combined productive power of society represented in capital'.[24] Marx writes in his notebooks:

> To the degree that labour time — the mere quantity of labour — is posited by capital as the sole determinant element, to that degree does direct labour and its quantity disappear as the determinant principle of production — of the creation of use values — and is reduced both quantitatively, to a smaller proportion, and qualitatively, as an, of course, indispensable but subordinate moment, compared to general scientific labour, technological application of the natural sciences, on the one side, and to the general productive force arising from social combination in total production on the other side — a combination which appears as the natural fruit of social labour (although it is a historic product). Capital thus works towards its own dissolution as the form dominating production.[25]

Cutler and Co. say that value relations thus become irrelevant — 'The social product is less due to the direct labours of men than to the associated scientific knowledge and technical application of humanity'.[26]

The implication is that this is already happening on a large scale and that capitalism is virtually displacing itself. However, when we read on in the *Grundrisse* it is apparent that Marx means something different and that in any case, his remarks are not inconsistent with the analysis in *Capital*. For instance, Marx writes:

> *Fixed capital,* in its character of means of production, whose most adequate form [is] machinery, produces value, i.e. increases the value of the product, in only two respects: (1) in so far as it *has* value; i.e. is itself the product of labour, a certain quantity of labour in objectified form; (2) in so far as it increases the relation of surplus labour to necessary labour, by enabling labour, through an increase of its productive power, to create a greater mass of products required for the maintenance of living labour capacity in a shorter time. It is therefore a highly absurd bourgeois assertion that the worker shares with the capitalist, because the latter, with fixed capital (which is, as far as that goes, itself a product of labour, and of *alien labour* merely appropriated by capital) makes labour easier for him (rather he robs it of all independence and attractive character, by means of the machine), or makes his labour shorter. Capital employs machinery, rather, only to the extent that it enables the worker to work a larger part of his time for capital, to relate to a larger part of his time as time which does not belong to him, to work longer for another.[27]

Once again Marx emerges superior to his improvers. Anyone

who may be baffled by the quotation selected, with deliberation, by Cutler and Co., will surely be illuminated by the passage they did not quote, which dots the i's and crosses the t's in a way which every worker in modern large-scale industry will understand. It is often said, with reason, that Marx anticipated automation — and could only do so because he thought dialectically — but he never said that machines could create value in substitution for human labour power. Moreover, he was quite clear about the *contradiction* between the development of the productive forces made possible by modern science and technology and the barriers imposed by capitalist property relations (and thus the actual limits to the application of automation under capitalism, as shown in the last sentence of this quotation).

The method of Cutler and Co. leads in the opposite direction to that of Marx. They claim that 'the basis for the law of value . . . is rendered irrelevant by the system of production'.[24] They fraudulently argue that Marx said that the primacy of direct labour in the labour process had been displaced under capitalism by eliminating capital as a social power and with it the contradictions of the capitalist mode of production. Everything is to be settled by logical categories in their own heads, proving only once again the dangers of the separation of mental and manual labour. Abandoning the labour theory of value they are left with an insalubrious mishmash stated as follows: 'If it is recognised that the agency of transformation of the *raw material* is the complex *process* (including each of its necessary elements, machines, the collective labourer, techniques and knowledge) then the resulting product can be ascribed only to the process itself (and to all its effectivities in combination) and not to labour or labour-time alone.'

So they have to throw out the distinction between necessary and surplus labour; abolish surplus value at a stroke; and assert that 'the notion of "exploitation" becomes untenable'. A great victory indeed for sociological science, or rather bourgeois ideology. At least they are right in one thing: if the labour theory of value is abandoned then 'the concepts of "exploitation" and "surplus value" lose their theoretical foundations'. In fact we are back in Alice in Wonderland where all have won and all will get prizes, for we have truly 'passed a long way from *Capital*'.

This chapter has only taken up one, but a very basic, point raised by a book whose title might lead one to expect a serious attempt to grasp Marx's meaning or to seek to apply Marxist theory to the present day crisis of capitalism. We have seen that it is nothing of the kind. It passes quickly over Chapter One of *Capital* and thus fails to deal with Marx's dialectical method, for which it substitutes a logical formalism derived from modern sociology. The authors were at one time associated with the revisionism of the leading French Stalinist philosopher Althusser. Where this leads is amply demonstrated in the political conclusions of this book. Having abandoned the law of value — and thus surplus value, exploitation and the rest — it is not surprising that they seek a way out of the crisis through a reformed capitalism. This is made clear in the concluding chapter of the volume where they call for a 'reconsideration of the nature of socialist policies and the forms of socialist political practice that are possible'. They give their own response as follows:

> Socialist policies can no longer be conceived as necessarily oriented towards the one big push that finally knocks capitalism out of the way and clears the ground for something else. This means that socialists should be concerned with expanding areas of socialisation and democratisation in the social formation and that existing struggles to these ends cannot be judged diversionary merely because they fail to confront the overall structures of state power and the economy.[29]

There is no doubt about the reactionary connotation of Althusserian thought, which lines up behind the 'peaceful road' policy of the Communist Party. As for our native breed they return unashamedly to that special English brand of reformism known as Fabianism — the inevitability of gradualness. In their time the first Fabians, like George Bernard Shaw, did battle with the law of value as the foundation for their reformist practice. Now history repeats itself, as a farce, where, dressed up in a pretentious learning, and after excursions into pseudo-Marxist theorising, we are offered another reformist recipe. But while Fabianism came during a period of capitalist expansion, the rapidly developing crisis of world capitalism is dealing daily blows at such 'thinkers' and their insipid attacks on Marxism.

Notes

[1] *Marx's Capital and Capitalism Today*, Volume 1, by Antony Cutler, Barry Hindess, Paul Hirst and Athar Hussain. Routledge and Kegan Paul, paper, price £3.15.

[2] I.I. Rubin, *Essays on Marx's Theory of Value*, Black & Red, p.71

[3] Cutler et al, *op.cit.*, p.71

[4] Cutler et al, *op. cit.*, p.19. What they mean by this is not clear; presumably it means that they are claiming to present an economic theory neither 'bourgeois' nor Marxist. From that standpoint, for all its pretensions, their work is a lamentable failure.

[5] Indeed, the question had been taken up still earlier in the *Grundrisse*, as Rosdolsky shows. For the relevant part of Volume III of *Capital* see Chapter X, Equalisation of the general rate of profit through competition. Bourgeois critics and some Marxists have made an enormous problem out of the 'transformation' of values into prices.

[6] *Capital*, Volume I (Progress Publishers edition), p.80.

[7] *Capital*, Volume I, p.164. It is worth emphasising, as Marx does, that a thing can be useful and the product of human labour without being a commodity; and while only labour produces *value* the contribution of Nature is required for the production of wealth (see opening sentences of the *Critique of the Gotha Programme*).

[8] Cutler et al, p.33; a remark typical of the rubbishy presumption of these gentlemen.

[9] *op.cit*. There is no place for entrepreneurial 'risk' in Marx's account, they complain.

[10] Roman Rosdolsky, *The Making of Marx's 'Capital'* Pluto, p.266.

[11] *ibid*. See the chapter 'On the actuality of the law of value'.

[12] Cutler et al, *op.cit.*, p.35.

[13] See Engels' Supplement to *Capital*, Volume III, p.868 in the FLPH edition.

[14] *ibid*

[15] *ibid*, p.172.

[16] Rosdolsky, *op.cit.*, p.173.

[17] *Capital*, Volume II (Progress Publishers ed.) p.389.

[18] *ibid.*, p.390.

[19] *ibid.*, p.392.

[20] Marx's *Capital*, Volume I. The passage cited here is the Moore-Aveling translation in the Progress Publishers edition, p.366; in the book the Penguin translation is used, p.510 in that edition.

[21] Cutler et al, *op.cit.*, p.40.

[22] *Capital*, Volume I, p.366, emphasis added.

[23] *Capital*, Volume I, p.365, note i.

[24] Cutler et al, *op.cit.*, p.41.

[25] Marx's *Grundrisse*, p.700. Penguin edition.

[26] Cutler et al, *op.cit.*, p.41.

[27] *Grundrisse*, p.701.

[28] Cutler et al, *op.cit.*, p.42.

[29] *ibid.*, p.44.

Chapter 4
Marx on the labour-process

Laying in wait for the unwary student of Marxist political economy are a number of commentators ready to take him by the throat and explain what Marx *really* meant. Indeed, in recent years, a veritable industry has grown up precisely to do this. The old hands are still probably the best known and the most dangerous and it would be well worthwhile to deal in detail some time with the contributions of the major revisers of the old school such as Paul Sweezy, Maurice Dobb, Ronald Meek and, last but not least, Ernest Mandel. What these gentlemen have in common is a contempt for dialectics and a total subservience to fashionable trends in bourgeois economics as well as to the Soviet bureaucracy. They thus ignore or distort Marx's method into some kind of model-building after the style of that indulged in by bourgeois economists and emasculate the substance of Marx's theoretical thought.

These writers, and others, have, in effect, turned Marx into an 'economist', a Ricardian perhaps or an anticipator of Keynes. Hence an abundant and growing literature about Marx's 'economics' trying to translate the language and concepts of *Capital* into a form more palatable for digestion by their university colleagues and an academic audience. Thus there are no end of articles and books on Marx and Keynes which contrive in most cases to debase Marxism. Bits and pieces are prised away from the whole structure of Marx's thought and examined in isolation to see whether they can fit into the more familiar categories of academic analysis. Thus while there has been some interest in the theory of value or the law of the declining rate of profit, it has often been from a one-sided point of view: an attempt to prove or disprove a prognostication or a 'prophecy' (one American professor succeeded in writing a book on these prophecies). The crisis-ridden history of capitalism in this century has not unnaturally produced a revived interest in Marx's 'theory of crisis', as though this was something separable from the whole structure of *Capital* to be put into a separate compartment of the medicine chest. Perhaps old Marx had some recipe which the others didn't know about? With the new plunge into crisis in this decade this tendency has been intensified. But while we may note that the turn to Marx confirms the bankruptcy of academic economics in the face of the crisis — the last economist to have a remedy for it is the now largely discredited Lord Keynes — it is nonetheless the case that most of those who do so distort or ignore the lessons of *Capital*.

One result of the failure to grasp Marx's *critique* of political economy even by those claiming to be Marxist is that many questions dealt with in *Capital* are overlooked or dealt with scantily. Here we shall try briefly to indicate some of them, notably the difference between *Capital* and 'economics', the labour-process (including man and nature) and the vital distinction between abstract and concrete labour. Most of these come up in the first volume (much superior in most respects to the notes in the *Grundrisse*) and are thus taken for granted in the later volumes. In fact, on these questions Marx writes with a masterly touch and it can be said that his treatment of them is the summing up, the quintessence of his dialectical method, derived from Hegel. It is to be hoped that others will take up these questions at greater length than can be done in an article having necessarily an introductory and tentative character.

The gap between *Capital* and mere 'economics' is evident from the very first chapter, beginning as it does with the commodity. The crucial breakthrough which this represented has been stressed in a previous article, as has the fetishism inherent in commodity production where 'a definite relation between men . . . assumes, in their eyes, the fantastic form of a relation between things'.[1] In fact, throughout this chapter, Marx is concerned with social relations, not with their fetishised representation in market dealings which is the sum and substance of 'economics'. A few quotations will suffice to emphasise Marx's concern with the *social* — the whole network of human relations of which the economic is, under capitalism, the key.

The relations between people take the form of commodities they produce and values are the social relations between them. Value, writes Marx, 'is something purely social'. This arises from the dual nature of the commodity, that is the fact that it is simultaneously a use-value and an exchange value. 'To discover the various uses of things is the work of history', writes Marx, 'So is the establishment of socially-recognised standards of measure for the quantities of these useful objects.' When the useful qualities of commodities are put out of sight there remains 'the same unsubstantial reality in each, a mere congelation of homogenous human labour, of labour power expended without regard to the mode of exploitation. All that these things now tell us is, that human labour is embodied in them. When looked at as crystals of this social substance, common to them all, they are — Values'. The measure of value is 'socially necessary labour time', 'that required to produce an article under the normal conditions of production and with the average degree of skill and intensity prevalent at the time'. This value cannot be measured by the producer or estimated by looking at it: 'value can only manifest itself in the social relation of commodity to commodity'.[2] Commodity production cannot be carried on without an intricate system of division of labour and relations between individuals are regulated through the market in a complex network of exchanges between commodities. Hence the enigmatic character of the 'forms of value' which Marx explores, amongst other things, to unravel the mystery of the money form.

As Marx puts it:

A commodity can acquire a general expression of its value only by all other commodities, simultaneously with it, expressing their values in the same equivalent; and every new commodity must follow suit. It thus becomes evident that, since the existence of commodities as values is purely social, *this social existence can be expressed by the totality of their social relations alone*, and consequently that the form of their value must be a *socially* recognised form [emphasis added].[3]

This is not at all to the liking of 'economics' which totally abstracts from the social. It assumes that 'consumers' have different amounts of money in their pockets without asking where it comes from and even before deciding what money is! It takes for granted that some own the means of production and others have to work for wages. It assumes, in other words that the forms of property existing under the capitalist mode of production are sacrosanct and, so to speak, eternal ('in the long run we are all dead', said the greatest modern pundit of bourgeois economics, Lord Keynes; so it doesn't matter any way).*

Marx, on the contrary (how often do the vulgarising textbooks describe him as an economic determinist?), emphasises all the time the social character of labour. The particular form taken at a certain stage of history in capitalist commodity production is the general form of value developed in Chapter One which is 'the social resumé of the world of commodities. That form consequently makes it indisputably evident that in the world of commodities the character possessed by all labour of being *human* labour constitutes its specific social character.'[4] (Marx's emphasis) How often does human labour figure in the economics textbooks except as a 'thing', a mere factor of production along with capital and land? The contrast with Marx can scarcely be greater than on this point; Marx is for man, economics is for capital, that is the only conclusion that can be drawn from the comparison. It was here that all the preliminary work carried out in collaboration with Engels or with his support (*The German Ideology*, the *Economic and Philosophical Manuscripts*, the *Grundrisse* and the *Critique of Political Economy*) bore its fruits. Like the academic economists, many of the so-called Marxist economists are caught up in the fetishism of commodity production. They do not see the meaning of the forms of value, or bother very much with them in their writing, or understand, therefore, the significance of the money form.

'It is just this ultimate money form of the world of commodities', writes Marx, 'that actually conceals, instead of disclosing, the social character of private labour, and the social relations between individual producers'.[5] All these categories, and the others dealt with in *Capital*, hold sway in 'a state of society, in which the process of production has the mastery over man, instead of being controlled by him'.[6] For the historical denouement that Marx expected from this, the revolutionary overthrow of capitalism, one has to wait, of course, until the later chapters, especially Chapter XXXII on the Historical Tendency of Capitalist Accumulation —

---

* Or, as Marx said, '*Après moi le deluge* is the watchword of every capitalist and every capitalist nation.'

a nasty sting in the tail for Marx-idolators as well as Marx-denigrators.

Marx could not have demonstrated the social character of value without the concept of human labour in the abstract, and thus the two-fold character of labour. Modest as he was in making claims to have discovered new principles, nevertheless he insisted that 'I was the first to point out and to examine critically this two-fold nature of the labour contained in commodities' — that is, the difference between concrete and abstract labour. And Marx went on: 'As this point is the pivot on which a clear comprehension of political economy turns, we must go into more detail.'[7] Here is another question on which economics has nothing to say and many 'Marxists' are equally silent.

According to Marx a commodity is both a *use value* — it satisfies a particular want — and an *exchange value*. Its use value rests upon the expenditure of labour of a specific kind (that of the weaver or the tailor, for example). This is what Marx calls concrete labour. But the products of different forms of labour can be exchanged (in a commodity capitalist system) because 'the value of a commodity represents human labour in the abstract, the expenditure of human labour in general'.[8] All labour, skilled and unskilled, qualified or unqualified, more intensive or less intensive, can be reduced, in a given society, to simple average labour. The more skilled, qualified or intensive labour can thus be regarded as a multiple of this simple average labour. Although this is a theoretical concept 'experience shows that this reduction is constantly being made'.[9] Products of more highly skilled labour expended in a given time will exchange for a greater number of products made by less skilled labour in the same time, and so on. It is only by making this reduction to abstract labour that Marx is able to go on to reveal the various forms of value, leading up to the money form.

The question of abstract labour has often been misunderstood and its significance not appreciated. In fact it is the necessary complement to the analysis of the social relations of the capitalist mode of production without which Marx could not have embarked. Rubin is one of the few commentators to have discussed abstract labour at length.[10] He rightly emphasises that abstract labour is not simply a physiological question, as though all work could be reduced to the expenditure of so much human energy and muscle. While this was, indeed, a presupposition it would be wrong to conclude that this is the end of the matter. On the contrary, like the other basic concepts of *Capital* abstract labour is a social phenomenon, not a material thing which is measureable as such. It has to be considered in a precise social, and thus historically-determined, context. There can be no abstract labour without the expenditure of physiological energy, but physiological energy in itself does not create value. The point Marx is making is precisely that only abstract labour creates value; concrete labour only creates use values. Abstract labour is the 'content' or 'substance' of value. When Marx ranked this a genuine discovery it was because it enabled him to overcome the contradiction in the labour theory of value of his predecessors, particularly Ricardo.

It was only in the period of capitalism that labour could be seen in this way. In previous modes of production labour inhered very strictly to individuals and generally produced use-values, not commodities for exchange. Marx explains that Aristotle was unable to reach the concept of value as a means of expressing all labour as equal human labour because he lived in a slave society.

'The secret of the expression of value' writes Marx, 'namely, that all kinds of labour are equal and equivalent, because, and so far as they are human labour in general, cannot be deciphered, until the notion of human equality has already acquired the fixity of a popular prejudice. This, however, is possible only in a society in which the great mass of the produce of labour takes the form of commodities, in which, consequently, the dominant relation between man and man, is that of owners of commodities.[11]

The abstract labour with which Marx is concerned is thus specific to the property relations of the capitalist mode of production, where labour power itself has become a commodity bought and sold at around its value. As Rubin puts it: 'The concept of abstract labour expresses the characteristics of the social organisation of labour in a commodity-capitalist society'.[12] The particular labour of all the many different workers only becomes social labour through its equalisation with all other forms of labour through the commodities (things) in which the social relations are expressed in fetishised forms. Abstract labour is that social side of labour, pre-supposing a given division of labour and particular social relations of production. Connection between the different producers is not made directly by personal contact, but impersonally through exchange. The employer buys labour power because it has use value for him but he is indifferent as to the use values in which it is embodied. He is interested only in the exchange value of the commodity and in production it is not concrete labour which interests him, but whether the labour produces exchange value, i.e. whether the commodities can be turned into money.

Just as the crisis is inherent in the commodity, so the category of abstract labour is the basis for the class struggle between the employers and the working class. Where production is governed by profit only as much labour will be employed as can be incorporated in commodities for sale at the acceptable rate of profit regardless of the use-values it could produce. If exchange value, or more accurately, value dominates in society, abstract labour dominates at the point of production. Thus unemployment on a mass scale while the needs of the masses go unsatisfied. The concept of abstract labour is a constant reminder of the fact both that the productive forces conflict inexorably with the social relations of capitalist production and that at the same time there grows the revolt of the working class, 'a class always increasing in numbers, and disciplined, united, organised by the very mechanism of the process of capitalist production itself'.[13]

The distinction Marx makes between concrete and abstract labour and the establishment of the latter as a social phenomenon inseparable from the capitalist mode of production is fundamental to the whole of his subsequent analysis. It is particularly relevant to what he calls 'the labour-process' which forms the subject matter of Chapter Seven. A number of important points are made at this stage in the discussion which are, again, often passed over or taken for granted. Simple as they may appear to be, however, they are actually as subtle in their significance for Marx's approach as they are clear in their mode of presentation. Perhaps some commentators do not dwell upon them because of their uncomfortable, i.e. revolutionary, connotations. In fact, this is a pivotal chapter upon which the whole subsequent structure of *Capital* turns. It also sums up in a very concrete and precise way essential elements of Marx's thought, at once materialist and dialectical.

Because Marx has already established the distinction between concrete and abstract labour he is able to separate the content of the labour-process from its particular form under the capitalist mode of production.

> The fact that the production of use-values, or goods, is carried on under the control of a capitalist and on his behalf, does not alter the general character of that production. We shall, therefore, in the first place, have to consider the labour-process independently of the particular form it assumes under given social conditions.[14]

The subject of Marx's book is the particular historically-determined form which the labour-process takes under the capitalist mode of production. The revolutionary core of *Capital* lies in the separation established between concrete labour as a human activity and the form it takes under capitalism, i.e. the production of surplus value.

The value-creating ability of labour is graphically summed up by Marx as follows:

> In order to be able to extract value from the consumption of a commodity, our friend, Moneybags, must be so lucky as to find, within the sphere of circulation, in the market, a commodity, whose use-value possesses the peculiar property of being a source of value, whose actual consumption, therefore, is in itself an embodiment of labour, and, consequently, a creation of value. The possessor of money does find on the market such a special commodity in capacity for labour or labour-power.[15]

The worker is obliged to sell his labour power in order to exist because he has no other commodity for sale — he owns no means of production. This fact, of course, is no part of nature but has a social-historical origin in the actual physical separation of the mass of the producers from the means of production and their concentration in the hands of the capitalist class. The worker sells his labour-power as exchange value in return for a definite quantity of the means of existence. The employer buys labour power as a use value: in fact he enjoys its use before he pays for it because the worker 'everywhere gives credit to the capitalist'.

Marx does not stop at this exchange, in appearance an exchange of equivalents (and that is what it really is) but proceeds to the essence, 'into the hidden abode of production on whose threshold there stares us in the face "No admittance except on business". Here we shall see, not only how capital produces, but how capital is produced. We shall at last force the secret of profit-making.[16]

Marx then analyses the most elementary factors of the labour-process: work itself, the subject of that work and its instruments. To begin with labour itself he squarely sets it as a process in which both man and Nature participate,

> ... and in which man of his own accord starts, regulates an controls the material reactions between himself and Nature. He opposes himself to Nature as one of her own forces, setting in motion arms and legs, head and hands, the natural forces of the body, in order to appropriate Nature's productions in a form adapted to his wants. By thus acting on the external world and changing it, he at the same time changes his own nature. He develops his slumbering powers and compels them to act in accordance with his sway.[17]

Thus a deeply dialectical process is involved: the unity and interpenetration of opposites, man is part of Nature, in conflict with it and both changes himself and his environment (Nature) in the process of production. Man turns Nature to his devices. Work also demands the strict attention of man. The different instruments of labour man fashions to extract a living from Nature bear witness to the stages of human evolution. 'It is not the articles made, but how they are made, and by what instruments, that enables us to distinguish different economical epochs. Instruments of labour,' writes Marx, 'not only supply a standard of the degree of developments to which human labour has attained, but they are also indicators of the social conditions under which that labour is carried on.'[18] In any case the labour-process is purposeful; unlike the spider or the bee 'the architect raises his structure in imagination before he erects it in reality'. Man annexes Nature to himself and 'with the help of the instruments of labour, effects an alteration, designed from the commencement, in the materials worked upon'.[19]

For Marx labour was not the source of all wealth. In the *Critique of the Gotha Programme* he insisted on this: 'Labour is *not the source* of all wealth. *Nature* is just as much the source of use values (and it is surely of such that material wealth consists!) as labour, which is only the manifestation of a force of nature, human labour power'.[20] The same point was made by Engels in *The Part Played by Labour in the Transition from Ape to Man:* 'Labour is the source of all wealth, the political economists say. It is this — next to nature which supplies it with the material that it converts into wealth. But it is actually infinitely more than this. It is the prime basic condition for all human existence, and this to such an extent that, in a sense, we have to say that labour created man himself.'[21] What Marx and Engels are concerned with here, besides opposing the mistakes of the Ricardian Socialists in Britain and the Lassallians in Germany with their talk about the right to the whole product of labour, was to reveal the true essence of man, cribbed, cabined and confined by capitalist social relations. As materialists they found this in the relationship between man and Nature and particularly in the definition of man as a tool-making animal. Of course, under capitalism Nature's productive powers are appropriated as private property and appear as the productiveness of capital, not to speak of the fact that capital squanders them on a gigantic scale. But that is another story.

The labour-process forms a continuous chain linking previous production in the shape of instruments of labour, raw materials, etc. with new production: 'Products are therefore not only results, but also essential conditions of labour'.[22] Thus even animals and plants in their present form are not products of Nature but of man's transformation of nature. The sheep we see in the fields are different creatures from those sheep which were 'great devourers of men' in the time of Sir Thomas More. The high-yield cereals of modern farming are not the same as the seeds used by European peasants only two or three generations ago which were lucky to produce three or four times their own volume in grain.

The labour-process is thus a continuous one, using up and consuming products even while it produces more in what Marx calls 'productive consumption'. 'The product . . . of individual consumption,' he says, 'is the consumer; the result of productive consumption is a product distinct from the consumer'.[23] The labour-process as Marx first describes it says nothing about class relations; it is

> . . . human activity with a view to the production of use-values, appropriation of natural substances to human requirements; it is the necessary condition for effecting exchange of matter between man and Nature; it is the ever-lasting nature-imposed condition of human existence, and therefore is independent of every social phase of that existence, or rather is common to every such phase.[24]

But without this basic concept it is impossible to define and comprehend the development of human society as different stages in man's relationship with Nature. This is something that 'economics' again takes for granted because of its uncomfortable implications for the status quo, that the present relations of production have outlived their historic usefulness.

Having made these basic points about the relationship between man and Nature Marx returns to the capitalist purchasing in the market all the necessary factors in the labour-process (the end product of a lengthy historical process). Under the capitalist mode of production the labour-process is turned into a process by which the capitalist consumes labour power, and it is this sense that Marx subsequently gives it in later parts of *Capital*. The specific characteristic of the labour-process is thus given by the separation between capital and wage-labour. The capitalist owns the means of production, therefore 'the labourer works under the control of the capitalist to whom his labour belongs' and 'the product is the property of the capitalist and not that of the labourer, its immediate producer'.[25] In return for the right to consume the worker has to surrender the use-value of his labour power.

> From the instant that he steps into the workshop, the use value of his labour-power, and therefore also its use, which is labour, belongs to the capitalist. By the purchase of labour-power, the capitalist incorporates labour, as a living ferment, with the lifeless constituents of the product.[26]

This is what the bourgeoisie calls the 'freedom of labour' which means in reality only freedom for the worker to sell his labour power if he can find an employer able to make a profit from it. This is the freedom which employers everywhere today, in the wake of Grunwick, are trying to make unfettered and unshackled by destroying the trade union rights by which workers have tried to even up their essential inequality in the wage bargaining and limit the extent of their exploitation.

But let us pursue Marx's chain of reasoning as he follows the capitalist in his operations. The latter produces use-values only because they are 'the material substratum, the depositaries of exchange value'. He wants to produce a commodity for sale and to do so aims 'to produce a commodity whose value shall be greater than the sum of the values used in production . . . His aim is to produce not only a use-value, but a commodity also; not only use-value, but value; not only value, but at the same time surplus-value.'[27] Value is determined by the quantity of labour materialised in the commodity. This labour is, of course, abstract labour as already defined and its quantity should not exceed the amount necessary under the given social conditions, i.e. socially-necessary labour time.

As for the worker his motions are transformed into an object without motion, the thing produced. Definite quantities of labour-time have thus been crystallised into something separate from the worker and not belonging to him. Moreover, the whole secret resides in the fact that in a day the worker is able to produce more value than the value of the labour power he has advanced on credit to the employer and that this additional value, or surplus value, belongs to the capitalist. Having paid for each constituent at its value he enjoys possession at the end of the labour-process of more value than he started with.

> By turning his money into commodities that serve as the material elements of a new product, and as factors in the labour process, by incorporating living labour with their dead substance, the capitalist at the same time converts value, i.e., past, materialised and dead labour, into value big with value, a live monster that is fruitful and multiplies.[28]

Under the capitalist mode of production the creation of value in the labour process becomes necessarily the creation of surplus value and the worker creates continually and afresh the means for his continued exploitation. There is no way of escape within the capitalist mode by wage increases or reforms; they can, at best, only lengthen the golden chain or lighten it a little as Marx shows towards the end of Volume I.[29] We may conclude, therefore, by referring to this summing up after other aspects of the labour process had been examined concretely and in detail in the intervening chapters.

Capitalist production is essentially the production of surplus value and only that labour is productive for capital which produces surplus value and contributes to the self-expansion of capital. The worker purchases the right to existence by paying for it in surplus labour (by producing profit for the capitalist). Labour-power not only produces value in the labour-process, it also transfers value from the instruments of production to the product and thus perpetuates the social relation which perpetuates this state of affairs. 'The labourer therefore constantly produces material, objective wealth, but in the form of capital, of an alien power that dominates and exploits him . . .'[30] Of course the worker must have time for rest and repose otherwise he could not constantly be at the disposal of capital, so even in his 'leisure time' he is not free. 'Within the limits of what is strictly necessary, the individual consumption of the working class is, therefore, the reconversion of the means of consumption given by capital in exchange for labour-power into fresh labour-power at the disposal of capital for exploitation', Marx writes. And he goes on:

> The individual consumption of the labourer, whether it proceed within the workshop or outside it, whether it be part of the process of production or not, forms therefore a factor of the production and reproduction of capital; just as cleaning machinery does, whether it be done while the machinery is working or while it is standing. The fact that the labourer consumes his means of subsistence for his own purposes has no bearing on the matter. The consumption of food by a beast of burden is none the less a necessary factor in the process of production, because the beast enjoys what he eats. The maintenance and reproduction of the working class is, and must ever be, a necessary condition for the reproduction of capital.[31]

No wonder 'economics' conveniently reduces everybody to the consumer and deals with consumption much more readily than with the labour-process. Lost in these fetishised forms it is thus able to avert its gaze from the class realities of the production process until forcibly reminded of them by the revolt of the working class against the conditions of its exploitation.

Notes

[1] *Capital* Volume I (Allen and Unwin ed.). p.43
[2] All these quotations are to be found in Chapter 1 of *Capital*
[3] *Capital*, p.36
[4] *ibid*, p.37
[5] *ibid*, p.47
[6] *ibid*, p.53
[7] *ibid*, p.8
[8] *ibid*, p.11
[9] *Ibid*
[10] I.I. Rubin. *Essays on Marx's Theory of Value* Black & Red, 1972 Chapter 14
[11] *Capital*, Volume I, p.29
[12] Rubin, *op.cit.*, p.141. He goes on to say: 'Abstract labour is the variety of social labour or socially equalised labour in general. It is social or socially equalised labour

in the specific form which it has in a commodity economy. Abstract labour is not only socially equalised labour, i.e. abstracted from concrete properties, impersonal and homogeneous labour, it is labour which becomes social labour only as impersonal and homogeneous labour. The concept of abstract labour presupposes that the *process of impersonalisation or equalisation of labour is a unified process through which labour is "socialised", i.e. included in the total mass of social labour.*'

[13] *Capital*, Volume I p.156
[14] *Capital*, Volume I p.789
[15] *ibid*, p.145
[16] *ibid*, pp.154-155 and see the whole of Chapter VI.
[17] *ibid*, pp.156-157
[18] *ibid*, p.159
[19] *ibid*, p.157. These passages should be studied as part of the practice of cognition in connection with the theory of knowledge of Marxism.
[20] Indeed, Marx had already made this point early in *Capital*: 'If we take away the useful labour expended upon them [i.e. use-values], a material substratum is always left, which is furnished by Nature without the help of man. The latter can work only as Nature does, that is by changing the form of matter. Nay more, in this work of changing the form he is constantly helped by natural forces. We see, then, that labour is not the only source of material wealth, of use-values produced by labour. As William Petty puts it, labour is its father and the earth its mother,' p.10
[21] The importance of Engels' contribution should be stressed.
[22] *Capital*, p.160.
[23] *ibid*, p.163
[24] *ibid*, pp.163-164
[25] *ibid*, p.165
[26] *ibid*, p.166
[27] *ibid*, p.166
[28] *ibid*, p.176. See also, p.216: 'Capital is dead labour, that vampire-like, only lives by sucking living labour, and lives the more, the more labour it sucks. The time during which the labourer works, is the time during which the capitalist consumes the labour-power he has purchased of him.'
[29] 'A rise in the price of labour, as a consequence of accumulation of capital, only means, in fact, that the length and weight of the golden chain the wage-worker has already forged for himself, allow of a relaxation of the tension of it'. *Capital*, p.631
[30] *ibid*, p.583
[31] *ibid*, p.585

Chapter 5

Marx's Theory of Capital Accumulation: an introduction

In the reproduction cycle of capitalism after World War II enormous contradictions built up behind the appearance of the boom. This period had apparently negated the slump conditions of the 1930s only finally overcome by re-armamament and war. But appearances were deceptive; 'in capitalist production', Marx once wrote, 'everything seems and in fact is contradictory'.[1] The movement of capital accumulation was now operating in a different form from that which it had taken in the pre-war period, but it was still the same process which was at work and the contradictions gathering beneath the surface and expressing the real essence of capital were to break through and bring the boom to an end in the later 1960s. These contradictions were driven forward by the revolutionary struggles of the working class and the oppressed masses. As the capitalists suffered one defeat after another they tried to buy time by a series of expedients — each of which rapidly made matters worse for their system. The collapse of the world monetary system and the spreading world economic crisis have fully confirmed the Marxist analysis of the contradictions of capitalism. The events of the past few years, and the looming prospect of a 'world Black-Friday' which will put October 1929 in the shade, demonstrate the unity of the accumulation process of which the slump of the 1930s, the war of 1939-45, the 'boom' of the 1950s and 1960s and the current drive toward deeper crisis and collapse are only different expressions.

At the time when bourgeois economists are as bereft of explanations for the crisis as they are bankrupt of solutions, Marx's analysis is being forcibly vindicated. The new theories of the reformists and the revisionists devised during the boom to 'prove' that it could go on for ever have been blown sky-high. Some, like Ernest Mandel, are still gazing into the future in search of a coming upturn or are trying hastily to re-adjust their sights without much success. What was lacking in all these theories, whether of avowed supporters of capitalism or self-proclaimed 'Marxists', was an understanding of the nature of capital, of the process of accumulation through which it was expressed and its conformity with the dialectical laws of motion. It is necessary to return to Marx's own work on these questions to develop the practice of the revolutionary party through the enrichment of its theory. In this article attention will be paid to Marx's concept of capital and to the basic conditions of capital accumulation. It will be followed by an examination of the accumulation process as a whole and the laws governing it, especially the law of the falling rate of profit.

The bourgeois economists, and the revisionists in their train, begin with a false, 'ideological' concept of capital and thus of accumulation. Pick up any economics textbook and turn to what it says about capital and one finds a retreat even from the position elaborated in the early nineteenth century by the Classical political economists and particularly David Ricardo and his school. For the sake of convenience let us take the definition proferred in the *Penguin Dictionary of Economics* under Capital. It reads:

> The stock of goods which are used in production and which have themselves been produced. A distinction is normally made between *fixed capital* consisting of durable goods such as buildings, plant and machinery; and *circulating capital* consisting of stocks of raw materials and semi-finished goods, components etc., which are used up very rapidly . . . In addition, the word capital in economics generally means *real capital* — that is, physical goods. In everyday language, however, capital may be used to mean money capital, i.e. stocks of MONEY which are the results of past savings. Two important features of capital are that it entails a sacrifice, since resources are devoted to making non-consumable capital goods instead of goods for immediate consumption; and that it enhances the PRODUCTION of the FACTORS OF PRODUCTION, LAND and LABOUR, and it is this enhanced production which represents the reward for the sacrifice involved in creating capital. Hence we can surmise that new capital is only created as long as its product is at least sufficient to compensate those who make the sacrifice involved in its creation. [Capitals and italics in the original.][2]

CAPITAL ACCUMULATION

Within the limits of a dictionary definition this is representative of how bourgeois economists see 'capital'. It is a thing, articles used in production, and has presumably existed since man began making digging sticks and flint axes. It is not indicated whose 'sacrifice' is entailed in its production and the ugly word 'profit' is not mentioned. Presumably it is the owner of this thing who makes a 'sacrifice' (of what sort is left to the reader's imagination), but has anyone known a capitalist to go without? The mention of factors of production and the bringing in of money (a result of past saving?) only adds to the confusion or rather the comforting conclusion that Moneybags is getting his reward and that everything is for the best in the best of all possible worlds. So much for the concept of capital in bourgeois economics. It could be dismissed as a schoolboy's misunderstanding if we did not know that is the generally held view of eminent professors, governors of banks, big industrialists, financial journalists and cabinet ministers. It was precisely this view, held by the 'vulgar economists' of his day, that Marx tore to shreds; let us look at how he did it.

Marx aimed many of his sharpest blows against the political economists and even more their epigones, 'the vulgar economists', for their failure to understand the nature of capital and, as for the latter, their deliberate confusion of the issue. As he puts it in one place:

> ... the more economic theory is perfected, that is, the deeper it penetrates into its subject matter, the more it develops as a contradictory system, the more it is confronted by its own, increasingly independent, vulgar element, enriched with material which it dresses up in its own way until it finally finds its most apt expression in academically syncretic and unprincipled eclectic compilation. To the degree that economic analysis becomes more profound it not only describes contradictions, but it is confronted by its own contradictions simultaneously with the development of the actual contradiction in the economic life of society. Accordingly, vulgar political economy becomes increasingly *apologetic* and makes strenuous attempts to talk out of existence the ideas which contain the contradictions.[3]

With uncanny accuracy Marx foretold the history of economic thought since his own day. All attempts to develop an objective law of value were given up when it was clear where they would lead: that capital itself contained the contradiction. Subsequently the apologetic doctrines of the marginal utility school held the field with the result that terms like 'capital' were defined in the 'academically syncretic and unprincipled eclectic' way already quoted. Economists like Keynes have tried to resolve the contradictions but 'the actual contradictions in the economic life of society' have overtaken them and thrown their once highly praised ideas onto the scrap heap. Today more than ever the economic crisis plunges economics into crisis: not only can it propose no remedies for the crisis, it cannot even explain it.

Even the most lucid of today's economists, like Ricardo before them 'cannot admit that the bourgeois mode of production contains within itself a barrier to the free development of the productive forces, a barrier which comes to the surface in crises and, in particular, in *over-production* — the basic phenomenon in crises'.[4] To understand why this is so it is necessary to refer in more detail to Marx's analysis of capital and to the process of accumulation to which it inevitably gives rise.

The whole purpose of *Capital* and other writings was to show that capital is not a thing, simply means of production for example, but is a social relation. In one of the earliest of his 'mature' works, a simple exposition of ideas on which he was to work for many years, he expressed it as follows, with a sting in the tail:

> Capital consists of raw materials, instruments of labour and means of subsistence of all kinds, which are utilised in order to produce new raw materials, instruments of labour and new means of subsistence. All these are component parts, are creations of labour, products of labour, *accumulated labour*. Accumulated labour which serves as a means of new production is capital.
>
> So say the economists.
>
> What is a Negro slave? A man of the black race. The one explanation is as good as another.
>
> A Negro is a Negro. He only becomes a slave in certain relationships. A cotton-spinning machine is a machine for spinning cotton. Only in certain relationships does it become *capital*. Torn from these relationships it is no more capital than gold in itself is *money* or sugar the price of *sugar*.[5]

Leaving aside the fact that economists today, as we have seen, even refuse to accept that capital is a product of labour (unlike Ricardo, for example), the basic concept is here which Marx was to worry throughout all his writings on political economy. It comes up in many forms in different places as he struggles to pull out all

CAPITAL ACCUMULATION

the richness of the concept of capital as a social relation. In this connection we can recall the analysis of the commodity itself in its form as use value and exchange value, the distinction between abstract and concrete labour and the fetishism of commodities in which social relations take the form of the relationship between things. To go back to the labour-process, under the particular conditions of the capitalist mode of production this becomes a process for the production of surplus value and thus of capital.

What does Marx mean by 'capital'? No one quotation can do justice to the richness of his conception, but let us consider a few examples. A connecting link with the point made in *Wage-Labour and Capital* is the following: 'The means of production become capital only in so far as they have become separated from the labourer and confront labour as an independent power'.[6] Capitalist relations exist only where labour power itself has become a commodity, an exchange value for the worker, a use value for the purchaser, the capitalist employer. Marx repeatedly refers to the 'social power' of capital. For instance, he says:

> Capital comes more and more to the fore as a social power, whose agent is the capitalist. This social power no longer stands in any possible relation to that which the labour of a single individual can create. It becomes an alienated, independent social power, which stands opposed to society as an object that is the capitalist's source of power.[7]

If capital is a social relation, a social power, it takes different forms. Someone may ask whether capital is not money, means of production, commodities and so forth. Marx's answer to that is clear enough, though it is often overlooked even by those who consider themselves Marxists because they see only the formal side and do not grasp the dialectical quality of Marx's thought. Thus, already in *Capital* Volume I, he emphasises that 'the circulation of commodities is the starting point of capital' and that 'we have no need to refer to the origin of capital in order to discover that the first form of appearance of capital is money. We can see it daily before our very eyes. All new capital, to commence with, comes on the stage, that is, on the market, whether of commodities, labour, or money, even in our days, in the shape of money that by a definite process has to be transformed into capital'.[8] Money is thus a form of appearance of capital, one of the many forms it assumes in the course of production, circulation and accumulation. Each of these forms, expressing a social relation in the shape of a relationship between things, demonstrates also the social power of capital. The capitalist first of all throws money into circulation in order to carry on production. He buys commodities in order, in turn, to sell them for money. He would not do this at all unless he expected to realise a larger sum of money at each period in the process. Hence his original money, call it M, is used to buy commodities C which are then sold for M', a larger sum than M.[9]

All commodities must pass through the money form, money being the independent form of value and thus indispensable for the production of commodities. Value becomes value in process, money in process and as such, capital. But behind these transitions are all the time social relations: the crucial relationship being that between the owner of the means of production, the capitalist, and the workers who have nothing to sell but their labour power.

To quote Marx again:

> Capital is no *Thing*, as little as money is a *thing*. In capital just as in money, it is particular social relationships of production of persons that are displaying themselves as *relationships of things* to persons, or it is particular social relationships that are appearing as *social natural properties* of things.[10]

We will look at the continuation of this quotation later; for the present it speaks for itself. Marx is talking about different forms of appearance of the self-movement of capital, a particular social relationship which developed in a particular historical epoch and saw on the one side the concentration of the ownership of money and commodities in one class and on the other the separation of another class from the ownership of anything but their labour power. Thus we come back all the time to the essential social relationship of the capitalist mode of production.

When Marxists talk about capital they mean, or should mean, this relationship and its different forms of appearance. In this relationship the capitalist has no independent role and is subject to definite laws independent of his will. As Marx insist many times, he *personifies* capital in the process of production (we mean, here, the industrial capitalist). 'As capitalist, he is only capital personified.' But before looking more closely at what Marx means by this a digression is necessary to examine the nature of these laws.

Marx recognises the objective character of laws reflecting real processes in nature and society independent of human consciousness. Men are able to acquire knowledge of these laws and precisely in *Capital* Marx's task was 'to lay bear the economic law of motion of modern society'. As capital personified, the capitalist is subject specifically to the laws of the market, the laws of competition. For Marx competition was not used, as in bourgeois economics today, to define a particular market situation, i.e. of many sellers and many buyers in which no single seller or buyer is able to influence the price determined by the forces of supply and demand. In any case, this situation, beloved of the textbooks even today, is in practice of the rarest. Characteristically, it was not until the 1930s that economics got round to examining the much more usual market situation in which a few sellers dominate the scene (so-called 'imperfect' or 'oligopolistic' competition). Marx was not oblivious to supply and demand, but in themselves they could not explain very much. What he did know was that 'competition' is not a stable state which can be taken for granted but a dynamic situation which turns into its opposite as the rival capitalists try to eliminate the competition of each other so that 'one capitalist kills many.'

In other words, the competitive struggle results in the elimination of the weaker firms, bringing about what Marx called the concentration and centralisation of capital, i.e. the growth of monopoly or monopolistic tendencies. As he put it 'Free competition brings out the inherent laws of capitalist production in the shape of external coercive laws having power over every individual capitalist.'[11] To understand these laws it was necessary to grasp 'the inner nature of capital', i.e. to go from appearance to essence.

The point about the capitalist, as the 'personification of capital' is that he 'does not produce in order to satisfy his needs with the product; he produces with absolutely no direct regard for consumption. He produces in order to produce surplus value.'[12] Here we reach the nub of the matter. Capitalist production is not production for consumption, it is the self-expansion of capital, its 'valorisation', the production of surplus value. We can thus complete an earlier quotation by adding:

> Without the existence of wage workers, there is no production of surplus value; without production of surplus value, there is no capitalist production and thus no capital and no capitalist![13]

In another place Marx writes:

> ... as personified capital he (the industrial capitalist) produces for the sake of production, he wants to accumulate wealth for the sake of wealh. In so far as he is merely a functionary of capital, that is, an agent of capitalist production, what matters to him is exchange value and the increase of exchange value, not use value or its increase. What he is concerned with is the increase of abstract wealth, the rising appropriation of the labour of others.[14]

The aim and compelling motive of the capitalist mode of production is the self-expansion of value, the making of money, accumulation. The entire character of this mode of production is determined by the self-expansion of the advanced capital value.

But as we know, the passage from M to M' requires the extraction of surplus value from living labour; there is no other source from which it can come. Thus the embarrassment of all those who try to define capital in accordance with the requirements of bourgeois ideology. The social relationship they endeavour to conceal is precisely that between capital and the wage-labourer who has nothing to sell but his labour-power. 'All capitalist production' Marx insists, 'rests upon the purchase of labour power in order to appropriate part of what it produces without payment, this part (surplus value) is sold in the product . . . *this is the basis of existence of capital, its very essence*'[15] — as opposed to its forms of appearance.

The production of surplus value is the absolute law of the capitalist mode of production. It is a law which imposes itself upon every capitalist on pain of extinction from the competitive struggle on the market. However, the industrial capitalist, having extracted surplus value from the workers he employs and realised it in the sale of the commodity in which it is incorporated on the market cannot simply sit back and enjoy the proceeds. In the first place he has to pay away part of 'his' surplus value to other capitalists, rent to landlords, dividends to shareholders, interest to the banks, payments to directors, rates and taxes to public authorities.[16] From the total pool of surplus value comes the material means for the support of the whole bourgeoisie as a class and for its state apparatus, the payment of many 'non-productive' workers. Thus, while the capitalists are in competition with each other and different sections of the bourgeoisie may enter into conflict they

CAPITAL ACCUMULATION

preserve their essential class solidarity in the face of the working class. They fight to maintain and increase their share of the total product in the form of surplus value. Marx is able to show scientifically that each individual capitalist and the class as a whole nd the class as a whole takes a direct part in the exploitation of the total working class. The average rate of profit (which tends to equalise itself over the different spheres) depends on the intensity of exploitation of the sum total of labour by the sum total of capital'.[17]

It is, however, not only the case of raising the total of surplus value accruing to the capitalist class as a whole. Always it is necessary that part of the surplus value should be thrown back into circulation in the form of money to buy more labour power and augment the means of production. Each capitalist has to do this as part of the competitive struggle; it is forced upon him by the nature of the capital (social relationship) he personifies.

In *Capital* Volume I Marx deals with accumulation as it concerns the individual capitalist. In Volumes II and III he considers accumulation as a function of the total social capital in the course of which its contradictions are revealed. These questions will be taken up in the next chapters; for the present accumulation will be examined mainly from the standpoint Marx adopts in Volume I.

Two points already made can be repeated for a start: the capitalist is 'personified capital' and 'competition makes the immanent laws of capitalist production to be felt by each individual capitalist, as external coercive laws'.[18] And Marx adds, 'It compels him to keep constantly extending his capital, in order to preserve it, but extend it he cannot, except by progressive accumulation.'[19] There is no way out for the capitalist, he must accumulate or perish (as we shall see later the same is true for the capitalist system as a whole). The idea of the economists that accumulation takes place through the thrift and abstinence of the capitalist is, of course, a myth, though one still widely believed, or at least propagated, by present-day economists.[20] It takes for granted that consumption is the aim of capitalist production and that accumulation takes place at the expense of consumption, whereas the reverse is true. Accumulation is the compelling motive and the capitalist's 'own private consumption is a robbery perpetrated on accumulation.'[21]

Generally speaking, of course, the capitalists do not deprive themselves of the good things of life, but it is not in their excessive expenditure that the historically determined character of capitalism resides. It is not in capitalist consumption but precisely in and through accumulation that the most profound contradictions of the capitalist mode of production express themselves. In fact, ever since Malthus, if not earlier, those economists who discerned the self-destructive potentialities of capitalism saw in consumption a way out of its crisis; mistakenly, of course. J.M. Keynes himself was only the last line of these false saviours.

'Accumulate, accumulate! That is Moses and the prophets!' The drive to reconvert the greatest possible amount of surplus value into capital is the driving force of the capitalist mode of production; the individual capitalist is simply the instrument through which it takes place. At the same time, the accumulation of capital is specific to this mode. In many forms of society part of production is converted into new means of production:

> This process, however, does not present itself as accumulation of capital, nor as the function of the capitalist, so long as the labourer's means of production, and with them, his product and means of subsistence, do not confront him in the shape of capital.[22]

Those economists who are caught up in the commodity fetishism of the bourgeois system are unable to 'think of the means of production as separate from the antagonistic social mask they wear today, as a slave-owner to think of the worker as distinct from his character as a slave.'[23] Thus orthodox definitions of 'capital' find it in all societies except those of the most primitive kind. They make the power of labour to create surplus value a natural and intrinsic property of capital because they dwell intellectually in a topsy-turvy world, while trying to present it as the only world which can exist. As Marx says, 'we have the complete mystification of the capitalist mode of production, the conversion of social relations into things, the direct coalescence of the material production relations with their historical and social determination. It is an enchanted, perverted, topsy-turvy world, in which Monsieur le Capital and Madame la Terre do their ghost-walking as social characters and at the same time directly as mere things.'[24]

The process of accumulation has as a necessary result the formation of larger aggregates of capital. One aspect of this is that the organic composition of capital rises, that is to say that the amount of value incorporated in constant capital (instruments of production, raw materials, etc.) rises relative to the variable capital (the amount laid out in wages). This reflects, but is not the same thing as, the technical change in the conditions of production — in short, the substitution of machinery for labour. It means also a rise in the productivity of labour and enables the capitalist to realise the economies of large-scale production. Accumulation also results in individual firms growing larger, what Marx calls the concentration of capital, an the transformation of many small into a few large capitals (i.e. the growth of 'monopoly'). It is thus an historical law of accumulation that 'an ever increasing part of capital is turned into means of production, an ever decreasing one into labour power.'[25] Other factors besides technology speed up this process, notably the growing concentration of financial (money) power in the banks and financial institutions.

While productive power grows labour tends to be made superfluous. Furthermore, as we shall see in the next chapter, the drive to accumulate, by forcing up the organic composition of capital, tends to bring about a falling rate of profit and thus turn into its opposite. Accumulation must not be seen, therefore, as a process which takes place in a smooth, untroubled way, leading to permanent expansion. Because for special reasons after World War II the capitalist world system embarked on a long phase of expanded reproduction based upon accumulation many so-called Marxists assumed that the contradiction had been overcome. Mistaking appearance for essence, they were unable to recognise that below the surface the contradictions were building up even more powerfully than before. What was at issue was not a new phase of capitalist development but a continuation of the same process as had been in operation before the world war. In the 1960s the contradictions began to break through in inflation, monetary breakdown, unemployment, overproduction and intensified trade war.

It is through the constant study of Marxism and the enriching of Marx's inheritance and of Lenin's analysis of imperialism that the revolutionary party can arm itself to prepare for the sharp turns in the crisis today.

Notes

[1] *Theories of Surplus Value*, Part I, p.212

[2] *The Penguin Dictionary of Economics*, entry under *Capital*. The book is edited by G. Bannock, R.E. Baxter and P. Rees. First published in 1973, it was recently reprinted. In Palgreave's *Dictionary of Political Economy*, first published in 1894, it was at least admitted that 'there is probably no term in economics which has given rise to so much controversy as capital'. A selection was given and the view that all capital was the result of labour was seriously discussed and not absolutely excluded. Without doubt economics has degenerated in the intervening period.

[3] *Theories of Surplus Value*, Part III, p.501.

[4] *Theories of Surplus Value*, Part II, pp.527-528.

[5] *Wage Labour and Capital*, Various editions.

[6] *Theories of Surplus Value*, Part I, p.396

[7] *Capital* Volume III, p.259. This 'social power' is a result of accumulation.

[8] *Capital* Volume I (Allen and Unwin edition), p.123. It comes in the second paragraph of Chapter IV, 'The General Formula for Capital'. The whole chapter, which introduces some basic concepts, should be studied.

[9] 'As the conscious representative of this movement, the possessor of money becomes a capitalist. His person, or rather his pocket, is the point from which the money starts and to which it returns. The expansion of value, which is the objective basis or mainspring of the circulation M-C-M′, becomes his subjective aim, and it is only so in so far as the appropriation of ever more and more wealth in the abstract becomes the sole motive of his operations, that he functions as a capitalist, that is as capital personified and endowed with consciousness and will, Use-values must never be looked on as the real aim of the capitalist; neither must the profit of a single transaction. The restless never-ending process of profit-making alone is what he aims at.' *ibid.*, p. 130.

[10] Marx, 'Results of the Immediate Process' in *Value: Studies by Marx*, edited by Albert Dragstedt, New Park Publications 1976, pp.104-105. The whole of this should be studied.

[11] *Capital*, Volume I, p.255. Again Marx speaks of 'laws, immanent in capitalist production [which] manifest themselves in the movements of individual masses of capital, where they assert themselves as *coercive laws of competition*, and are brought home to the mind and consciousness of the individual capitalist as the directing motives of his operations', *ibid.*, p.305.

[12] *Theories of Surplus Value*, Part I, p.88. The same point is made in various other places, e.g. in 'Results of the Immediate Process'.

[13] *Value . . .* p.105.

[14] *Theories of Surplus Value*, Part I, p.273.

[15] *ibid.*, p.284, emphasis added.

[16] Marx wryly observes: 'What the industrial capitalist has to surrender to landlords, the State, creditors of the State, the Church and so forth, who only consume revenue, is an absolute diminution of his wealth, but it keeps his lust for enrichment going and thus preserves his capitalist soul'. *ibid.*, p.274.

[17] See *Capital*, Volume III, pp.191-195. As Marx says 'capital becomes conscious of itself as a *social power* in which every capitalist participates proportionally to his share in the total social capital.'

[18] 'Except as personified capital, the capitalist has no historical value . . . But, so far as he is personified capital, it is not values in use and the enjoyment of them, but exchange value and its augmentation that spur him into action. Fanatically bent on making value expand itself, he ruthlessly forces the human race to produce for production's sake . . .' *Capital*, Volume I, p.603.

[19] *Capital*, Volume 1, p.603.
[20] As the quotation from the *Penguin Dictionary of Economics* shows.
[21] *Capital*, Volume I, p.603.
[22] *ibid.*, p.609.
[23] *ibid.*, p.621.
[24] *Capital*, Volume III, p.809.
[25] *Capital*, Volume I, p.630.

Chapter 6

Marx on the formation of an average rate of profit

The objective laws of the capitalist mode of production impose upon the individual capitalist, as upon the system as a whole, the imperative demand to accumulate or perish. As Marx sums it up:

> *Accumulation* by means of the reconversion of profit, or surplus product, into capital now becomes a continuous process as a result of which the increased products of labour which are at the same time its objective conditions, conditions of reproduction, continuously confront labour as *capital* — which are alienated from labour and dominate it. Consequently it becomes a specific function of the capitalist to accumulate, that is, to reconvert a part of the surplus product into conditions of labour.[1]

Not only does this mean that dead labour — the existing means of production, the result of past labour — acquires the power continuously to extract a surplus from the unpaid labour of living labour. The very process of accumulation itself, in its working out, demonstrates that this mode of production is a determinate historical category, not embodying eternal relations of production but only those of a given epoch.

The rate of accumulation, which has yet to be studied, does, to be sure, determine the rate of growth of the system as a whole: it may expand, stagnate or contract. The whole period since World War II has been nothing but a particular stage of accumulation and flagging accumulation brought the expansion phase to an end. In this a basic economic law, a fundamental contradiction of the capitalist mode of production, is revealing itself: continued accumulation tends to drive down the rate of profit even though the mass of profit may continue to grow.

Accumulation means that the capitalists are compelled to throw back into production part of the surplus value extracted from the working class to create more means of production. They must produce commodities as exchange values and realise them by sale in order to make a profit on their capital for the process to continue. But in doing so, by their collective action, they tend to push down the rate of profit and are driven to other steps in order to prevent this happening. The declining rate of profit was, as Marx observed, the terror of the classical political economists because they half perceived in it the nemesis of capitalism. Marx himself saw it as in inescapable law, expressing the deepest contradictions of the capitalistic mode of production. He set out to provide an explanation of this law, which he described as 'in every respect the most important law of modern political economy, and the most essential for understanding the most difficult relations. It is the most important law from the historical standpoint. It is a law which, despite its simplicity, has never been grasped, and even less, consciously articulated.'[2]

In the Rough Draft for *Capital* known as the *Grundrisse* and in the manuscripts which Engels published as Volume III of *Capital* Marx attempted this articulation. Indeed, the understanding of the declining rate of profit was one of the most significant of Marx's achievements and one which, despite his reference to its 'simplicity', required an enormous methodological leap attributed by him to having 'leafed through Hegel's Logic'.[3] There have been many expositions and commentaries on the declining rate of profit based on Marx's work, by critics as well as self-styled Marxists. Few have recognised the method by which Marx proceeded and many have tended to go straight to the third part of Volume III without a study of the whole theory in which it is embedded. In fact it forms part of a new stage in Marx's analysis of the 'movements of capital as a whole'. In the first volume, as he points out, he was concerned with the immediate process of capitalist production.[4] The focus was on the law of value and the production of surplus value, taking to a large extent the individual capitalist (Moneybags) and his wage-workers as the starting point. This was, of course, justifiable, because the primary question was value and its production: the social relations and fetishism it involved. For this purpose it was necessary to assume that values and prices were generally identical and that, therefore, what Marx called the organic composition of capital was the same in all branches of production.

Of course, Marx well knew that the assumptions he was making were not realistic. Contrary to some vulgar critics, he did not make a mistake which then had to be corrected in the third volume. The drafts which made up this volume dated from the same period as the writing of Volume I. In any case all the main features of the analysis he wanted to present are to be found, at least in embryonic form, in the *Grundrisse* sketched out some years before.

The concept of the organic composition of capital, essential for Marx's theory of accumulation, including the tendency for the rate of profit to fall, is worked out in Volume I.[5] The important step forward here was the distinction between *constant* capital (c) and *variable* capital (v). Constant capital included that part of the means of production used up in producing a commodity, the raw materials, fuel, instruments of production that do not undergo any quantitative alteration in value during the labour process. This is the objective factor. Variable capital is that part of capital laid out on the purchase of labour power which does undergo an alteration in value in the labour process, the subjective factor. While the physical form of constant capital is changed its value form is not; it adds no new value. Labour power, on the other hand, both reproduces the equivalent of its own value and also produces an excess, surplus value (s).

The value of every commodity, C, is represented in the formula c + v + s. The *organic composition of capital* is given by the formula c/v and it has both a technical and value form. Technical improvements involving the increasing productivity of labour usually mean a greater amount of means of production, e.g. machinery employed to a given amount of labour power. The effect of the value composition will be in the same direction but not necessarily in the same proportion, since it will depend on the changing values of the two forms of capital. It is the value relationship which Marx generally means.

Also to be noted is the *rate of surplus value* or s/v; this indicates the ratio between that part of the working day (week, year, etc.) in which the worker works to produce surplus value (s) and that part in which he produces the value of his own labour power. On the scale of an industry or economy these symbols will represent all the surplus value and all the variable capital concerned. In all these operations, of course, value has a purely social reality but manifests itself in the relationship of commodity to commodity and commodity to money. Surplus value (profit) can only be extracted at the point of production, but this presupposes capitalist relations of production and thus also private property rights and the bourgeois state to uphold the laws. This is the product of a lengthy historical process establishing the capitalist mode of production.

In much of Volume I, as has been said, Marx establishes the law of value and shows how it imposes itself on the individual capitalist through what he calls competition. He notes, for example, that this spurs the capitalists to accumulate and that in doing so they employ more constant capital in proportion to variable capital. In other words, the organic composition of capital rises. The growing productivity of labour 'appears, therefore, in the diminution of the mass of labour in proportion to the mass of means of production moved by it, or in the diminution of the subjective factor of the labour process as compared with the objective factor'. Marx goes on to say that 'with the growth of the total capital, its variable constituent or the labour incorporated in it, also does increase, but in a constantly diminishing proportion'.[6] This change does not take place evenly in the different branches of production; on the contrary, it is subject to the law of uneven development, taking place more rapidly in some than in others, causing violent fluctuations and shifts in the distribution of labour.[7]

Marx does not take up the detailed analysis of the consequences of either the increasing organic composition of capital or its unevenness between industries or the changes taking place in the course of accumulation until Volume III.[8] In particular there is the problem of working out how firms and industries with a high organic composition of capital survived, or even came into being, given that only variable capital produced new value. Yet these were precisely the most advanced technologically, the product of capital accumulation and the most subject to centralisation and concentration of capital. It was here, in showing how the law of value asserted itself through the apparently conflicting manifestations of appearance, that Marx's dialectical method proved its superiority over classical political economy and its epigones, including the various brands of revisionism. Unfortunately, Marx did not live to complete the analysis he was carrying out in the manuscripts which Engels edited and prepared for publication as Volume III. The loose ends, brief summaries and incomplete trains of thought to be found in these writings were seized upon by the critics. In other cases, as with the so-called 'transformation problem', itself integrally connected with the law of the declining rate of profit, the tendency, even among 'Marxists', has been to see these as separable problems susceptible to some kind of formal solution in the best tradition of 'economics'. The dialectical thought proved too much to stomach, the 'Hegelian language' has been studiously avoided. The contention is, on the contrary, that the understanding of these new questions which Marx introduced in Volume III must be dialectical. An attempt will be made here to indicate some of the main lines for study.

Always we must return to the question of fetishism and the need to penetrate from appearance to essence. The appearance taken by the capitalist property relations is well described by Marx in an important passage in *Theories of Surplus Value* from which the following extract is taken:

> The bourgeois sees that the product continually becomes the condition of production. But he does not perceive that the production relations themselves, the social forms in which he produces and which he regards as given, natural relations, are the continuous product — and only for that reason the continuous prerequisite — of this specific social mode of production. The different relations and aspects not only become independent and assume a heterogeneous mode of existence, apparently independent of one another, but they seem to be the direct properties of things; they assume a material shape.

Thus, as under commodity fetishism, 'a definite social relation between men . . . assumes in their eyes the fantastic form of a relation between things'.

Marx goes on:

> Thus the participants in capitalist production live in a bewitched world and their own relationships appear to them as properties of things, as properties of the material elements of production.[9]

In the first chapter of Volume III Marx takes the way the capitalist perceives the commodity and contrasts it with how its value is really made up. 'What the commodity costs the capitalist and its actual production costs are two quite different magnitudes.'[10] Instead of $C = c + v + s$, the capitalist takes constant and variable capital together as his cost price, call it k. The value thus appears as $k + s$. The capitalist measures the cost of the commodity in capital, while the actual cost is measured by the expenditure of labour. For the capitalist, therefore, cost price is less than value but 'in capitalist economics the cost-price assumes the false appearance of a category of value production itself.'[11]

The variable part of the capitalist's advanced capital appears as wages and as full payment for the labour expended in production and this is no different from the constant capital. The capitalist habitually thinks not of constant and variable capital but of fixed capital (plant and machinery, for example) and circulating capital (wages, cost of raw materials and other things used up in production). The specific value-creating capacity of labour is thus denied. The excess received for the commodity when it is sold and added to the total capital appears to spring from all the different elements that contribute to cost price (k) and is regarded as profit (p). Thus $C = c + v + s$ *appears* as $C = k + p$. As Marx puts it: 'The profit, such as it is represented here, is thus the same as surplus value, only in a mystified form that is nonetheless the outgrowth of the capitalist mode of production.'[12]

When the capitalist sells the commodity the price obtained should include a profit otherwise he will soon be out of business. However, he may still make a profit by selling it below its value, or he may make an additional profit by selling it above its value; in other words p need not be equal to s. The fluctuations in prices occurring on the market seem to confirm the opinion of the capitalist, or the bourgeois economist, that the cost price is the true inner value and that profit is a reward for the capitalist's own contribution, or that of 'capital'. On the contrary, as Marx sees it:

> The fundamental law of capitalist competition, which political economy has not hitherto grasped, the law which regulates the general rate of profit and the so-called prices of production determined by it, rests, as we shall see later, on this difference between the value and the cost-price of commodities, and on the resulting possibility of selling a commodity at a profit under its value.[13]

We leave aside here the endless attempts of economic theory to explain the origins of profits, the mystery of how more value comes out of production than goes into it which Marx solved with the theory of surplus value. Marx discussed and exposed such theories many times and the more sophisticated theories put forward since his time only create a still more bewitched world of fantasy. What remains for Marx is to explain how a general, or average, rate of profit arises despite the different amounts of surplus value contained in the value of different commodities produced by capitals of different organic composition. To do this, however, it was first necessary to make clear the distinction between profit and surplus value.

For the individual capitalist the proportions in which he lays out capital on wages and constant capital is a matter of indifference: he is only interested in the relation between surplus value and total capital. Moreover he is concerned in a continuous process of circulation, purchasing inputs of various sorts which then pass through the various stages of production for a more or less lengthy period of time before he realises his outlays by sale, apparently according to the formula $k + p$. Thus if a given capital can be turned over in a shorter time that will be equivalent to a higher rate of return, or profit. Part of the surplus value may in fact have to be paid away to merchant capitalists who sell the product and so on. Capital is constantly being metamorphosed, as Marx brilliantly describes. In the course of this, 'Surplus value does not appear as the product of the appropriation of labour-time, but as an excess of the selling price of commodities over their cost price, the latter thus being easily represented as their actual value (*valeur intrinsèque*), while profit appears as an excess of the selling price of commodities over their immanent value.'[14] The real relations of capitalist production, especially the exploitation of the workers, is thus obscured because surplus value takes the form of profit on capital.

How this occurs is dialectically described by Marx:

> The way in which surplus-value is transformed into the form of profit is ... a further development of the inversion of subject and object that takes place already in the process of production. In the latter, we have seen, the subjective productive forces of labour appear as productive forces of capital. On the one hand, the value of the past labour, which dominates living labour, is incarnated in the capitalist. On the other hand, the labourer appears as bare material labour-power, as a commodity. Even in the simple relations of production this inverted

relationship necessarily produces certain correspondingly inverted conceptions, a transposed consciousness, which is further developed by the metamorphoses and modifications of the actual circulation process.[15]

As an example of the latter we only have to consider the explanations of capital, profit and value offered by present-day economics. Thus it remains a mystery where surplus value comes from.

As we have seen, the rate of surplus value is different from the ratio between surplus value and total capital, what Marx calls the *rate of profit*. The former is s/v, the latter is s/c + v. Given the rate and amount of surplus value, however, the rate of profit expresses a different way of measuring the surplus value, that is to say it will be greater the larger the proportion of new value created to the capital paid out in wages. What appears on the surface is not, however, the essence of the matter, as Marx insists.

> If, as Hegel would put it, the surplus re-reflects itself in itself out of the rate of profit [he writes], or, put differently, the surplus is more closely characterised by the rate of profit, it appears as a surplus produced by capital above its own value over a year, or in a given period of circulation.[16]

In this concentrated formula based on Hegel's *Logic* Marx suggests that surplus value as the essence can only appear as profit. The semblance is that profit is a surplus produced by capital, while the essence is that profit is surplus value determined in a certain way. 'That which shows itself is essence in *one* of its determinations, in one of its aspects. *Essence* seems to be just that. Semblance is the showing of essence in itself' is how Lenin summarises Hegel's thought on this point.[17]

Marx goes on:

> Although the rate of profit thus differs numerically from the rate of surplus value, while surplus value and profit are actually the same thing and numerically equal, *profit is nevertheless a converted form of surplus value, a form in which the origin and secret of its existence are obscured and extinguished*. In effect, profits is the form in which surplus value presents itself to the view, and must be stripped by analysis to disclose the latter.[18] [Emphasis added.]

Thus, 'In surplus value, the relation between capital and labour is laid bare', while in the form of profit it appears as a relation of capital to itself. In other words profit can be considered as a fetishised form of surplus value, part of the bewitched world of capitalist property relations. As Marx puts it: 'The further we follow the process of self-expansion of capital, the more mysterious the relations of capital will become, and the less the secret of its internal organism will be revealed.'[19] But it was precisely Marx's object to reveal this secret, hence his investigation of the famous transformation of value into prices and the law of declining rate of profit.

The significance of the points established by Marx in the first two chapters of Volume III becomes more fully apparent in the second part concerned with the conversion of profit into average profit. Without grasping this section it is impossible to understand the law of the tendency of the rate of profit to decline which makes up the third part according to the arrangement of the manuscripts adopted with good reason by Engels.

Marx's task here is to show 'precisely the way in which a general rate of profit takes shape in any given country'.[20] He makes certain assumptions, such as that the rate of surplus value and the length of the working day remain constant, in order to isolate the main operating factors in the situation. It is also assumed that commodities are sold at their value. In that case technical conditions will impose different ratios of constant to variable capital, on the average, in different branches of production or different organic compositions of capital. It is, of course, the value relations and not the technical compositions as such which concern Marx in this analysis. It is then not difficult to show that if these conditions prevail the rate of profit $s/c + v$ will differ in the different spheres of production alhtough capitals of similar magnitude are involved and allowing for differences in the turnover period of the different capitals.

In what would be regarded by modern economists, no doubt, as an 'elegant' demonstration, Marx shows, on the one hand that capitals of different organic compositions produce different rates of profit and, on the other hand, 'that differences in the average rate of profit in the various branches of industry do not exist in reality, and could not exist without abolishing the entire system of capitalist production'.[21]

However, Marx had assumed that products were sold at their value; now it is clear that they cannot be sold at their value. This contradiction, taken by superficial critics to show that Marx had been wrong about the law of value, or that he had to 'correct' Volume I in Volume III, is precisely the contradiction of capitalism Marx had revealed in the previous analysis of the relationship between surplus value and profit. It now takes the form of the relationship between value and price.

From his analysis of the different compositions of capital Marx had therefore drawn the conclusion that 'it would seem that here the theory of value is incompatible with the actual process, and that for this reason any attempt to understand these phenomena should be given up'.[22] In fact he was able to show that the law of value did assert itself through this contradiction. He begins by drawing from his analysis what is the appearance: 'The cost-prices are the same for equal capitals in different spheres, no matter how much the produced values and surplus values may differ. The equality of cost-prices is the basis for competition among invested capitals, whereby an average profit is brought about.'[23] That is how it must be.

Various economists, some claiming to be Marxists, others not, have dealt with the problem of the transformation of values into prices as though it was a question of the correct mathematics. We shall not proceed in this way and it does not appear from a reading of *Capital* that Marx saw it in this way. It was more a philosophical problem of appearance and essence and it was not in any case to be separated from the whole analysis of the working out of the law of value in the development of the capitalist mode of production. Certainly for Marx it was never seen as an enormous problem in itself but only part of the explanation of the self-movement of capital as a process reflecting the dialectical laws.

Thus the rate of profit accrues to capital in accordance with its magnitude regardless of its organic composition. Competition between capitals brings about an average rate for the simple reason that an abnormally high profit in one sphere would attract capitals until the rate was brought down to the average. The average rate of profit ensures that each capital receives its share of the total surplus value produced by the social capital in all spheres of production. In the aggregate the total profit must be the same as the total surplus value; thus for the system as a whole the rate of profit, given the rate of surplus value, will be determined by the organic composition of capital. In other words, this will be divided up according to the amount of capital in each firm or industry. This does not mean that there will not be deviations from the average rate of profit; for example, firms may be more or less efficient and prices of inputs and outputs as well as general market conditions, technology, etc. are in a constant state of change and flux. At any particular time, therefore, a particular capital may receive too much or too little surplus value. 'Under capitalist production,' writes Marx, 'the general law acts as the prevailing tendency only in a very complicated and approximate manner, as a never ascertainable average of ceaseless fluctuations.'[24]

Each particular capital does not merely receive the simple average rate of profit, it also contributes to the formation of that average. The general or average rate of profit in a given economy will depend upon the organic compositions of capital in the different spheres and the different rates of profit in them and upon the relative amounts of capital invested in the different spheres. For example, an industry in which the organic composition of capital is particularly high may not involve a very large part of the total social capital. In making these points it should be borne in mind that Marx is assuming a competitive situation such that the movement of capitals tends to equalise the rate of profit for capitals of different magnitudes. The point about a monopoly is that it is able to attract more than its aliquot part of the total profit at the expense of other spheres of production.

In order to understand the formation of the general rate of profit Marx had to distinguish cost price from value and develop what he called the 'price of production' as its converted form. The removal of the assumption that cost-price is equal to the value of a commodity means that this must be less than the value. This is because 'the cost price of a commodity refers only to the quantity of paid labour contained in it while its value refers to all the paid and unpaid labour contained in it. The price of production refers to the sum of the paid labour plus a certain quantity of unpaid labour determined for any particular sphere of production by conditions over which it has no control.'[25]

The development of Marx's thought proceeds dialectically from the abstract to the more concrete and in this case marks a great step forward in revealing the laws of motion of capitalism, Marx's goal when he began work on *Capital*.

AVERAGE RATE OF PROFIT

On the basis of the distinction made between value and cost-price and profit and surplus value and the formation of an average rate of profit Marx moves towards a closer approximation to the understanding of how these laws actually work themselves out. He proceeds by a process of abstraction and successive approximations, tracing out a theoretical development according to dialectical laws. He is not describing what takes place because that could only result in remaining at the level of appearance; he therefore has to penetrate to essence. This is surely what Lenin meant when in referring to *Capital* he wrote in the *Philosophical Notebooks*:

> If Marx did not leave behind him a '*Logic*' (with a capital letter), he did leave the *logic of Capital* and this ought to be utilised to the full in this question. In *Capital* Marx applied to a single science logic, dialectics and the theory of knowledge of materialism [three words are not needed: it is one and the same thing] which has taken everything valuable in Hegel and developed it further.[26]

This point made by Lenin has never really been fully investigated by students of *Capital* and in particular in the case of the sections of Volume III now being discussed.

To return to Marx's thought. He is now able to say: 'It is then only an accident if the surplus-value, and thus the profit, actually produced in any particular sphere of production, coincides with the profit contained in the selling price of a commodity.'[27] The surplus value produced in any given sphere or by a firm goes to swell the aggregate surplus value at the disposal of the capitalist class. Whatever its amount, assuming competition and a given degree of exploitation, each capitalist or each branch of production will tend to receive the average profit on the capital engaged in production. The difference between profit and surplus value can now be seen in a fresh light. Marx defines the position as follows:

> The actual difference of magnitude between profit and surplus value — not merely between the rate of profit and the rate of surplus value — in the various spheres of production now completely conceals the true nature and origin of profit not only from the capitalist, who has a special interest in deceiving himself on this score, but also from the labourer. The transformation of values into prices of production serves to obscure the basis for determining value itself. Finally, since the mere transformation of surplus value into profit distinguishes the portion of the value of a commodity forming the profit from the portion forming

its cost-price, it is natural that the conception of value should elude the capitalist at this juncture, for he does not see the total labour put into the commodity, but only that portion of the total labour for which he has paid in the shape of means of production, be they living or not, so that his profit appears to him as something outside the immanent value of the commodity. Now this idea is fully confirmed, fortified and ossified in that, from the standpoint of his particular sphere of production, the profit added to the cost-price is not actually determined by the limits of the formation of value in his own sphere, but through completely outside influences.[28]

What bewitched the practical capitalist equally baffled the political economist, as it does the present-day economists. As Marx says, they abandoned the search for the determination of value 'and with it all vestiges of a scientific approach, in order to cling to the differences that strike the eye in the phenomenon [i.e. surface appearances — T.K.] — this confusion of the theorists best illustrates the utter incapacity of the practical capitalist, blinded by competition as he is, and incapable of penetrating its phenomena, to recognise the inner essence and inner structure of this process behind its outer appearance'.[29] In fact this point is not only true of bourgeois economics but also of many self-styled Marxists of the Stalinist and revisionist schools. For example, their preoccupation with the transformation of values into prices and their apologetic tone indicates that they do not know or deliberately conceal what Marx was about. There is absolutely no need to be apologetic or to make a mystery of this question: it demonstrates the superiority of Marx's dialectical method over the narrow, ideologically-determined conceptions of his opponents and critics.

The conditions under which the average rate of profit is determined mean that capitalists will see new techniques using more constant capital in relation to variable capital as a profitable affair. And Marx asks the question:

> How could labour be the sole source of profit in view of the fact that a reduction in the quantity of labour required for production appears not to exert any influence on profit? Moreover, it even seems in certain circumstances to be the nearest source of an increase of profits, at least for the individual capitalist.[30]

It should be borne in mind that Marx is setting the stage here for the presentation of the law of the declining rate of profit.

Thus, however profit is distributed among the different spheres of production and firms, 'the sum of the profits in all spheres of production must equal the sum of the surplus-values and the sum of the prices of production of the total social product equal the sum of its value'.[31] It may happen that in some spheres profits equal surplus value, indicating that its organic composition of capital was the same as the average social capital, but this would be exceptional. As has been seen capital in each sphere receives not the amount of surplus value generated in it but a share of the total surplus value proportionate to its total capital regardless of its organic composition of capital. Surplus value is thus transmuted into profit just as the prices obtained by adding average profit to cost price transmutes values into prices.

Under the capitalist mode of production commodities are not exchanged simply as commodities (as assumed in the first part of *Capital*) but as products of capital claiming a proportion of the total surplus value produced proportionate to its magnitude. This movement is not simply a logical one, it is the result of an historical process from simple commodity production to a purer and more advanced form of capitalism.

As Marx puts it:

> The exchange of commodities at their values, or approximately at their values, thus requires a much lower stage than their exchange at their prices of production, which requires a definite level of capitalist development.
>
> Whatever the manner in which the prices of various commodities are first mutually fixed or regulated, their movements are always governed by the law of value. If the labour-time required for their production happens to shrink, prices fall; if it increases, prices rise, provided that other conditions remain the same.[32]

Historically values come first, prices of production emerge as part of a lengthy and complex process of development. However developed the form of capitalism prices of production gravitate around values. 'The law of value dominates price movements with reduction or increases in the required labour-time making prices of production fall or rise', Marx says.[33] The law of value always asserts itself though not instantaneously or directly. The more advanced the form of capitalism the more complex the process. Moreover actual market prices diverge from prices of production, being determined by day-to-day conditions. At any one time, for a particular commodity there is no necessary coincidence between value, price of production and market price. Much of bourgeois economic theory is concerned with market price as determined by supply and demand, not with what determines either value or price of production. But supply and demand cannot explain anything unless the social conditions on which they rest are known. Marx does not ignore supply and demand, on the contrary they are assumed in the very fact that the commodity represents a unity of use value and exchange value and would not be produced at all if it was not expected that it would satisfy a social need and should represent socially necessary labour. Social demand thus regulates the distribution of labour time, but it does so 'subject to the mutual relationships of the different classes and their respective economic position, notably therefore to, firstly, the ratio of total surplus value to wages, and, secondly, to the relation of the various parts into which surplus value is split up (profit, interest, ground-rent, taxes etc.). And thus this again shows that absolutely nothing can be explained by the relation of supply and demand before ascertaining the axis on which this relation rests.'[34] It is this which the economics textbooks take for granted.

A study of the relationship between social demand and the distribution of social labour and consequently between market-values, prices of production and values shows that the whole process is governed by the latter. 'The exchange, or sale, of commodities at their value is the rational state of affairs, i.e. the natural law of their equilibrium. It is this law that explains the deviations, and not vice versa, the deviations that explain the law'.[35] What Marx is looking for, 'the real inner laws of capitalist production cannot be observed in their pure state, until supply and demand cease to act, i.e. are equated'.[36] The rational state of affairs, equilibrium (to which some economists have devoted an enormous amount of mathematical ingenuity), is never realised, nor is it really possible to say what it is. The economic system works as a continuous movement of contradiction and incessant fluctuation and reciprocal and interrelated changes. Supply and demand are not independent of each other as has been assumed by economic theory but mutually determine each other and production determines the market as much as the market determines production. The task is to discover regularities, or laws, in the process as a whole.

AVERAGE RATE OF PROFIT

In the case of capital it moves from those spheres with a lower rate into those with a higher one (creating a demand for inputs as well as a supply of commodities).

> Through this incessant outflow and influx [writes Marx], or briefly, through its distribution among the various spheres, it creates such a ratio of supply and demand that the average profit in the various spheres of production becomes the same, and values are, therefore, converted into prices of production.[37]

In this process, however, 'the values that lie beneath the prices of production and that determine them in the last instance' are concealed. It appears quite differently because 'everything appears reversed in competition'. And Marx goes on:

> The final pattern of economic relations as seen on the surface, in their real existence and consequently in the conceptions by which the bearers and agents of these relations seek to understand them, is very different from, and indeed, quite the reverse of, the inner but concealed essential pattern and the conception corresponding to it.[38]

Marx's method enabled him to reveal the 'inner but concealed essential pattern' by which capitalist development took place and also to make a stringent critique of political economy, 'the conception corresponding to it'. This chapter has tried to indicate how this was done in the sections of Volume III of *Capital*, clearing the ground for the exposition of the law of the tendency of the rate of profit to fall. Without an understanding of Marx's method it is impossible to appreciate the significance of this law.

Notes

[1] *Theories of Surplus Value*, Part Three, p.272.

[2] *Grundrisse* (Pelican edition), p.748. It is following on from the declining rate of profit that Marx makes the point, differently expressed in various other writings that 'Beyond a certain point, the development of the powers of production becomes a barrier for capital; hence the capital relation a barrier for the development of the productive powers of society', *ibid*, p.749.

[3] The exact quotation comes in a letter to Engels, dated January 14, 1858, 'I am getting some nice developments, e.g. I have overthrown the whole doctrine of profit as previously conceived. In the *method* of working it was of great service to me that by mere accident I leafed through Hegel's *Logic* again.'

[4] See the first paragraph of Chapter I, Volume III, p.25. Rosdolsky, in *The Making of Marx's Capital* takes up the questions to be dealt with mainly from the *Grundrisse*. In the present article only the more thoroughly worked out theory in Volume III will be considered. Obviously a working over and coordination of both versions is necessary.

[5] Especially at the beginning of Chapter XXV where a number of paragraphs were added to the third edition from which the English translation was made.
[6] *Capital*, Volume I, p.636 (Allen & Unwin ed.). 'The law of the progressive increase in constant capital, in proportion to the variable, is confirmed at every step by the comparative analysis of the prices of commodities, whether we compare different economic epochs or different nations in the same epoch'. *ibid*.
[7] *Capital*, Volume I, p.640.
[8] Though he does deal with the consequences of the fact that 'an ever increasing part of capital is turned into means of production, an ever decreasing one into labour-power' leads to the concentration and centralisation of capital, i.e. the growth of monopoly. See *Capital*, pp.639 seq.
[9] *Theories of Surplus Value*, Part Three, p.544.
[10] *Capital*, Volume III, p.26.
[11] *ibid.*, p.28
[12] *ibid*, p.36
[13] *ibid*, p.37
[14] *ibid*, p.44.
[15] *ibid*, p.45.
[16] *ibid*, p.47.
[17] V.I. Lenin, *Collected Works*, Vol. 38, p.103.
[18] *Capital*, Volume III, p.47.
[19] *ibid*, p.48.
[20] *ibid*, p.141.
[21] *ibid*, p.151.
[22] *ibid*, p.151.
[23] *ibid*, p.151.
[24] *ibid*, p.159.
[25] *ibid*, p.163.
[26] Lenin, *op.cit*, p.319.
[27] *Capital* Volume III, p.165.
[28] *ibid*, pp.165-166.
[29] *ibid*, p.166.
[30] *ibid*, p.168.
[31] *ibid*, p.170.
[32] *ibid*, p.174.
[33] *ibid*, p.178.
[34] *ibid*.
[35] *ibid*, p.184.
[36] *ibid*, p.186.
[37] *ibid*, p.192.
[38] *ibid*, p.205.

Chapter 7

Marx on the declining rate of profit

Before Marx could provide an explanation of the tendency of the rate of profit to fall he had to establish the conditions for the formation of a general, or average, rate of profit. As we have seen, this, in turn, is integrally related to the operation of the law of value and the derivation of profit from surplus value.[1] It is therefore impossible to separate the falling rate of profit from the whole body of Marx's analysis of the capitalist mode of production. As we see later in subsequent articles, it leads on directly to the question of capitalist crisis and the drive of capitalism towards collapse. The extraction of these laws represented at the highest level the working out of the method of dialectical materialism.

The founders of classical political economy, notably Adam Smith and Ricardo, had been very much aware of the falling rate of profit as a tendency inherent in capitalism but the explanations they offered were incorrect. Marx had to begin with a critique of his predecessors and then develop new tools of analysis which had been beyond their grasp. Before working out the more finished exposition of the law which appears in Volume III of *Capital* he dealt exhaustively with the question in the manuscripts making up *Theories of Surplus Value* and the *Grundrisse*.

This is how Marx sums up the errors of Smith and Ricardo in one passage:

> Thus Adam Smith says that the rate of profit falls with the accumulation of capital, because of the growing competition among the capitalists; Ricardo says that it does so because of the growing deterioration of agriculture (increased price of necessaries). We have refuted his view, which would only be correct if rate of surplus-value and rate of profit were identical, and therefore the rate of profit could not fall unless the

rate of wages rose, provided the working day remained unchanged. Adam Smith's view rests on his compounding value out of wages, profits and rents (in accordance with his false view which he himself refuted). According to him, the accumulation of capitals forces the reduction in *arbitrary* profits — for which there is no inherent measure — through the reduction in the price of commodities; profits, according to this conception, being merely a nominal addition to the prices of commodities.[2]

Ricardo made the fall in the rate of profit depend on so-called diminishing returns from land and consequent rise in rents. He failed to reach an accurate conception of the average rate of profit because he failed to distinguish between values and cost prices and confused the rate of profit with the rate of surplus value. Marx was able to solve the problem of the transformation of values into prices as well as demonstrate the difference between surplus value and profit and thus establish the conditions for the formation of an average rate of profit. At the same time, he was able to do what the classical political economists had failed to do, namely to distinguish constant from variable capital. Without these important theoretical conquests it would have been impossible to explain the law of the declining rate of profit as a permanent *tendency* in capitalism.

Once the concepts of a general rate of profit and variable and constant capital have been established it is not difficult for Marx to show that a rise in the organic composition of capital must bring about a fall in the rate of profit, assuming that the rate of exploitation remains the same. Thus if the rate of profit is represented by $s/c + v$ and s/v remains the same, as the ratio of c to v rises so the rate of profit will decline.

The continual relative decrease in variable capital (i.e. labour power) to constant capital (means of production, raw materials, fuel etc), or the rising organic composition of capital, is the same thing as continued accumulation or the rising productivity of labour. The compelling motive of capitalist production is not the satisfaction of human wants but the production of surplus value, part of which must be accumulated — incorporated in new means of production. Thus in the very process of its self-expansion and the development of the productive power of labour capitalism tends to bring about the fall in the rate of profit upon which its continued expansion depends. In other words: 'Beyond a certain point, the development of the powers of production becomes a barrier for capital; hence the capital relation a barrier for the development of the productive powers of labour.'[3]

In presenting the law in its simplest form and without qualification Marx proceeds from the abstract to the more concrete. He leaves out of account other influences which may depress profit rates or those which work in the opposite direction so that this basic underlying force inherent in the capitalist mode of production can be clearly defined and emphasised. Likewise, the analysis is made independently of the division of the profit subsequently to it coming into the hands of the industrial capitalist. Marx insists that: 'The profit to which we are here referring is but another name for surplus-value itself, which is presented only in its relation to total capital rather than to variable capital from which it arises.'[4]

If we refer to the section of the *Grundrisse* in which Marx was working on this question we find that he points to 'two immediate laws' arising from the transformation of surplus value into profit. The first of these was that 'Surplus value expressed as profit always appears as a smaller proportion than surplus value in its immediate reality actually amounts to.' He underlined this sentence, by which he meant to emphasise that $s/c + v$ is always smaller than s/v, i.e. the rate of profit is always smaller than the rate of surplus value. Consequently, 'the rate of profit never expresses the real rate at which capital exploits labour, but always a much smaller relation'.[5]

The second of these laws was an earlier formulation of what was to be more simply expressed in Volume III, namely that 'the rate of profit declines to the degree that capital has already appropriated living labour in the form of objectified labour hence to the degree that labour is already capitalised and hence also acts increasingly in the form of fixed capital in the production process or to the degree that labour is already capitalised and hence also acts increasingly in the form of fixed capital in the production process or to the degree that the productive power of labour grows.' As he puts it later in the same paragraph, 'The profit rate is therefore inversely related to the growth of relative surplus value, to the development of the powers of production, and to the magnitude of the capital employed as (constant) capital within production.'[6] Thus in its insatiable drive for surplus value and in the development of the productive forces capitalism inevitably brings about the tendency for the profit rate to decline.

The relative decrease in variable capital relative to constant capital is 'but another expression for greater productivity of labour'. Every capitalist strives to increase the productivity of labour, the amount produced by a worker in a given time. The main way in which this can be done is to increase the amount of machinery used; but this raises the organic composition of capital and tends to bring down the rate of profit.

This law does not mean that the absolute mass of exploited labour falls. On the contrary, the historical tendency has been for the scale of production to grow with a rise in the labour force and for production to be concentrated into a smaller number of large units. 'The drop in the rate of profit [writes Marx] is not due to an absolute, but only to a relative decrease of the variable part of the total capital, i.e., to its decrease in relation to the constant.'[7] In other words, the absolute mass of profit continues to grow despite the tendency for the rate of profit to fall. Individual capitalist firms try to overcome the operation of the law through larger investments of capital. The operation of the law bears down most harshly upon the smaller and weaker firms, driving them into bankruptcy or inducing them to sell out to their more powerful rivals. The operation of the law thus hastens the break up of the old free competition and speeds up the growth of monopoly, another tendency already foreshadowed in *Capital* although in Marx's day the transition to monopoly capitalism had scarcely begun. Nevertheless it represented the working out of the 'laws of motion' of the capitalist mode of production elucidated by Marx.

There is, however, little consolation for the supporters of capitalism in the growth of the *mass* of profits. This arises from the same causes as produce the tendency for the rate of profit to decline. It only means that a relative decrease of variable capital and profit can be accompanied by an absolute increase in both owing to the increasing scale of production based upon continued accumulation. As Marx puts it:

> The same causes that bring about a tendency for the general rate of profit to fall necessitate an accelerated accumulation of capital and, consequently, an increase in the absolute magnitude, or total mass, of the surplus-labour (surplus-value, profit) appropriated by it. Just as

everything appears reversed in competition, and thus in the agents of competition, so also this law, the inner and necessary connection between two seeming contradictions.[8]

For example, a powerful capitalist may deliberately accept a lower rate of profit for a time in order to drive a rival out of business. The fall in the profit rate sometimes appears as the effect of an increase in capital and as a calculation on the part of the capitalist (so-called small profits, high returns). Such conceptions arise from the wrong idea that profits are simply added to the true value of commodities (what businessmen call the mark-up). Marx says: 'Crude as such ideas are, they necessarily arise out of the inverted aspect which the immanent laws of capitalist production represent in competition.'[9]

It is a difference once again between appearance and essence and the fetishised forms which the different categories of capital assume. Thus when the productivity of labour increases and prices of commodities fall, with a reduction in the amount of profit on each individual commodity 'it then appears as if the capitalist adds less profit to the price of the individual commodity of his own free will, and makes up for it through the greater number of commodities he produces.'[10]

> The fall in commodity prices and the rise in the mass of profit on the augmented mass of the cheapened commodities is, in fact, but another expression for the law of the falling rate of profit attended by a simultaneously increasing mass of profit.[11]

In considering the tendency for the rate of profit to fall it should be remembered that Marx speaks of it as a law of tendency. This does not mean that it is sometimes in abeyance, though the force with which it operates may vary at different times, for example with the ups and downs of the economic cycle. More properly it does not appear on the surface, it does not necessarily show itself in an actual falling rate of profit, in the manner, of course, in which Marx calculates profits which is not the same as that of the businessman or the accountant.

In fact as Marx points out the problem is rather to explain why the rate of profit had not fallen more, and more rapidly. A century or so after Marx it is still more important to be able to explain why this law of tendency has not brought about a collapse of capitalism.

Marx ascribes this to what he calls 'counter-acting tendencies', making up Chapter XIV of Volume III. However, this is a brief chapter, scarcely more than notes, and there is not much help to be obtained from Marx's other writings on this question. In fact he had begun in the previous chapter showing that there were conditions under which the law might not show itself as an actual fall in the rate of profit. Although the tendency was for the increase in the productivity of labour brought about by a higher organic composition of capital to lower the price of individual commodities, containing less materialised labour and absorbing less living labour, the profit contained in them could increase. That would be so if the rate of surplus value could be raised either by prolonging the working day (absolute surplus value) or by more intensive work (relative surplus value). In either case, however, there are strict limits to the extent to which this can be done (for example, under modern conditions, resistance from the trade unions). Likewise, Marx says:

> The rate of profit could even rise if a rise in the rate of surplus-value were accompanied by a substantial reduction in the value of the elements of constant, and particularly fixed, capital (i.e., plant and machinery). But in reality, as we have seen, the rate of profit will fall in the long run.[12]

At this stage Marx offers no explanation of how such a fall in the value of constant capital could come about. Later he suggests the increased productivity of labour as a factor which could reduce the value of the constant capital transferred to the product, despite the continued increase in its volume. Thus the same influences which tend to bring about a fall in the rate of profit could, paradoxically, moderate this tendency.

Other counter-acting factors mentioned by Marx are relative over-population, foreign trade and the increase in the capital stock. The former may occur because labour is displaced by machinery and thus becomes cheaper, leading to the growth of industries in which the organic composition of capital is relatively low such as luxury production. However such industries will also be subject to the general law for the organic composition of capital to increase. The existence of such industries, by acting on the average rate of profit, will tend to moderate its fall. It should be noted that Marx here is obviously thinking of productive labour (that which produces surplus value) and does not discuss the growth in the unproductive labour force (services, distribution, armed forces, etc.) which may occur. This will have to be supported out of the surplus or out of revenue and has nothing to do with the formation of the general rate of profit and thus with its tendency to decline.

Foreign trade may act to counter the rate of profit's falling tendency by increasing the rate of surplus value and cheapening the elements of constant capital. This is so, notably, where more advanced countries secure gains from trade with less developed ones in the shape of surplus profits. Capital invested in less developed countries, where the organic composition of capital is lower, will also yield a higher rate of profit than if it were invested in the capital-exporting country. In this way Marx comes near to formulating a theory of imperialism as the product of an attempt to stave off the operation of the tendency of the rate of profit to fall. The development of industry in certain less developed countries, mainly by multinational corporations, or in partnership with them to take advantage of cheap labour is a current example. Of course, all such counter-acting tendencies have their limits and in this case it is clear that the organic composition of capital will tend to rise in these less developed countries, wages will also rise and the rate of profit will come down nearer to that in the capital-satiated countries.

Marx also mentions, clearly for more detailed consideration later, the fact that with the progress of capitalism 'a portion of capital is calculated and applied only as interest-bearing capital.'[13] From a reading of this paragraph it would seem that Marx does not think that this has any bearing on the average rate of profit because it is paid out of the total surplus value. Rather does he mean that some capital is satisfied with a lower rate of interest in such investments as railways, without entering into the determination of the average rate of profit. This aggravates the contradictions in the system, drives the capitalists into an onslaught on the working class to raise the total of surplus value in opposition to the tendency of the rate of profit to fall and helps to account for such developments as wage controls, corporatism and fascism.

Once more, it should be remembered that Marx speaks of the declining rate of profit as a law of tendency 'i.e. a law whose absolute action is checked, retarded and weakened, by counteracting circumstances.'[14] The force with which it operates may vary at different times and in different countries, for example with the ups and downs of the economic cycle. More properly it operates in the same way as the law of value, not openly and on the surface, but nonetheless in a determinate way. Thus attempts to measure the rate of profit to show whether it has been falling or not are futile even if data can be obtained to enable the calculation to be made according to what Marx defined as the rate of profit (which was different from what the businessman or the accountant means by that term).

Marx's formulation of the law has been criticised for depending too exclusively upon the rising organic composition of capital and for not having an empirical basis. What is involved in such criticisms are completely opposite methods. Marx does not begin with what appears on the surface, but extracts what is the most essential, the driving force of the capitalist mode of production which is precisely 'self-expansion of capital, i.e. appropriation of surplus value, of profit.'[15] In this process part of surplus-value must be accumulated and there is a drive to increase the productivity of labour. At the same time, and inescapably, this tends to bring about a fall in the profit rate as well as depreciating the value of existing capital (for example, that part invested in means of production which become obsolete).

That there is an empirical trend for the organic composition of capital as defined by Marx to increase can scarcely be disputed as the outcome of the continuous application of science and technology to production. The question is that Marx proceeded dialectically from the abstract to the concrete; on the basis of the inner necessity of capital in its self-expansion he was able to establish in *Capital* Volume I that constant capital would grow proportionately to variable capital. The chapters on the tendency of the rate of profit to fall in Volume III are the working out of the General Law of Capital Accumulation in that volume, and Marx's rough draft in the *Grundrisse* shows that he had struggled with this problem for years and was probably not completely satisfied with the formulation in the manuscripts used by Engels in compiling Volume III. But there is a consistent chain of thought in all Marx's writings which suggests that he felt that the main problem had been solved at the theoretical and especially the methodological level. It is this which the economists fail to understand. They try to derive laws from surface phenomena; hence the old true saying, two economists, three opinions — and what is more, opinions which change as rapidly as a weather vane, as is to be seen in the present crisis.

Marx could not deduce such a law from observing what happened in the economy only. He began rather with what was wrong with the explanations offered by Adam Smith and Ricardo. In any case, as Marx showed, the counter-acting tendencies are part of the law-governed process and are normally powerful enough to ensure that the fall in the rate of profit does not appear on the surface at all; on the other hand, its remorseless operation contributes in a powerful way to the actual behaviour of the capitalist mode of production. In fact, it is impossible to understand this mode of production without a study of this law: that was the major point which came out of Marx's researches, carried out with the dialectical method.

As has been said, Marx went from the abstract to the more concrete. In working out this law he had to operate at a high level of abstraction, with 'unrealistic' assumptions, such as a 'chemically pure' capitalism. It was only in this way that the law could be exposed in all its force just as in a laboratory experiment certain conditions have to be kept constant in order that a particular reaction can be observed. Thus, for instance, Marx says nothing about the role of the State, trade unions, monopoly power or the use of force and fraud by capitalists to influence the rate of profit. Likewise, Marx says, there may be other factors which tend to push the rate of profit down, but he leaves them out of account in order to demonstrate the main one more clearly. He does this not because all these factors are of no importance in the real world of capitalism. On the contrary, it is because of the role of the State, the action of trade unions, the activities of monopolies, banks and multinational corporations can only be understood in relation to the laws of motion of the capitalist mode of production of which they are themselves products. High among these laws is precisely the tendency for the rate of profit to fall; Marx called it the most important law. The counter-acting tendencies form part of this law and are conscious or unconscious attempts to avert its effects, though it always exerts itself imperatively in the long run.

To repeat, then, the law is part of the self-expansion of capital taking place dialectically. As Marx puts it: 'The average profit does not obtain as a directly established fact, but rather is to be determined as an end result of the equalisation of opposite fluctuations.'[16] The profit rate at any given time in a particular capitalist country is thus a manifestation of the unity and conflict of opposites; out of their interpenetration comes the predominant tendency at the given moment. This is not a stable rate because it is all the time subject to the forces tending to drive the rate of profit down as well as to counteracting tendencies working in the opposite direction. It is the product of contradictions, giving rise to new contradictions, not to a state of equilibrium and repose. Marx was always hostile to the harmonists and respectful towards Ricardo who, although a supporter of capitalism, fearlessly revealed its contradictions. It is only from a dialectical standpoint that the law can be grasped and used as a tool of analysis of an actual, contradictory and dynamically changing economic situation. Any other point of view would mean turning Marx into one of the harmonists he so despised. He saw the law as expressing all that was contradictory in capitalism; driving it towards convulsions, crises and self-destruction.

A number of other aspects of Marx's exposition of the tendency for the rate of profit to fall remain to be considered but they will best be dealt with in relation to this latter point: the crisis of capitalism. Before leaving this question, however, it is worth pointing out that the formation of an average rate of profit and even the falling rate of profit have suffered neglect or misinterpretation even by self-styled Marxists. Much more interest has been displayed in what came to be called 'the realisation problem'. This was true, for instance, of Lenin's early theoretical contributions to Marxism in the 1890s (to be found in the first four volumes of his *Collected Works*)[17] as well as of Rosa Luxemburg in her famous book *The Accumulation of Capital* and those who engaged in polemic with them. It was true again during the period of theoretical blight for which Stalinism was responsible and continued under the pressure of the predominant bourgeois theories such as those of J.M. Keynes after World War II.

It was, of course, true that the commodities embodying surplus value have to be sold in order that surplus value can be realised and

DECLINING RATE OF PROFIT

make its contribution to the rate of profit. It was an essential part of Marx's argument, to which reference will be made later, that a fall in the rate of profit is accompanied by an increase in the mass of surplus value. Realisation comprised what Marx called 'the second act of the process'. As he wrote:

> The entire mass of commodities, i.e. the total product, including the portion which replaces the constant and variable capital, and that representing surplus value, must be sold. If this is not done or done only in part, or only at prices below the prices of production, the labourer has indeed been exploited but his exploitation is not realised as such for the capitalist, and thus can be bound up with a total or partial failure to realise the surplus-value pressed out of him, indeed even with the total or partial loss of capital. The conditions of direct exploitation, and those of realising it are not identical. They diverge not only in place and time, but also logically. The first are only limited by the productive power of society, the latter by the proportional relation of the various branches of production and the consumer power of society. But this last-named is not determined either by the absolute productive power, or by the absolute consumer power, but by the consumer power based on antagonistic conditions of distribution, which reduce the consumption of the bulk of society to a minimum varying within more or less narrow limits. It is further more restricted by the tendency to accumulate, the drive to expand capital and produce surplus value on an extended scale. This is a law for capitalist production, imposed by incessant revolutions in the methods of production themselves, by the depreciations of existing capital always bound up with them, by the general competitive struggle and the need to improve production and expand its scale merely as a means of self-preservation and under penalty of ruin. The market must, therefore, be continually extended, so that its interrelations and the conditions regulating them assume more amd more the form of a natural law working independently of the producer, and become ever more uncontrollable. This internal contradiction seeks to resolve itself through expansion of the outlying field of production.[18]

In the context of the discussion of the tendency for the rate of profit to fall, the dialectical approach expressed in passages like the one just quoted gives no licence for abstracting a so-called 'realisation problem' from the whole network of capitalist contradictions in which the falling rate of profit plays a central role. This will be the theme of the next chapter.

Notes

[1] See previous chapter 'Marx on the formation of an average rate of profit'. It is worth emphasising that the rate of profit in question is the general, or average, rate of profit on the total productive social capital. It therefore determines the aggregate income of the bourgeoisie as a whole and ensures its solidarity in the face of the working class, the producers of surplus value. Marx is thus dealing with profit in its purest form, that is, as surplus value and before its division among the different sections of the ruling class. Under the capitalist mode of production the average rate of profit acts as a regulator of production.

[2] *Theories of Surplus Value*, Part Two, p.467. This sums up a lengthy critique of the two authors.

[3] *Grundrisse* (Pelican ed.), p.749; 'The *real barrier* of capitalist production is *capital itself*,' *Capital*, Volume III, p.245.

[4] *Capital* Volume III, p.210.

[5] *Grundrisse* (Pelican ed.), pp. 762-3.

[6] *ibid*.

[7] *Capital*, Volume III, p.213.

[8] *ibid*, p.220.

[9] *ibid*, p.221.

[10] *ibid*, p.225-226.

[11] *ibid*, p.226. An important aspect of the declining rate of profit is how it is influenced by the attempts of the individual capitalist to escape is operation by adopting new methods, so-called 'innovations'. This enables him to sell below market prices while still making more than the average rate of profit until competitors catch up. The Austro-American economist J.A. Schumpeter built a whole theory of economic development in opposition to Marxism on this simple point, see his two-volume opus *Business Cycles*.

[12] *Capital*, Volume III, p.225.

[13] *ibid*, p.235.

[14] *ibid*, p.229. Also 'the same influences which tend to make the rate of profit fall, also moderate the effects of this tendency', p.231 and 'the law acts only as a tendency. And it is only under certain circumstances and only after long periods that is effects become strikingly pronounced', p.233.

[15] *Capital*, Volume III, p.246.

[16] *Capital*, Volume III, p.360; it is characteristic that Marx makes this quite fundamental point when he is explaining something else, namely how profit (surplus value) is divided.

[17] There was, of course, a good reason why Lenin should have taken up this angle since he was engaged in a polemic with the Narodniks who claimed that capitalism could not develop in Russia. Lenin bases himself on the reproduction schemas in *Capital* Volume II to show that this view was wrong.

[18] *Capital*, Volume III, pp.239-240.

Chapter 8

Marx and the theory of capitalist crisis

The new stage of capitalist crisis, now the driving force for revolution on an international scale, gives a new relevance to Marx's *Capital*. It is not enough, however, to claim that his analysis is being confirmed; we need to examine it afresh in the light of contemporary developments, determine its inadequacy and carry forward into our time the task Marx set himself over a century ago. First, however, it is necessary to know how Marx approached the theory of crisis by a study of his work and that is the aim of the present chapter: an ambitious one which can clearly only be carried out in a tentative way.

Marx's purported theory of crisis has been a subject of controversy ever since the second and third volumes of *Capital* appeared. It is understood that we are here referring only to interpretations of Marx's writings and not the various popular and often spurious 'Marxist' theories of crisis. A number of different views have been expressed about whether Marx had a theory of crisis at all. There is no chapter or heading in *Capital* with such a title and that may seem surprising at first sight. Views on the question may be summarised as follows:

1) That there is a more or less complete theory of crisis in Marx's work which has only to be extracted and put together;

2) That Marx had not fully worked out a theory of crisis, but in the event left only the outline and notes for such a theory scattered in different parts of his work;

3) That the theory of crisis forms an integral part of Marx's work but remains incomplete and thus has to be interpreted in the light of the method of *Capital* and Marx's scientific analysis of the capitalist mode of production as a whole.

The last of these views seems to be the soundest. Certainly Marx did not write out a theory of crisis in the manner of bourgeois economists. For the latter crises are an aberration which really should not happen at all, so they give rise to separate chapters in their textbooks and a special branch of economics concerned with what is often euphemistically described as 'the business cycle'. Study of crises is based on the notion that if their cause can be discovered then a crisis-free capitalism can be developed. Crises are thus seen as untoward events, disturbing an otherwise harmonious progress towards equilibrium. The theory merely becomes an exercise in totting up the innumerable possible causes, taking refuge in sophisticated models employing mathematical and econometric techniques and throwing in a mass of empirical data to provide some contact with reality. When it comes to explaining crises the upshot is complete theoretical bankruptcy. It is, for example, impossible to find in the literature of economics a convincing theoretical explanation of the world economic depression of the 1930s. Although there are now vastly more economists around, many in official positions in national governments and international organisations, they are completely at sea in explaining the crisis now gripping the capitalist world, let alone in prescribing remedies.

Marxism is not a superior form of economics with more correct answers. It is wholly different methodologically and scientifically in that it sees the capitalist mode of production as an historically determinate system, driving irrevocable to crisis and destined to be overthrown by the revolutionary class it produces. From that standpoint a separate theory of crisis was not required; for Marx crisis inhered in the capitalist mode of production from the time that it came onto the scene. In fact he introduces it in *Capital* Volume I at an early stage in the course of analysing the commodity and money.

Thus commodity exchange involves two separate and antithetical acts, sales and purchase. The seller receives money in exchange for the commodity, 'but no one is obliged to purchase because he has just sold'.

> To say that these two independent and antithetical acts have an intrinsic unity [writes Marx], are essentially one, is the same as to say that this intrinsic oneness expresses itself in an external antithesis. If

the interval of time between the two complementary phases of the complete metamorphosis of a commodity becomes too great, if the split between the sale and the purchase becomes too pronounced, the intimate connection between them, their oneness asserts itself by producing — a crisis. The antithesis, use-vale and value; the contradictions that private labour is bound to manifest itself as social labour, that a particularised concrete kind of labour has to pass for abstract human labour; the contradiction between the personification of objects and the representation of persons by things; all these antitheses and contradictions, which are immanent in commodities, assert themselves, and develop their modes of motion, in the antithetical phases of the metamorphosis of a commodity. These modes therefore imply the possibility, and no more than the possibility of crises. The conversion of this mere possibility into a reality is the result of a long series of relations, that, from our present standpoint of simple circulation, have as yet no existence.[1]

It is clear, therefore, that for Marx the *possibility* of crisis was to be found in the basic contradiction between use-value and exchange value (or value), concrete and abstract labour, purchase and sale, the commodity and money, the very stuff of *Capital*. In his notes criticising Ricardo's theory of accumulation Marx explains how 'the most complicated phenomenon of capitalist production — the world market crisis' is denied by the economists because they deny 'this first condition of capitalist production, namely, that the product must be a commodity and therefore express itself as money and undergo the proces of metamorphosis'.[2]

In this metamorphosis is contained the antithesis between exchange-value and use-value and the transformation of the commodity into money as an essential and necessary form of its existence. It is not a question of products but of commodities and of money which is independent of commodities and yet an essential aspect of them. Again, the sale of a commodity does not oblige the seller to purchase another with the money he receives, so the chain of commodity circulation can be broken. In the same way, if commodities are produced which cannot go through the metamorphosis into money the possibility of crisis exists. In these transactions money is not simply an intermediary, a neutral thing, but plays a role of its own. 'Money,' writes Marx, 'is not only "the medium by which the exchange is effected" but at the same time the medium by which the exchange of product with product is divided into two acts, which are independent of each other, and separate in time and space.'[3] As he says later, under the capitalist mode of production direct production for personal needs does not take place:

> Crisis arises from the impossibility to sell. The difficulty of transforming the *commodity* — the particular product of individual labour — into its opposite, money, i.e. abstract general social labour, lies in the fact that *money* is not the particular product of individual labour, and that the person who has effected a sale, who therefore has commodities in the form of money is not compelled to buy again at once, to transform the money again into a particular product of individual labour.[4]

If the possibility of crisis arises from the separation of purchase and sale, which could not happen under a barter economy, the crisis itself 'is nothing but the forcible assertion of the unity of phases of the production process which have become independent of each other'.[5] Of course, in these notes Marx simplifies considerably and emphasises that he only intends to show how commodity production itself contains the possibility of crisis, or as he puts it 'the most abstract form of crisis'.[6]

In writing these passages against Ricardo, and in other places, Marx was clearly impressed by the periodical crises occurring in his own time, notably those of 1857 and 1866. They were preceded by speculation on the commodity markets and were heralded by financial panics, a mad rush out of commodities into money. Everything went well as long as commodities were being transformed into money and money being re-transformed into commodities, i.e. the circulation of capital was taking place through these metamorphoses. As Marx puts it: 'This intertwining and coalescence of the process of reproduction or circulation of different capitals is on the one hand necessitated by the division of labour, on the other it is accidental; and thus the definition of the content of crisis is already fuller.'[7] In fact the relations between the different producers and merchants through whose hands the commodities passed were governed not so much by cash payments as by credit, by promises to pay which depended upon confidence and the completion of various transactions as expected by each participant. If one or another could not replace his capital this would rebound onto the others because of the complexity of the chain of mutual claims and obligations, sales and purchases through which the possibility of crisis could develop into actuality.[8] Although Marx does not deal with it at this point, this brings onto the scene the possibility of crises arising in the banking and credit system. His main purpose is to emphasise the possibility and actual predisposition to crisis of the capitalist process of reproduction analysed more fully elsewhere.

These passages in *Theories of Surplus Value* show Marx's thought in course of elaboration. He worries the basic concept of the division of purchase and sale and shows how this can lead to a crisis in the means of payment but he rejects the latter as a cause of crises. Showing how crisis can arise, or establishing the general conditions for crisis, is not the same thing as tracing causes. On the causes of crisis Marx remains circumspect and to follow his thinking more closely we have to turn to other sections of his work.[9]

In Volume I of *Capital* he assumes the existence of periodical crises without venturing far into their explanation. 'The life of modern industry,' he writes, 'becomes a series of periods of moderate activity, prosperity, overproduction, crisis and stagnation.'[10] He insists that causes must be sought in the system of production and circulation to which capitalism gives rise and not in the expansion or contraction of credit, 'which is a mere symptom of the periodic changes of the industrial cycle'. He shows how the ups and downs of industry bring into existence 'an industrial reserve army' growing in periods of depression and diminishing in periods of prosperity. It is in Volume II that Marx develops new concepts for the analysis of crisis following from the alteration in perspective in this volume and its successor. The subject now is the reproduction and circulation of the aggregate social capital as explained in the important introduction to Part III of Volume II. The focus is no longer on the individual capitalist but on the self-expansion of capital as a whole.

The individual capital now forms but a part of the aggregate social capital. 'The movement of the social capital consists of the totality of the movements of its individualised fractional parts, the turnovers of the individual capitals. Just as the metamorphosis of the individual commodity is a link in the series of metamorphoses of the commodity-world — the circulation of commodities — so the metamorphosis of the individual capital, its turnover is a link in the circuit described by social capital,' Marx writes.[11] The emphasis is now on the process of reproduction of capital as a whole while in the earlier part of the work it had been on some individual capital. 'However,' Marx points out, 'the circuits of individual capitals interwine, presuppose and necessitate one another, and form, precisely in this interlacing, the movement of the total social capital.'[12] From this standpoint it was also possible for Marx to distinguish more sharply the distinctive features of money capital.

Money capital is necessarily the first form in which every capital appears upon the scene. A portion of the advanced capital value must, in addition, constantly appear and re-appear in order to set productive capital in motion, its proportion depending on the scale of production and the length of time taken in turning over the capital. In short, 'the entire advanced capital-value . . . must be bought over and over again with money'.[13]

In other words, what was true of the individual capital (the antithesis and unity of sale and purchase dealt with in Volume I) is also true, on the scale of the whole economy, of the aggregate social capital. There is consequently need for money capital on the scale required by the growth of production and the period of turnover of capital. Hence the development of banking and credit and the substitution of joint stock companies for the individual capitalist and consequently a further possibility of crisis through disturbances in the money market. Production on a larger scale also means that labour-power and means of production are required, tying up money in capital for a greater or lesser period, but not immediately producing commodities which can be converted into money. Thus a further hiatus between purchase and sale, this time on the scale of the aggregate social capital.

To go behind the question of the reproduction and circulation of capital as a whole Marx had to make an important breakthrough in theory. This could only be done on the basis of the scientific concepts already developed in Volume I: the law of value, the two-fold nature of the commodity and of labour, the distinction between constant and variable capital and the source of surplus-value. All these discoveries had to be carried forward to make possible others and to contribute towards the understanding of the capitalist mode of production as a regime of crisis. This mode of production produces commodities: the commodity contains surplus value — the new value created by the workers — as well as constant capital and variable capital. The compelling motive of this system is thus the extraction and realisation of surplus value through the conversion of commodities into money. The capitalist has then to reconvert the money into productive capital by renewed purchase of the elements of constant and variable capital on the market. This assumes other capitalists producing these elements of capital and workers, having nothing to sell but their labour power, receiving wages spent on consumption. Marx shows how this takes place, assuming only capitalists and workers and the exchange of commodities at their values, first of all under conditions of simple reproduction where values are simply replaced and there is no accumulation.

This assumption, as Marx adds, is an abstraction since capitalism cannot work without accumulation. However, simple reproduction is contained in reproduction on an extended scale, where accumulation does take place, and the simplification enables Marx to explain the process of reproduction as such without the complicating though vital element of accumulation.[14]

Marx's major breakthrough here was the division of total social production into two major departments: Department I producing means of production and Department II producing articles of individual consumption.[15] The aggregate capital in each department can then be divided (as with the individual commodity) into three parts: variable capital, constant capital and surplus value. Department I has thus to produce means of production for its own consumption as well as for Department II while Department II produces means of individual consumption for the capitalist and worker in both departments. We will not follow the lengthy explanations and mathematical examples which Marx provides to illustrate the relationships between these two departments. It is here that what he had earlier described as the intertwining of the different individual capitals takes on a more concrete form. The process involves the constant transformation of money into commodities and commodities into money and the extraction and realisation of surplus value if it is to continue smoothly.

Under expanded reproduction part of the surplus value is used to increase production. This means first of all the expansion of Department I producing means of production setting in motion an increased demand for variable capital and thus production of consumer goods. At the same time, the accumulated surplus value, with corresponding amounts of money capital, should correspond to the value of the new means of production in one or both departments. Clearly, if reproduction is to take place over time a definite proportionality must be maintained, or imposed. As Marx says about these relationships:

> The fact that the production of commodities is the general form of capitalist production implies the role which money is playing in it not only as a medium of circulation, but also as money-capital, and engenders certain conditions of normal exchange peculiar to this mode of production and therefore of the normal course of reproduction, whether it be on a simple or an extended scale — conditions which change into so many conditions of abnormal movement, *into so many possibilities of crisis*, since a balance is itself an accident owing to the spontaneous nature of this production. [Emphasis added][16]

or again

> The constant supply of labour-power on the part of working class I, the re-conversion of a portion of commodity-capital I into the money-form of variable capital, the replacement of a portion of commodity-capital II by natural elements of constant capital IIc — all these necessary premises demand one another, but they are brought about by a very complicated process, including three processes of circulation which occur independently of one another but intermingle. *This process is so complicated that it offers ever so many occasions for running abnormally*. [Emphasis added][17]

It has to be emphasised that capitalism does not produce products but *commodities* and that its aim and compelling motive is the snatching of surplus value and its accumulation. These are the dominating motive forces of the process of expanded reproduction. There is no mechanism other than the spontaneous interplay of capitals on the market and the forces of competition to keep the whole process moving and in balance. As Marx says, 'this process is so complicated that it offers ever so many occasions for running abnormally'. In other words, lack of proportionality in the process of reproduction may be a precipitating cause of crisis or may result from a cause produced elsewhere. Some Marxists, notably Rosa Luxemburg, have taken Marx's reproduction schema (the division into two Departments and of each department into variable and constant capital and surplus value) as the starting point for the theory of crisis. What they claim, in short, is that the conditions for continued reproduction cannot be maintained, or not without continued possibilities for realisation outside the capitalist system, i.e. in colonies. Without going into what has become a rather arid controversy here, it can be said that Marx did not intend the schemas to be a model of the real world. They were essentially an abstraction to illustrate certain fundamental aspects of the reproduction process — but only *certain* aspects. These passages from Volume II cannot be understood apart from what Marx had previously written about the possibility of crisis existing in the most general form in the separation of purchase and sale from the theory of the tendency of the rate of profit to decline. Certainly Marx never hinted in Volume II that anything inherent in the reproduction schemas *alone* could cause the breakdown and collapse of capitalism. For his mature views on this question we surely have to turn to other parts of his work and this will be done in the concluding part of this chapter.

What Marx says about the division of purchase and sale remains fundamental to his whole analysis of the capitalist process of production and reproduction and thus of the crisis. It is contained in the question of realisation as its essence: i.e. 'the entire mass of commodities . . . must be sold', if not, out of the contradiction between production and consumption, crisis inevitably results. Constantly expanding production thus requires constantly growing markets, a struggle between the capitalists themselves to realise surplus value, if necessarily at each other's expense. The failure of the market to expand brings about what Marx calls the crisis of overproduction.

The term overproduction, however, needs to be carefully defined. In a sense, Marx points out, there is constant *underproduction* under capitalism in the sense that the needs of the producers themselves, not to speak of the reserve army of labour, go unsatisfied even in periods of 'prosperity'.[18] That is because there are not enough products to satisfy these needs; but capitalism produces commodities — entirely different things. The character of this mode of production is determined by the fact that the direct producers have nothing to sell but their labour power and can only sell it as long as the purchasers hope to be able to appropriate, in the sale of the product of their labour, the unpaid labour or surplus value, which they produce. In other words production is carried on in order to make a profit and will cease more or less immediately if profits fall below the average, signifying an overproduction of *commodities*.

It is in this respect that Marx speaks of the bourgeois mode of production as containing 'within itself a barrier to the free development of the productive forces, a barrier which comes to the surface in crises, and, in particular, in *over-production* — the basic phenomenon in crises'.[19] If accumulation is carried beyond a certain point, under given conditions, it will result in too much capital (potential production of commodities) seeking for a share of surplus value and driving down the rate of profit. Although the whole purpose of the capitalist mode of production is the accumulation of capital, the more it is successful in this the more it brings about the conditions for crisis. In that sense every boom is only the creation of surplus capital leading the way for overproduction. All sorts of contradictions and struggles are contained in this process which cannot be gone into here. As Marx sums it up: 'Since the aim of capital is not to minister to certain wants, but to produce profit, and since it accomplishes this purpose by methods which adapt the mass of production to the scale of production, not vice versa, a rift must continually ensue between the limited dimensions of consumption under capitalism and a production which forever tends to exceed this imminent barrier.'[20]

Put still more concisely: 'The *real barrier* of capitalist production is *capital itself*.'[21] It was this thought which haunted Ricardo, that capitalism had no way of escape but was historically doomed. It is a point which Marx makes many times in different forms, that the self-expansion of capital leads to contradictions. Only 'a general devaluation or destruction of capital,' the destruction of productive forces, provides again the conditions for renewed accumulation.[22] 'The contradiction of the capitalist mode of production,' writes Marx, 'lies precisely in its tendency towards an absolute development of the productive forces, which continually come into conflict with the specific *conditions* of production in which capital moves, and alone can move.'[23] Even a period of expanded reproduction such as capitalism enjoyed following the immense destruction of capital values as a result of World War II and the depression which had preceded it could only prepare the way for a new crisis of historic dimensions (and not merely the old-style cyclical crisis). The break with Marx of the various schools of revisionists under the pressure of the boom was based on the view (implicit or explicit in their theories) that capitalism had changed and that *capital* (the social relationship) no longer constituted a barrier to the development of the productive forces. These were impressionistic views based upon appearances, capitulating to those bourgeois theories derived from the fetishised forms of capitalism itself; a decline into vulgar economics and apologetics for bourgeois society. 'It should not astonish us,' Marx once wrote, 'that vulgar economy feels particularly at home in the estranged outward appearances of economic relations in which these *prima facie* absurd and perfect contradictions appear and that these relations seem the more self-evident the more their internal relationships are concealed from it, although they are understandable to the popular mind. But all science would be superfluous if the outward appearances and the essence of things directly coincided.'[24] This may stand as an epitaph on those schools of revisionists who told us during the boom that Marx was out of date and should be rejected or 'improved' in the light of Keynesianism and other fashionable theories.

One of the favourite revisions of Marx to which such theories led was the claim that he was an underconsumptionist. This fitted in very well with Keynesianism which was only a sophisticated form of underconsumptionism, saying, in effect, that crises were a result of lack of effective demand and thus that if demand in some form (based on government spending on public works, armaments or space research) could be injected into the system expansion could be maintained (the so-called 'full employment' policies now thrown on the scrap-heap when, in theory, they should be most applicable!).

An examination of Marx's theory shows that it is completely scientific and has no place for such superficiality. If we refer to the division of production into the two departments it is obvious, for example, that the majority of workers cannot consume their own products whether they are steel ingots or Rolls Royces. As we have seen, Marx says that in a sense, under the capitalist mode of production, there is always underproduction: wants are not satisfied because capital is only interested in demand backed by ability to pay. By definition part of the product of labour, surplus value, goes into hands other than those of the direct producers so, once more, the workers cannot buy back what they produce. And it is useless to see a way out by raising wages or re-distributing income because this merely hits profits and thus the capitalists' incentive to produce and to accumulate. In any case they employ workers not to give them a job, or to permit them to consume, but to extract surplus value from their unpaid labour.[25]

Marx's tersest and most effective dismissal of the notion of 'under-consumption' comes in *Capital* Volume II where he writes:

> It is sheer tautology to say that crises are caused by the scarcity of effective consumption, or of effective consumers. The capitalist system does not know any other modes of consumption than effective ones, except that of *sub forma pauperis* or of the swindler. That commodities are unsaleable means only that no effective purchasers have been found for them, i.e. consumers (since commodities are bought in the final analysis for productive or individual consumption). But if one were to attempt to give this tautology the semblance of a profounder justification by saying that the working class receives too small a portion of its own product and the evil would be remedied as soon as it receives a larger share of it and its wages increase in consequence, one could remark that crises are always prepared by precisely a period in which wages rise generally and the working class actually gets a larger share of that part of annual product which is intended for consumption. From the point of view of those advocates of sound and 'simple'(!) common sense, such a period should rather remove the crisis. It appears, then, that capitalist production comprises conditions independent of good or bad will, conditions which permit the working class to enjoy that relative prosperity only momentarily, and at that always only as the harbinger of a coming crisis.[26]

This is very relevant to developments over the past decade. The growth of working class consumption standards, within definite confined limits, during the boom, only prepared the way for crisis, e.g. by raising labour costs, strengthening the working class as a class in resistance to capitalism and jeopardising profits. Thus far from the crisis revealing the need to raise consumption as a way out, exactly the opposite is the case. Keynesiansim is now discredited and the apologists for capitalism call not for the raising of consumption but for the cutting of living standards, social services, public spending on education, welfare, etc. The real nature of

CAPITALIST CRISIS

capital is thus nakedly exposed and with it the revolutionary confrontation between the classes.

There is no contradiction between this passage, with its unequivocal condemnation of the theory of underconsumption and the equally famous one in Volume III in the course of which Marx claims that: 'The ultimate reason for all real crises always remains the poverty and restricted consumption of the masses as opposed to the drive of capitalist production to develop the productive forces as though only the absolute consuming power of society constituted the limit.'[27] This 'ultimate reason' is only another way of looking at capital itself, i.e. the relationship between the owners of the means of production and the working class. It is the other side of what Marx spoke of as under-production. Capitalism is incapable of raising the consuming levels of the masses beyond certain limits, and when it does so, as we have just seen, it only creates the conditions for crisis. The danger in underconsumption theories is both that they are scientifically wrong — they are unable to explain how capitalism works — and they lead to reformist political conclusions, creating the illusions that a crisis-free capitalism is possible based on raising consumer standards. This was the road followed in the past by people like John Strachey in Britain and Louis Corey in the United States who, after attempting a Marxist analysis of the crisis of the 1930s, succumbed to underconsumptionism and became orthodox Keynesians, the former as a Minister in the Attlee government.[28]

Of course, we are far from having presented a full account of Marx's theory of crisis, but enough has been said, perhaps, to encourage a study of his texts and the carrying out of further work on the subject in line with current political tasks. Before concluding, however, it is necessary to return again to the declining rate of profit dealt with in the previous chapter. This question has not been forgotten; on the contrary, it has always been in the background and its significance can now be more fully appreciated. In fact, when Marx talks about the real barrier to capitalist production being capital itself it is precisely this law which he has in mind. The tendency for the rate of profit to fall is an inevitable consequence of the capitalist process of development; it is the other side of the growth in the productivity of labour brought about by accumulation and thus the rise in the organic composition of capital. Together with the counter-acting forces it brings into play it, like the law of value, operates as a blind law of nature governing the whole process. If this law is analysed, however, it can be seen that it is also another aspect of the self-expansion of capital, of the continuous chain of purchase and sale, of the transformation of commodities (including labour-power) into money and of money into commodities. In the striving of capitalists to overcome the operation of this law, weaker capitalists are driven to the wall, the concentration and centralisation of capital goes on apace. Capitalists in each country strive for markets abroad and seek colonies and spheres of investment (i.e. imperialism) to counteract the tendency. Insofar as, in seeking to oppose the operation of the law, they have to produce at lower cost, this means the further substitution of constant for variable capital and only contributes to further pressure on the profit rate. The drive for profit is the other side of the need to realise the commodities produced, to turn them into money. Note that Marx emphasises as a cause of crisis the fact that a purchase does not lead necessarily to a sale. Even if the commodity is sold and realisation takes place on the scale of social capital as a whole, this does not mean that the tendency for the rate of profit to fall ceases to operate. Capitalism is thus crisis-prone from two sides, from that of the need to realise the commodity-product and from that of the tendency for th rate of profit to fall.

At the same time, the whole complexity of the relationships betweem the multitudinous individual capitals, as demonstrated in the two departments of production and their relations, raises the possibility of disproportions as a source of 'overproduction'. It always has to be borne in mind that the capitalist mode of production produces *commodities*, not products to satisfy human wants. The contradictions it contains expose it to crisis at many points. The immense complexity of the chain linking production and sale, with its counterpart in money transactions and credit relations, adds to the fragility of the system as a whole, making it susceptible to all kinds of shocks. Apart from laying out the general conditions for crisis, their possibility, Marx is cautious about specifying any one or a number of *causes* as being decisive. Moreover, in studying his writings on the subject of crisis it is necessary to take into account the level of abstraction at which he

CAPITALIST CRISIS

proceeds (there is also observation and comment on contemporary crises, of a different order from those we confront today). Marx does not provide a recipe book but a scientific guide to knowledge which has to be applied and built upon.

Finally, it should be recalled that Marx is frequently writing about the recurrent crises of a cyclical character rather than about the crisis of capitalism as a whole. It is clear, however, that he assumes that the capitalist mode of production is historically doomed and was driving towards breakdown or collapse. As he put it in the *Grundrisse*:

> The growing incompatibility between the productive development of society and its hitherto existing relations of production expresses itself in bitter contradictions, crises, spasms. The violent destruction of capital not by relations external to it, but rather as a condition of its self-preservation, is the most striking form in which advice is given to it to be gone and to give room to a higher state of social production . . . These contradictions lead to explosions, cataclysms, crises, in which by momentaneous suspension of labour and annihilation of a great portion of capital the latter is violently led back to the point where it is enabled to go on fully employing its productive power without committing suicide. Yet, these regularly recurring catastrophes lead to their repetition on a higher scale, and finally to its violent overthrow.[29]

In this epoch Marx's words assume a prophetic character.

Notes

[1] *Capital*, Volume I (Allen and Unwin ed.), pp. 87-88.
[2] *Theories of Surplus Value*, Part II, pp. 492-535 contains Marx's most sustained discussion of crises, aimed against Ricardo and his school who denied the possibility of general overproduction. These notes have been used for the present chapter, but a good deal more can be extracted from them.
[3] *ibid.*, p.504 — the quote is from Ricardo. In fact, as Marx says, '*money* is an essential aspect of the commodity and . . . in the process of metamorphosis it is independent of the original form of the commodity', p.502.
[4] *ibid.*, p.509.
[5] *ibid*. Again: 'Crisis is the forcible establishment of unity between elements that have become independent and the enforced separation from one another of elements which are essentially one', *ibid.*, p.513.
[6] The *content* of any particular crisis thus remains to be determined; the abstract form of crisis is not its cause. Marx lists a number of possible causes.
[7] *ibid.*, p.511
[8] *ibid.*, p.511
[9] But see his notes 'On the Forms of Crisis' *ibid.*, pp. 513-517.
[10] *Capital*, Volume I p.455.
[11] *Capital*, Volume II, pp. 351-352.
[12] *ibid.*, p.353.

[13] *ibid.*, p.355.
[14] *ibid.*, Ch.XX *passim*.
[15] *ibid.*, p.395
[16] *ibid.*, p.495
[17] *ibid.*, p.495
[18] *Theories of Surplus Value*, Part II. p.527. 'The word *overproduction* in itself leads to error. So long as the most urgent needs of a large part of society are not satisfied, or *only* the most immediate needs are satisfied, there can of course be absolutely no talk of *over-production of products* — in the sense that the amount of products is excessive in relation to the need for them. On the contrary, it must be said that on the basis of capitalist production, there is constant *underproduction* in this sense. The limits to production are set by the profit of the capitalist and in no way by the needs of the producers. But over-production of products and over-production of *commodities* are two entirely different things.'
[19] *ibid.*, p.528
[20] *Capital*, Volume III, p.251
[21] *ibid.*, p.245. 'The fact that bourgeois production is compelled by its own immanent laws, on the one hand, to develop the productive forces as if production did not take place on a narrow restricted social foundation, while on the other hand, it can develop these forces only within these narrow limits, *is the deepest and most hidden cause of crises*, of the crying contradictions within which bourgeois production is carried on and which, even at a cursory glance, reveal it as only a transitional, historical form.' *Theories of Surplus Value*, Part III, p.84 (emphasis added).
[22] *Grundrisse* (Pelican edition), p.446.
[23] *Capital*, Volume III, p.252.
[24] *ibid.*, p.797.
[25] 'What the workers in fact produce, is surplus value. So long as they produce it, they are able to consume. As soon as they cease to produce it, their consumption ceases, because their production ceases.' *Theories of Surplus Value*, Part II, p.519.
[26] *Capital*, Volume II pp. 410-411.
[27] *Capital*, Volume III, pp. 472-473
[28] While still claiming to be Marxists Strachey wrote *The Nature of Capitalist Crisis* and Corey, *The Decline of American Capitalism* (both containing concessions to underconsumption).
[29] *Grundrisse*, p.750.

Chapter 9

Marx and the theory of rent

What the theory of rent sets out to do is to explain why and how, under the capitalist mode of production, landed property is in itself a source of revenue, acquiring as a right part of the surplus value extracted from the working class. At one time the revenue from landed property was socially honourable and respected while interest-bearing capital carried the stench of usury and even of sin. For the rising bourgeoisie of Britain in the late eighteenth and early nineteenth century, however, rent was the unjustified and unearned income of the landed aristocracy whose predominance it was challenging. The theory of rent developed by Adam Smith and David Ricardo, the leaders of the classical school of political economy, was a battle slogan showing, in the words of the latter, that the interests of the landowners are always and everywhere opposed to those of the rest of the community. But as the bourgeoisie grew richer and won social acceptance from the old ruling class of landowners and their coalescence began the question of rent dropped out of the picture. Rent was now collected as often by new-rich bourgeois as by authentic scions of noble houses who now found their way onto the boards of banks and business houses. Both now faced a common enemy and threat to private property in general from the working class and the labour movement. The less said about rent, therefore, the better. The earlier bourgeois antipathy to rent and its receivers was kept feebly alive by Fabians like Bernard Shaw or people with one-track minds like the once famous Henry George, appealing to a dwindling audience of smaller capitalists and middle-class people.

It is nevertheless worthwhile to examine how Marx saw the

question of rent both for theoretical and practical political reasons. Rent is still a monstrous drain on the productivity of social labour, but it can only be collected because the working class is exploited as the producers of surplus value. Marx had to spend a good deal of time on the question of rent, first of all because of the central place it occupied in the teachings of the political economists and the errors in their particular theories of rent. He insisted, at the same time, that it was of secondary importance. As he put it:

> Capitalist production is based on the antithesis of two factors, materialised labour and living labour. Capitalists and wage-labourers are the sole functionaries and factors of production whose relationships and confrontation arise from the nature of the capitalist mode of production.[1]

The capitalist confronts the worker as the direct owner of surplus value and if he has to hand over part of it to the landowner that is not at all because the latter is a necessary agent for capital but rather a parasitic excrescence, as the militant ideologists of the rising bourgeoisie were not slow to point out. Landed property had, however, played a necessary role in the appearance and extension of capitalist property relations. Feudal in origin, it was transformed by the action of capital upon it. There could, indeed, have been no capitalist development without the formation of modern landed property.[2]

In Britain this took place in a really revolutionary way with the enclosures of the open fields and commons and the destruction of the peasantry as a class. This was part of the process Marx called 'primitive accumulation', bringing into being a landless proletariat while concentrating landed property into its typical English and Scottish form of the large landed estate leased out to tenant farmers.[3] This opened the way for capitalist agriculture and the so-called agrarian revolution of the eighteenth century which provided the food for a growing urban population based on factory industry manned by the new industrial working class. Thus without landed property the accumulation of capital could not have taken place and yet it still retained something of a feudal aura with the squireachy continuing to play a leading role in the countryside into the twentieth century. Some feudal tenures even continued into the late 1920s. In Marx's day, however, he could say:

English conditions are the only ones in which *modern landownership*, i.e., landownership which has been *modified* by capitalist production, has been adequately developed. For the modern — the capitalist — mode of production, the English view is here the classical view.[4]

If the fact that the capitalist, having extracted surplus value from the worker, had to share it with a third party, the landlord, was of secondary importance for Marx, he was nonetheless sure that for the sake of completeness, and because of the role of landed property in the transition from feudalism to capitalism, it was necessary to include rent in his analysis.[5] The manuscripts relating to the question were brought together by Engels to form Part VI of the third volume of *Capital*, running to close on 200 pages in the English translation. There are signs of incompleteness and duplication and a good deal of the text comprises the working out of numerical examples for different cases under which rent arose. Moreover, the section ends with an historical survey of the origins of capitalist ground-rent which might have been more logically placed after the introduction to the subject (Ch.XXXVII). In addition, Marx wrote extensive commentaries on the theory of rent of his predecessors, including a polemic against the Prussian landowner-economist Rodbertus and a close examination of the theories of Smith and Ricardo, stressing what was valid in them and revealing their faults. These appear in Part II of *Theories of Surplus Value* and shed useful light on the development of Marx's own thought on the subject. Both these major treatments of the theory of rent are rich in historical examples and shed light on the nature of capitalism today as well as in the past, as will be shown.

Before taking up the theoretical points it is worth remarking that Marx was no more tender towards the rent-receiver than towards the capitalist employer. In a particularly impressive passage, one of the kind to which his bourgeois detractors always object as being too subjective, he writes as follows: rent is distinguished:

> . . .by palpable and complete passiveness of the owner, whose sole activity consists (especially in mines) in exploiting the progress of social development, towards which he contributes nothing and for which he risks nothing, unlike the industrial capitalist; and finally by the prevalence of monopoly price in many cases, particularly through the most shameless exploitation of poverty (for poverty is more lucrative for house-rent than the mines of Potosi ever were for Spain) and the

monstrous power wielded by landed property, when united hand-in-hand with industrial capital, enables it to be used against labourers engaged in their wage struggle as a means of practically expelling them from the earth as a dwelling place. One part of society thus exacts tribute from another for the permission to inhabit the earth, as landed property in general assigns the landlord the privilege of exploiting the terrestrial body, the bowels of the earth, the air, and thereby the maintenance and development of life.[6]

Today landlordism is alive and well, waxing fat on human need and misery wherever capitalism rules. Marx's picture is by no means exaggerated or out-dated; if anything it has been surpassed by reality as town populations have grown and land values have soared. But now we must consider its scientific basis, how the theory of rent completed his analysis of the capitalist mode of production.

Before Marx could get to grips with the problem of rent it was necessary to establish how the general rate of profit was formed. This meant showing that commodities were sold not at their values but at their prices of production.[7] The general, or average, rate of profit assumed that competition between capitals distributed over the different spheres of production according to market demand, reflecting the use value of the commodities in question. This 'is indeed the effect of the law of value, not with reference to individual commodities or articles, but to each total product of the particular social spheres of production made independent by the division of labour; so that not only is no more than the necessary labour-time used up for each specific commodity, but only the necessary proportional quantity of the total social labour-time is used up in the various groups'.[8] This being so, each capital would receive a proportion of the total surplus proportionate to the amount of constant plus variable capital employed regardless of their proportions, i.e. the organic composition of capital. The selling price of commodities can be represented by the formula $c + v + p$, where p is the average rate of profit, and is assumed to be equal to prices of production. The total selling price in each sphere of production will equal the total value produced, but individual commodities do not sell at their value except by chance. Some will sell above, others below their value according to the efficiency of production in each case and the forces of competition will tend to reduce the socially necessary labour time and thus the value on the average.

The landowner now comes on the scene. Agricultural, and indeed other forms of production cannot be carried on without land and the forces of nature in general. 'Landed property' writes Marx, 'is based on the monopoly by certain persons over definite portions of the globe as exclusive spheres of their private will to the exclusion of all others'.[9] Landed property in the full sense of the right of use and abuse (although known to the Romans) came into existence under the influence of capital and the capitalist mode of production. It required the expropriation of the mass of the people from the land and the subordination of agriculture to capitalism. In Britain, where this assumed its classic form, it was carried out with the greatest ruthlessness.

> In this respect [wrote Marx] England is the most revolutionary country in the world. Wherever the conditions handed down from history were at variance with, or did not correspond to, the requirements of capitalist production on the land, they were ruthlessly swept away; this applies not only to the position of the village communities but to the village communities themselves, not only to the habitats of the agricultural population but to the agricultural population itself, not only to the original centres of cultivation, but to cultivation itself ... The Englishman meets with historical conditions of agriculture which have been progressively *created* by capital since the end of the 15th century ... English conditions are the only ones in which *modern landownership*, i.e. landownership which has been *modified* by capitalist production, has been adequately developed.[10]

Of course, since Marx's time other countries have followed a similar path, but the English land system, in which farmers rented land from big landowners and employed wage-labourers to produce for the market, was the model for the construction of the theory of rent both by Marx and his predecessors of the classical school of political economy.

Landlordism, or landed property as Marx calls it, means that the landowners acquire monopoly control of certain forces of nature without which production cannot be carried on, not only the land itself but waterfalls, mines, forests etc. By virtue of their ownership of portions of the planet they are able to appropriate a large and growing portion of the surplus value created by labour in the shape of rent. Ownership of land is thus a very special property right, but one which was at that time objectionable to the capitalists who had to hand over part of their profits (surplus value) to a leisure class of aristocrats. It also had strategic importance in another sense since work on the land, to produce the necessary means of subsistence for the population as a whole, is the basis of all surplus labour.[11] Unless agriculture is capable of producing such a surplus there can be no division of labour, the growth of industry, towns and social wealth. Under the capitalist mode of production the agricultural population not only diminishes proportionately but also in absolute numbers. This is because 'in industry (in the strict sense) the increase of constant capital in relation to variable capital goes hand in hand with an absolute increase, though relative decrease, in variable capital; on the other hand, in agriculture the variable capital required for the exploitation of a certain plot of land decreases absolutely . . .'[12]

Given landed property and the peculiarities of agriculture, it is now possible to see more clearly how rent arises. But it is first necessary to point out that the money handed over to the landlord and commonly called rent, is usually larger than rent in the economic sense used by Marx. This larger sum he calls 'lease-money'; it contains, for instance, interest on capital invested in the land or buildings for which the rent is paid; it may contain part of the profits of the capitalist or even part of what would otherwise have been paid out as wages. Rent in the strict sense is payment for the land as such, based upon its particular attributes such as fertility and location.[13]

What Marx calls *differential rent* is the rent exacted for a monopolisable force of nature, a piece of the earth which has become private property. According to its type and quality, this natural force makes labour more productive than where labour is carried on without it, or with an inferior form. This force of nature (unlike, say, air or steam) is not at the disposal of all capitals. By making labour more productive when in use it enables commodities to be produced whose individual prices of production are below those of the average social price (which they help to form) regulating market price. To put it more simply, they will be sold at the same price although they have cost less to produce. In terms of the formula already used $c + v$ will be smaller than the average but p will be larger. Capital employed with the use of this monopolisable natural force will thus attract more than the average profit, the difference being what Marx calls 'surplus profit', being 'equal to the difference between the individual price of production of these favoured producers and the general social price of production regulating the market in this entire production sphere'.[14] It is easy to see that if commodities indeed sold at their values, these commodities would be sold at a lower price, but clearly this is impossible because the total produced would be below the social demand. That is why the theory of rent could not have been brought into Volume I of *Capital* although the process whereby landed property was formed was dealt with in some detail as part of the process of primitive accumulation.

It should be emphasised that differential rent does not determine the price of commodities. Rent does not arise from the exceptional productivity of agriculture or anything special about the soil as a source of value as was held by the Physiocrats. Marx discovered from his reading of eighteenth century books and pamphlets that this important point had been made by a Scottish farmer, James Anderson, well before Ricardo who wrote: 'It is not . . . the rent of the land that determines the *price* of its produce, but it is the *price* of that produce which determines the rent of the land . . .'

The Physiocrats, early spokesmen of capital, had seen land as the only source of surplus in the form of rent. Following on from Anderson and others, Ricardo postulated the existence of capitalist relations in order to explain rent, taking as 'the starting-point for the physiology of the bourgeois system — for the understanding of its internal organic coherence and life process . . . the determination of *value by labour-time*.'[15] It was from this that it was possible to show that rent was equal to the excess of the value of the product of labour using a particular monopolisable force of nature over its average price, pocketed by the landowner. Thus rent cannot enter into the formation of price and 'landed property does not create the portion of value which is transformed into surplus-profit'.[16]

Marx spends a good deal of space on considering the various cases under which differential rent arises not only in relation to agricultural land but also from the private ownership of waterfalls, mines, etc. The reader can study these examples for himself in Volume III and Marx's critique of Ricardo in *Theories of Value*,

Part II. Marx's differences with the latter, the scientific value of whose discoveries he appreciated highly, mainly concerned Ricardo's unwillingness to recognise the existence of *absolute rent*. For Ricardo rent arose from the difference between the various grades of better land compared with that land which was just good enough to be brought into cultivation. This land did not give rise to rent although its output is necessary in order to satisfy social demand.

Marx shows that this position was untenable and does so theoretically, not from the point of view of commonsense which might say that no landlord is going to allow a farmer or tenant to use land without paying a rent. Marx is intent upon revealing the defects in Ricardo's reasoning; this is necessary in order to provide an accurate picture of the working out of the laws of motion of the capitalist mode of production.

Assume, therefore, that capital invested in the worst land yields the average rate of profit — for otherwise, under capitalist conditions, it would not be cultivated at all. The additional output will tend to bring down the price, though not to below the level before rising demand led to its cultivation. The hypothetical capitalist farmer cultivating the worst soil and not paying any rent would thus sell the product at a price covering the price of production plus the average profit. And he is a hypothetical figure. As Marx puts it:

> The fact that the tenant farmer could realise the usual profit on his capital did not have to pay any rent, is by no means a basis for the landlord to lend his land gratis to the farmer and to become so philanthropic as to grant *crédit gratuit* for the sake of a business friendship. Such an assumption would mean the abstraction of landed property, the elimination of landownership, and *it is precisely the existence of the latter that constitutes a limitation to the investment of capital and the free expansion of capital in land* [emphasis added].[17]

The existence of differential rent (according to Ricardo the only form) 'presupposes the existence of a monopoly in landownership, landed property as a limitation to capital' and this will be so on the worst land in cultivation.[18] So although this land pays no differential rent the landlord still exacts *absolute rent*; to assume the countrary would be to imagine that landed property had been abolished. Absolute rent is paid by the farmer, in this case, from the difference between the price of production and the market

THEORY OF RENT

price; the market price has to rise to a certain level before this land is cultivated at all. In other words, until it can pay rent it will not be brought into cultivation so that in the case of absolute rent the existence of landed property does push prices up to the point where rent can be exacted. The landlord will not permit his land to be used unless it can produce a surplus which he can collect in the form of rent. Thus, under capitalism, land remains uncultivated, shops, houses and offices are left empty because no one is able to pay the rent demanded by the landowner. He would rather leave them in that state than spoil the market by reducing the rent. Thus landed property constitutes a barrier to the investment of capital, giving rise to surplus-profit which the landlords collect as rent.

Of course, it will depend upon conditions of supply and demand, which are constantly fluctuating, and the relative bargaining powers of the parties whether the landowner does collect all the absolute and differential rent accruing to his property. In some cases he may exact more than this, as for example in nineteenth century Ireland and to some extent in England, too, where the bargaining position of tenants was weak. In other cases part of the rent proper may be retained by the tenant, for example where the rent has risen but the tenant has a lease based upon the old rent. And it should be recalled that the lease-money inludes payments other than either form of rent in the economic sense.

Whatever the particular conditions, however, rent accrues to the owners of monopolisable forces of nature. Absolute rent arises from the excess of the value of commodities produced with their use over their prices of production; differential rent arises out of the conversion of surplus-profit into rent.[19] Both assume the existence of landed property separate from capital. As long as the movements of capital are subject to the laws of competition, an average rate of profit will prevail over industry as a whole, regardless of the organic composition of capital in each case. Where landed property exists, however, such an equalisation is ruled out. Wherever land is required for production or other purposes, the landowners take hold of 'a portion of the surplus-value, which would otherwise take part in equalising to the general rate of profit. The rent, then, forms a portion of the value, or, more specifically, surplus-value of commodities, and instead of falling into the lap of the capitalists, who have extracted it from their labourers, it falls to the share of the landlords who extract it from the capitalists.'[20] This fact led in the nineteenth century to deep resentment on the part of the capitalists against the landowners, especially as the latter had a powerful and privileged position in the state apparatus. Thus from the point of view of promoting capitalist development at that time it would have been quite consistent to nationalise the land and to eliminate rent as a tax on capital.[21] Today, of course, the capitalists are as ferociously opposed to land nationalisation as they are to any other form, because the old distinction between landlords and capitalists has become blurred and they both stand in opposition as property-owners to the socialist revolution. It is not simply, therefore, that landed property has become a barrier to capital; capital itself is the main barrier to the development of the productive forces and the demand for the nationalisation of the land can only be part of a comprehensive programme for the nationalisation of the means of production without compensation and under workers' control.[22] It would be utopian to suppose that rent can be abolished without at the same time abolishing the profit system as a whole.

Early in his introduction to the discussion of ground rent Marx writes:

> As important as it may be for a scientific analysis of ground-rent — that is the independent and specific economic form of landed property on the basis of the capitalist mode of production — to study it *in its pure form free of all distorting and obfuscating irrelevancies*, it is just as important for an understanding of the practical effects of landed property — even for a theoretical comprehension of a multitude of facts which contradict the concept and nature of ground-rent and yet appear as modes of existence of ground rent — to learn the sources which give rise to such muddling in theory. [emphasis added][23]

His treatment of the question needs to be studied as an example of the method of *Capital*. The working out of the theory in the pure form is combined with a study of the appearance it takes so that what is essential can be abstracted and a real advance made in knowledge beyond what as previously possible. It is at the same time necessary for the reader not to mistake the pure form for what exists. The objection, for example, that things have changed since Marx's day, that capitalism is different and so on is not valid unless it can be shown that the essence of this mode of production has changed. We find no evidence for that, but rather that its practical effects have continued to develop, always, of course, in a contradictory way.

Thus the pure theory of ground rent as advanced by Marx conserves its validity, but the working out of the theory has to be examined in the light of the recent developments in capitalism. Marx wrote, for example, of 'the amazing vitality of the class of big landowners' and there is plenty of evidence of that today in all the capitalist countries. At the same time, much capital investment has now gone into land and natural resources attracted by the rent element in the return, parasitic in character. For example, while industry in Britain has been allowed to run down through lack of investment under the pressure of the declining rate of profit, British capitalists have invested vast sums in property not only at home but also in continental centres such as Brussels and Paris (sometimes with disastrous results). They were after the gains from rent, hoping to make speculative gains from the rise in property values consequent upon general social development during the boom of the 1960s. This underlines the parasitic and decaying nature of capitalism in general and British capitalism in particular that it now has to emulate landlordism, having abandoned its one-time mission to develop the productive forces.

Another point worth making in conclusion concerns one of the vital assumptions made by Marx in analysing rent in its pure form, that is that in the industrial sector competition prevails. Thus, while the existence of landed property giving monopoly control over certain forces of nature without which the labour process cannot be carried on enables it to attract part of the surplus value, industrial capital receives its share as profit proportionate to the amount of capital involved. Marx, therefore, was considering rent in relation to the competitive capitalism which prevailed in his day and, while the fundamentals of the theory could only have been grasped by considering rent in its 'pure form', for practical purposes its operation has to be seen in conjunction with finance capital and monopoly capital in the stage of imperialism. For instance, in a way analogous to rent monopoly capital is able to appropriate more than its proportionate share of the total surplus value, as Marx pointed out.[24] Moreover, a central feature of the giant corporations representative of monopoly capital is that they seize hold of natural resources on a global scale and make society pay monopoly profits made up in part of 'rent'. Generally speaking, and especially in the underdeveloped countries dominated by imperialism, resources such as oil-wells, mines and mineral deposits are a prime target for seizure by the multinational corporations. Where they cannot be seized outright, a 'rent' is paid to the local bourgeoisie or its state in the shape, for example, of oil revenues. The relative decline of landed property in the old sense thus sees its resurrection in new forms corresponding with technological development. The theory of rent thus retains its relevance and is still necessary to complete the analysis of the capitalist mode of production in its imperialist stage.

Notes

[1] But Marx goes on to say: 'The circumstances under which the capitalist has in turn to share a part of the surplus-labour or surplus value which he has captured, with a third, non-working person, are only of secondary importance.' *Theories of Surplus Value*, Part II, p.152.

[2] This point is often missed in the discussions of the transition from feudalism to capitalism and the reason why it took place first of all in Europe and especially in England. See what Marx says about this making England 'the most revolutionary country in the world', *ibid.*, p.237.

[3] See *Capital*, Volume I., Ch.XXVI. Marx means by 'primitive accumulation' the preparation of the ground for capitalist accumulation proper which included the forcible expropriation of the agricultural producer from the land and its concentration into a few hands: 'It appears as primitive, because it forms a pre-historic stage of capital and the mode of production corresponding to it.'

[4] *Theories of Surplus Value* (TSV), Part II, p.238. It is here, Marx says, that 'within a relatively small territory capital has farmed so ruthlessly and has for centuries mercilessly sought to adapt to its own needs all traditional relationships of agriculture'.

[5] 'Without this, our analysis of capitalism would not be complete,' *Capital*, Volume III, p.601.

[6] *ibid.*, p.754.

[7] See Chapter 6, 'Marx on the Formation of an Average Rate of Profit'. 'The average profit itself is a product formed under very definite historical production relations by the movement of social processes, a product which . . . requires very complex adjustment. To be able to speak at all of a surplus over the average profit, this average profit itself must already be established as a standard and as a regulator of production in general as is the case under capitalist production. For this reason there can be no talk of rent in the modern sense, a rent consisting of a surplus over average profit, i.e. over and above the proportional share of each individual capital in the surplus-value which performs the function of enforcing all surplus-labour and appropriating directly all surplus-value,' *Capital*, Volume III, p.764.

[8] *Capital*, Vol.III, p.620.

[9] *ibid.*, p.601.

[10] *TSV*, Part II, p.237.

THEORY OF RENT

[11] 'The natural basis of surplus-labour in general is that Nature must supply — in the form of animal or vegetable products of the land, in fisheries, etc. — the necessary means of subsistence under conditions of an expenditure of labour which does not consume the entire working-day. This natural productivity of agricultural labour (which includes here the labour of simple gathering, hunting, fishing and cattle-raising) is the basis of all surplus-labour, as all labour is primarily and initially directed towards the appropriation and production of food.' *Capital* Volume III, p.617. 'The Physiocrats . . . are correct in stating that in fact all production of surplus-value, and thus all development of capital, has for its natural basis the productiveness of agricultural labour.' *ibid.*, p.766.

[12] *Capital*, Volume III, p.622. This process in agriculture can be observed in advanced countries like the USA and Britain where the absolute reduction in an already relatively small labour force is still going on.

[13] '. . it is correct to say that rent is a payment for the "use" of natural things, irrespective of whether it is for the use of the "original powers" of the soil or of the power of the waterfall or of land for building or of the treasures to be found in the water or in the bowels of the earth,' *TSV*, Part II, p.246.

[14] *Capital*, Volume III, p.626.

[15] *TSV*, p.166. The context of this is high praise for Ricardo's scientific achievement and rigorous objectivity combined with a sharp critique of his shortcomings as a theorist.

[16] *ibid.*

[17] *Capital*, Volume III, p.732.

[18] *ibid.*, p.733.

[19] *ibid.*, p.746. '*Absolute* rent is the excess of *value* over the *average price* of raw produce. *Differential rent* is the excess of *market-price* of the produce grown on favoured soils over the *value* of their own produce.' *TSV*, Part II, p.142.

[20] *Capital*, Volume III, p.753.

[21] As Marx pointed out: 'Assuming the capitalist mode of production, then the capitalist is not only a necessary functionary, but the dominating functionary in production. The landowner on the other hand, is quite superfluous in this mode of production,' *TSV*, p.44.

[22] This barrier, Marx points out, is relative, not absolute: 'For as soon as the land has been rented, landed property ceases to act as an absolute barrier against the investment of necessary capital. Still, it continues to act as a relative barrier even after that, in so far as the reversion to the landlord of the capital incorporated in the land circumscribes the activity of the tenant within very definite limits,' *ibid.*, p.746.

[23] *Capital*, Volume III, p.610.

[24] For example, 'if equalisation of surplus-value into average profit meets with obstacles in the various spheres of production in the form of artificial or natural monopolies, and particularly monopoly in landed property, so that a monopoly price becomes possible, which rises above the price of production and above the value of the commodities affected by such a monopoly, then the limits imposed by the value of commodities would not thereby be removed. The monopoly price of certain commodities would merely transfer a portion of the profit of the other commodity-producers to the commodities having the monopoly price.' *Capital*, Volume III, p.839-840.

Chapter 10
Revisionism and the crisis

A reader of Ernest Mandel's recent book *The Second Slump* is bound to be struck by the modesty with which the author frequently points to the way in which his (or 'our') predictions have been confirmed.[1] In fact the book is a re-write and an up-dating of articles written between 1974-1976 so that any predictions which happen to have been wrong can be expunged. Since Mandel still refers with self-satisfaction to an article of his which appeared in 1964 entitled 'The Economics of Neo-Capitalism' one is bound to ask how far its main theme has been confirmed or otherwise and how it is that the term 'neo-capitalism' has been dropped by the riter who did most to give it currency in revisionist circles.[2]

Written while the boom was still perceptible and when revisionists like Mandel were struck by the appearances of prosperity to revise Marxism in all directions, the theory of 'neo-capitalism' was clearly enunciated. 'Neo-capitalism itself', wrote Mandel, 'is the new *modus operandi* of the capitalist system, whose distinctive characteristics flow from the organic needs of capital itself, as well as from the system's attempt to answer the challenge of the world-wide progress of anti-capitalist forces (the Soviet bloc and the colonial revolution).' After this categorical statement, he then put forward four characteristics of the new stage of capitalism. They included technological innovation, the increased importance of selling costs, the role of the state in evening out fluctuations and the use of planning techniques to 'rationalise' capital investment.

According to Mandel, therefore, capitalism had moved into a distinctly new phase for which a new term had to be coined. His theory was reminiscent of that of earlier revisionists, such as

Bernstein or Hilferding, who had written about 'organised capitalism' or 'regulated capitalism'. This is particularly the case in what he has to say about the role of the state.

> The necessity of avoiding at all costs a repetition of the 1929 type depression has become a life and death question for capitalism under the conditions of the Cold War and the rise of the anti-capitalist forces on a world scale [writes Mandel]. The techniques of anti-cyclical policies and the redistribution of purchasing power by each individual state now guarantees, directly and indirectly, private profit in ways that range from concealed subsidies to the 'nationalisation of losses', and this aspect of contemporary capitalism now becomes one of its most notable features.

There is little doubt that Mandel's belief in the relative success of Keynesian-type policies in controlling the business cycle was the key to his adoption of 'neo-capitalism'. He was speaking about a planned capitalism and the rationalisation of capital investment. 'Socialists,' he wrote, 'should view neo-capitalism as an essentially organic development of monopoly capitalism'. In his theory it was combined with the idea that a 'third industrial revolution' was in progress which made both for faster growth and greater efficiency in capitalist industry. At the same time he credited capitalist governments with a positive ability to prevent slumps. For instance, reviewing the world economic situation in 1969 he said:

> My own conviction is that whatever decisions the capitalists may take — and probably they will decide to continue the anti-inflationary measures; that is to say head towards a recession in 1970 — it seems hardly possible that they can view the perspective of five, six or seven million unemployed in the United States lightly. For that reason, I believe that as soon as the recession has reached a certain point they will revert to anti-recession measures in order to limit unemployment. And we must understand that they still have the resources needed to do this.[3]

So whatever he said about 'contradictions' building up inside 'neo-capitalism' he ends up with a vote of confidence in the ability of the capitalist state to spend its way out of a recession and especially to avert a repetition of 1929.

This point was made repeatedly by Mandel during his 'neo-capitalist phase' and nowhere more emphatically than in a pamphlet entitled *A Socialist Strategy for Western Europe* widely circulated in Britain in the early 1970s by the Institute for Workers' Control.[4] 'As far as an economic crisis or catastrophe is concerned,' he there insisted, 'it has been emphasised and re-emphasised that there are strong reasons why this can be avoided by neo-capitalism for a considerable period.' He then went over the ground covered in his 1964 article and repeated:

> The first problem for Marxists to face is the following: since we have established, as our initial hypothesis, that we cannot expect any catastrophic economic crisis comparable with 1929-32 . . . does this imply that there will be no crisis at all to threaten the capitalist economy, society and State?

As far as the economic crisis was concerned Mandel did think then, and presumably still does, that 'we consider that neo-capitalism is perfectly capable of converting serious overproduction crises into milder and briefer recessions' but not of 'suppressing its repeated short-term fluctuations'. Again he said, that there will be 'no catastrophic crisis of the 1929-33 type' so that 'the vanguard force within the workers' movement must put forward a whole series of objectives to galvanise the masses'. This un-Marxist 'galvanising' theory, which sees the working class as a kind of passive mass, led on to the notorious programme of 'structural reforms' later to be taken up by the Euro-Stalinists.

For Mandel, therefore, there can be no question of another 1929-32 (whatever that may mean). He passes a vote of confidence in the ability of capitalism to control the process of reproduction by state measures. 'To go over the principal points,' as he said, 'the size of the state budet and state intervention n the economy; the use of a whole arsenal of anti-crisis techniques; the use of "public investment" (particularly armaments) to compensate for any sagging in private investment, etc.' The 'etc.' was a stroke of genius worthy of Mandel. The capitalists today are still vainly searching for that 'etc.' which Mandel, from his later writings, is sure they have found.

For a man constantly claiming to have made correct predictions, in fact to have foreseen practically everything in the economic twists and turns of the last 20 years, some reckoning was surely due regarding the major prediction of all, namely that capitalism could control the process of reproduction and avert slumps (if not recessions). Unfortunately, nothing like a self-criticism has ever emanated from Mandel's facile pen or fluent lips. Like the veritable guru that his supporters in the revisionist camp have turned him into, he has never been wrong. Indeed, Mandel always takes out insurance policies in these matters — qualifications and asides enabling him to disclaim any predictions that went wrong. Like a clever fortune-teller, he makes so many predictions that some are bound to be right. From his many writings he could claim that he had foreseen the end of the boom (so had a great many other people, including many reputable bourgeois economists), but he steadfastly maintains that whatever has happened subsequently, not only is the situation of world capitalism not the same as in 1929 and after, but it must also be not so desperate. It is on these lines that while abandoning the term 'neo-capitalism' he clings to and reinforces his previous position on the nature of capitalist crisis in the 1970s.

Only a methodical and tedious search through all Mandel's voluminous writings would solve the mystery of when he dropped the term 'neo-capitalism', though not, it is necessary to add, the theory behind it. Only a few years after his famous 'neo-capitalism' article had been presented to the ageing sceptics of *Socialist Register*, in 1968 to be precise, Mandel addressed the Socialist Scholars Conference in the United States and said the following:

> I do not care very much for the term 'neo-capitalism' which is ambiguous, to say the least [then why had he used it without qualification in 1964? — T.K.]. When one speaks about 'neo-reformism of the Communist Parties in the West', one means, of course, that they are basically reformist; but when the term 'neo-socialist' was used in the thirties and forties to define such dubious figures as Marcel Deat or Henri de Man, one meant rather that they had stopped being socialists. Some European politicians and sociologists speak about 'neo-capitalism' in the sense that society has shed some of the basic characteristics of capitalism. I deny this most categorically, and therefore attach to the term 'neo-capitalism' the opposite connotation: a society which has all the basic elements of classical capitalism.[5]

The question arises of why, then, Mandel should ever have adopted the term so whole-heartedly previously, and even continued to use it later in other connections? The answer is given by

Mandel himself; he had to find some term to describe what he was convinced had taken place, that is to say that:

> Starting either with the great depression of 1929-32 or with the second world war [!?], capitalism entered into a third stage of development, which *is as different from monopoly capitalism or imperialism described by Lenin, Hilferding and others as monopoly capitalism was different from classical 19th century* laisser-faire *capitalism*. We have to give this child a name; all other names proposed seem even less acceptable than 'neo-capitalism'. [emphasis added — T.K.][6]

He then proceeded to reject a number of alternative terms, including *Spatkapitalismus*, or 'late capitalism', but was quite adamant that capitalism *had* entered a new stage and that a term was needed to describe it, so he decided to stick to 'neo-capitalism' after all. In other words there could be no doubt about the nature of the infant Mandel was carrying to the baptismal font, there was only doubt about what to call it. The child itself was pure Mandel, a revisionist product, still-born as far as its relation to reality was concerned.

Meanwhile Mandel was labouring at a somewhat heavy thesis first presented in German in 1972 under the title of *Der Spatkapitalismus*, rendered into English in 1975 and published as *Late Capitalism*.[7] Never lacking in modesty, Mandel claimed to be doing for 'late capitalism' what Marx and Lenin had done for previous stages. But he also explained that he was not suggesting that capitalism had changed 'in essence'; late capitalism was 'merely a further development of the imperialist, monopoly-capitalist epoch'. These warnings were obviously related to the changes in the economic and political situation. His US speech was made against the background of the events of 1968 when despite many revisionist 'predictions' to the contrary, the workers in advanced Europe had taken the lead in revolutionary struggle. As he was writing his new *magnum opus* the world economic crisis worsened daily, rendering increasingly obsolete Mandel's earlier predictions about the capacity of 'neo-capitalism' to avoid slump and crisis. As for the latter term, it now appeared to have been definitively dropped and 'late capitalism' — though meaning exactly the same thing — was substituted for it. As the great man explained:

Its superiority over the term 'neo-capitalism' is obvious — given the ambiguity of the latter, which can be interpreted to imply either a radical continuity or discontinuity with traditional capitalism. In the near future, perhaps, discussion will yield us a better term of synthesis. In the meantime, we have retained the notion of 'late capitalism', judging it to be the most serviceable term available, and above all believing that what is really important is not to name but to explain the historical development that has occurred in our age.[8]

So after a decade or so in which he had brandished the term 'neo-capitalism' as a great discovery, almost trade-marking it for his tendency, he now drops it like a hot potato, adopting an alternative no less ambigious to describe the same thing.

In his latest work, therefore, it is not surprising that there is no discussion of 'neo-capitalism'; and he is frugal in the use of 'late capitalism' as well. Perhaps a 'better term of synthesis' is gestating in Mandel's revisionist skull and will be used in his next book. For the present let us look at what this one has to offer.

In large part it is a commentary on the course of events of the years 1974-1975, the so-called 'generalised recession'. Already in November 1976 he had announced that this had come to an end in the previous year, 'earlier in the United States, later in West Germany, Japan and the other imperialist countries. It has since been followed by a phase of economic upturn.'[9] Presumably this upturn is still continuing and Mandel writes about a completed process, one economic cycle, purporting to analyse it in Marxist terms consistent with his theory of 'neo-capitalism' (re-baptised, 'late capitalism'). After all, from Mandel's 1964 standpoint the depth of the recession must have been a surprise (though that does not mean to say that he did not 'predict' it!).

In fact, the theoretical basis of Mandel's analysis comes not from Marx but from the Russian economist Kondratiev who worked in the 1920s and perished in Stalin's purges. He put forward the theory that economic development takes place through 'long waves' with an upturn and a downturn spanning in all about half a century. During the upswing booms are strong and depressions mild while during the downswing booms tail off early and depressions are deeper and more prolonged. Kondratiev imposed this pattern on the whole of capitalist development, finding empirical evidence to give it some kind of plausibility.

Kondratiev put forward his theory in two or three articles now virtually unobtainable.[10] In fact, by now Mandel has probably written more about 'long waves' than Kondratiev himself, including a long-winded and 'erudite' chapter in *Late Capitalism*.[11] It was never clear exactly what the 'long waves' referred to, whether it was prices, profits, rates of growth, how they were caused or whether it was the shorter industrial cycle which produced the 'long waves' or vice versa.[12] We do not need to tackle these problems or to question the empirical evidence claimed to exist in their support. It may be noted that the first economist to rescue Kondratiev's theory from obscurity was the Austro-American economist Joseph Aloysius Schumpeter. One of the few bourgeois economists to take the challenge of Marxism seriously, he made it his life work to produce an alternative theory of capitalist development and Kondratiev's 'long waves' formed an essential part of it. Mandel is travelling in his footsteps by making the 'long waves' a crucial part of his analysis of 'late capitalism'.

In fact the Kondratiev theory sees history repeating itself in cycles of faster and slower growth and thus denies the Marxist theory that the capitalist mode of production displays an inherent tendency towards breakdown and collapse. The downturns become explicable in quite different terms and, in any event, prepare the way for a new upturn after a given time, that is to say, about 25 years.[13] After that, with equal fatality, a new long period of expansion is generated. What is the significance, then, of Mandel's espousal of this theory? Not only does it provide a superficial explanation of the post-war boom and the current world economic crisis, but it presumably means that if capitalism survives into the 1980s or 1990s it will again be ripe for a long period of expansion. No Marxist can properly analyse the development of capitalism within such a mechanical framework however much lip-service he pays to *Capital* and however much he talks about revolution.

Mandel's espousal of the Kondratiev theory is extremely revealing about his impressionistic and empirical method. He seized on an entirely one-sided explanation of past trends which had assumed a fashionable role in bourgeois discussions of the business cycles and built it into his revisionist theory of 'neo-capitalism'. He then abandoned this term but clings all the more firmly to Kondratiev, well aware of the cautions uttered by

Trotsky. Writing soon after Kondratiev had put forward his theory, Trotsky insisted that:

> It is already possible to refute in advance Professor Kondratiev's attempt to invest epochs labelled by him as major cycles with the same 'rigidly lawful rhythm' that is observable in minor cycles; it is an obviously false generalisation from a formal analogy.[14]

Mandel drowns this point in a much longer quotation in which Trotsky summarises Kondratiev's theory and calls for further investigation. It would certainly be a misreading of Trotsky to see in his article an unqualified endorsement of Kondratiev and the tendency he warns against is precisely the path followed by Mandel. In his book the latter appropriates the 'long wave' as though it were his own invention:

> The generalised recession is thus a synthetic expression of the reversal of the 'long wave of expansion' . . . I had predicted this reversal as early as 1964, and my *Late Capitalism* is largely devoted to it.

And Mandel continued: 'The new "long wave" was to be characterised by a medium-to-long-term growth rate probably 50 per cent inferior to that of the fifties and sixties.'[15] This was about the extent of the 'crisis' as Mandel sees it.

In 1975 Mandel began writing periodical commentaries on the economic situation which appeared in the revisionist publications *Inprecor* and *Intercontinental Press*. These form the basis of his new book and to refer to the original articles is to blow sky-high his claims as a prophet. For example, although the book is called *The Second Slump* he studiously avoided the term 'slump' in his articles; it was always 'the generalised recession of the international capitalist economy'. It will be the most serious recession of the post-war period, he cautiously asserted in January 1975. How long will it last, he then asked? 'Much depends on government policies, that is, on political decisions. Will the governments "refloat" the economy or not? That is the crucial question.'[16] This was perfectly in line with the theory of 'neo-capitalism' which made the State and not objective laws the master of the economy. By June 1975 he was 'predicting' that 'an upturn towards the end of 1975 or the beginning of 1976 remains the most likely prospect'.[17] By the end of 1975 he was 'waiting for the upturn', predicting an early recovery based upon government deficit-spending and settling into a new Kondratiev 'long wave of reduced growth'.[18] Later in the following year he asserted confidently: 'There can be no doubt that the generalised recession of the international capitalist economy came to an end in 1975.' The upward turn in the cycle, he claimed was beyond dispute. 'If the causes of the turnabout of the cycle are examined,' he wrote, 'it becomes clear that the recession was halted and the upturn initiated by enormous deficit spending in 1975.'[19] In other words, Keynesian-type counter-cyclical policies had succeeded once again. Growth would slow down to about 50 per cent of its boom-time level.

By concentrating on the recession and the short-term ebbs and flows in investment and profits Mandel had effectively exorcised the real crisis in which the capitalist world system was plunged. To see only the ending of a recession in 1975 — even if it did end, a conclusion with which many bourgeois economists would disagree — however qualified, is to oppose the view that the capitalist mode of production is in a deep historic crisis actually worse than that of 1929-32, although manifesting itself in different ways. Always living off impressions, Mandel begins with appearances, the most obvious ones that he reads off from statistical tables. Few capitalist commentators have been deceived by indices of production or trade into thinking that the crisis has gone away. In fact capitalism is in a deep historic crisis which is endemic and insoluble. Attempts to deal with it by capitalist governments in resorting once again to inflationary policies have only made it worse by aggravating the contradictions. The crisis manifests itself within each capitalist country, though in different ways, and in relations between them — trade war, monetary chaos, the free fall of the dollar, the balance of payments deficits of some and the huge surplus of others. These problems have defied all efforts by governments, bankers and industrialists to resolve them. Every summit meeting ends in stalemate leaving the situation worse by further undermining confidence in the system and in its prospects for recovery. To speak about an 'upturn' in these circumstances, or to interpret the crisis through the arbitrary patterns of a Kondratiev is to lose all touch with the method of Marxism whatever formal use is made of its categories and its language. The mark of Mandel's revisionism is that he can make no analysis of the overriding crisis and can only repeat parrot-fashion that there will never be a repetition of 1929-1932.

It becomes evident that Mandel has more confidence in the viability of the world capitalist system than its own apologists. Take, for example, the state of European industry, whole sections of which are being forced to close down or contract, condemning whole areas to economic decay and mass unemployment. This is what *Time* had to say about that in its October 16, 1978 issue:

> The crisis is murky, eluding both easy definition and remedy. Morbid symptoms are only too familiar: lagging production in major industries, inflation in too many places still flickering at dangerous levels, joblessness alarmingly high and in many countries inching upward. Slight signs of general improvement next year do not fundamentally alter the grim outlook. Only gradually has the public begun to realise that what is happening is not merely a transitional aftermath of another cyclical recession: the Depression of the 1930s was a temporary collapse rather than a profound mutation of the existing industrial order. Today, a sea change is at work in Europe's old industrial patterns. It is no exaggeration to say that not since the Industrial Revolution has Western Europe confronted such a wrenching peacetime transformation in its economic life.

The writers of this article are no Marxists but strong adherents of the capitalist way of life and free enterprise. They are not shortsighted enough to talk about 'neo-capitalism' or recovery being round the corner. Nor do they, wisely, have any time for Kondratiev's theories. On the other hand they do state the nature of the crisis more clearly than Mandel has ever done and their comparison with the Depression of the 1930s — a 'temporary collapse' — is one up on his facile assumption that those years saw a capitalist nadir which will never be matched again because governments have some magic recipe to prevent it happening! As *Time* says, the crisis affects all industrial countries; once prosperous industries are now wallowing 'like helpless dinosaurs'. Unemployment piles up, protectionism raises its head and governments talk but can do nothing. Mandel's 'technological revolution' has gone the way of the one once promised by Prime Minister Harold Wilson; or rather it has turned into its opposite leaving large sections of the industrial economy of Europe high and dry.

Of course, this is only one side of the story. More than ever before capitalism is a world system and, under the aegis of the giant multinationals the international division of labour is changing as the imperialist seeks to counteract the tendency of the rate of profit to fall by turning to industrial investment in the less developed countries. Here the organic composition of capital is lower and wages are closer to the subsistence level in a backward agrarian economy. The giant firms are trying to maintain profits by shifting the more labour-intensive process to these areas, aggravating still further the crisis in the older industrial countries. In those countries large sections of the working class have become redundant, can no longer produce surplus value and are therefore superfluous as far as capital is concerned. But to impose this new division of labour completely the workers' organisations have to be attacked and defeated: this is the problem facing the capitalists in Britain and Europe.

This is only one aspect of the crisis, one which Mandel is bound to underestimate in his talk about 'neo-capitalism' and 'the third industrial revolution'. They reduce capitalist social relations and the class struggle itself to the small change of economic discourse. It is not surprising that Mandel has taken on the mantle of the old hands like Maurice Dobb and Paul Sweezy, commenting on the economic situation and turning Marxism into economics, deserting the method and ending up, like Mandel himself, as 'left-Keynesians'. Doesn't Mandel repeat many times in *The Second Slump* that the capitalists spent themselves out of the 'recession of 1972-1975'? And does not this mean that they can repeat the performance indefinitely?

Like earlier revisionists before him, Mandel sees no tendencies dominant in the capitalist mode of production towards its breakdown and collapse. He is thus always looking for a way out for the capitalists before they have found one for themselves: witnes his 'predictions' about the end of the recession in 1975. Thus he is unable to see any difference between the present situation of capitalism and 1929, except that the working class is undefeated; if anything, in his book, the situation for the capitalists is better. Isn't production at a higher level and technology more advanced? Meanwhile he has his eyes glued to short run trends, assuming that the long run is taken care of by the fatalistic and metaphysical Kondratiev theory of the long wave. Once again, let it be said, this is not Marxist method but the crudest empiricism masquerading as Marxism which characterises everything that Mandel writes, including and above all this book.

If we are not in a recession or crisis what are we in? According to Mandel there is now 'a hesitant and inflationary recovery'. 'The fragmented, hesitant, and uneven recovery' he goes as far as to say, 'constantly borders on a plunge into a new recession'. It is prevented from doing so by continued government expenditure and the piling up of debt. 'This was the price paid', he declares 'for averting a catastrophic crisis of the scope of the 1929-32 depression and for the efforts to transform it into a recession more limited in depth and breadth albeit the most serious since the Second World War.'[20] Always Mandel holds out the possibility that the capitalists have a way out. Having ventured to say that 'Hovering over the future recession is the triple threat of a major bank crash, the insolvency of some important dependent or semi-colonial countries, and a crisis or collapse of the dollar' he hastens to add, a few sentences later:

> The system is not at all at the end of its rope. It still commands significant reserves in most of the imperialist countries, enormous reserves in the richest one . . . And above all it combines these still considerable economic reserves and resources with an arsenal of political, ideological and military weapons to be used in the service of a cause it will pursue tenaciously for long years: a substantial new rise in the rate of profit through a sharp upturn in the rate of surplus value.[21]

Consistent with the whole theory of 'neo-capitalism' or 'late capitalism', Mandel remains convinced of the strength of capitalism, the power of the state to avert crises or turn slumps into recessions. As has been stressed before, he sees no tendencies driving the system towards breakdown and collapse, tendencies objectively stronger than Keynesian measures or the policies of the 'monetarists'. The renewed crisis in the capitalist world system, like the upsurge of the European working class in 1968, took Mandel unawares and he had hastily to make an adaptation. This book is really the consummate result of this process, driving the revisionists into further contradictions and double-talk and exposing their method in its true colours.

Notes

[1] *The Second Slump*, New Left Books, 1978.
[2] 'The Economics of Neo-capitalism', *Socialist Register*, 1964.
[3] *The Decline of the Dollar*, Monad Press, 3rd printing, 1974, p.72, from a talk originally given in December, 1969.
[4] *A Socialist Strategy for Western Europe*, Institute of Workers Control. No date, but third impression apparently made in 1974. It gives the baldest expression of Mandel's policy of 'structural reforms'.
[5] 'Workers under Neo-capitalism', *International Socialist Review*, Vol.29, No.6, November-December, 1968, p.2.
[6] *ibid.*, pp.2-3. Mandel went on to say: 'We shall define neo-capitalism in which a combination of factors — accelerated technological innovation, permanent war economy (*sic*), expanding colonial revolution — have transferred the main sources of monopoly profits from the colonial countries to the imperialist countries themselves and made the giant corporations both more independent and more vulnerable'.
[7] *Late Capitalism*, New Left Books, 1972.
[8] *op. cit.*, pp.10-11.
[9] *Inprecor*, November, 1976. 'If the causes of the turn-about are examined,' he wrote, 'it becomes clear that the recession was halted and the upturn initiated by enormous deficit spending in 1975.' This point is reiterated and expanded upon in *The Second Slump*.
[10] The most accesssible is in a book produced for the American Economic Association for students, *Readings in Business Cycle Theory*, first published by The Blakiston Company, 1944, 'The Long Waves in Economic Life'.
[11] *op. cit.* Ch.4.
[12] Mandel is sure that 'these "long waves" do not assert themselves in mechanical fashion through the articulation of the "classical cycles" . . . The "long waves" is conceivable only as the result of the cyclical fluctuations and never as some kind of metaphysical superimposition upon them'. But this makes it all the more difficult to explain why, for periods of 20-25 years the 'classical cycles' should display strong boom and weak slumps during the upward phase and the reverse during the downward phase. A plausible argument, and one more in line with Kondratiev's theory, would be that the long cycles themselves determine the intensity of the shorter cycles. Both views would be equally 'metaphysical' and Mandel cannot disarm criticism by claiming that his view is empirically based; there is no 'proof' one way or the other and no reason to think that the 'long wave' is part of the 'laws of motion' of the capitalist mode of production.
[13] According to Mandel the Kondratiev upswing ended about 1965; according to that the present downswing would end in the second half of the 1980s and presumably a new upswing would then be due. If not there is no point in talking about the present period as being part of a long wave of slower growth. Note also that Mandel says 'Long waves tending towards stagnation in no way imply a permanent depression of material production over a period of twenty or twenty-five years. They are characterised by a succession of over-production crises and periods of recovery and rise in production, exactly like the long waves tending towards expansion. The cycles continue to function as such . . .' *The Second Slump*, p.182. All this is pure Kondratiev, not Marxism.
[14] L. Trotsky, 'The Curve of Capitalist Development', first published in Russian in 1923, in *Problems of Everyday Life*, Monad Press, 1973, pp.273-280. Trotsky called Kondratiev's theory 'a symmetrically stylised construction' which should be subject 'to careful and not over-credulous verification in respect to individual countries and

the world market as a whole. (It is already possible to refute in advance Professor Kondratiev's attempt to invest epochs labelled by him as major cycles with the same "rigidly lawful rhythm" that is observable in minor cycles; it is obviously a false generalisation from a formal analogy.)' These warnings evidently did not deter Mandel.

[15] *The Second Slump*, p.13

[16] *Inprecor*, No.16-17, January 16, 1975. He went on to say: 'The recession is precisely a crisis of overproduction whose breadth and duration are limited by an injection of inflationary buying power. Thus, if the economy is refloated by means of such injections during coming months . . . the international capitalist economy will avert a grave depression.' Despite all his talk about a crisis of overproduction and various disclaimers Mandel's analysis is basically an underconsumptionist one with more affinities with Keynes than with Marx.

[17] *Inprecor*, No.27-28, June 5, 1975, p.9. Mandel attributed this to 'pump-priming', i.e. Keynesian-type policies of government spending. He opined that: 'It is not likely that the recession will continue to deepen through the rest of the year and into the beginning of next year . . . the downward trend of production will come to an end some time during the fourth quarter of 1976', *ibid.*, p.7. He speculated on the possibility of 'a new period of accelerated growth', in the same issue.

[18] *Inprecor*, December 18, 1975. 'Waiting for the upturn'. In this article he anticipated bravely that 'the economies of the imperialist countries will no longer experience the average growth rates they did during the 1950s an 1960s' . . . 'the economic atmosphere is coming closer to the atmosphere that prevailed at the beginning of the 1920s'. The relevance of the latter remark is not clear: the early 1920s saw the beginning of a boom which ended in 1929.

[19] *Inprecor*, November, 1976; *Intercontinental Press*, 1976, p.1700. All the points made in these articles are more or less reproduced in *The Second Slump* with some judicious pruning and rewriting and the addition of some new material.

[20] *The Second Slump*, pp.92-93.

[21] *ibid.*, pp.191-192.

Chapter 11

The unknown 'Capital': Marx's second volume[1] Part 1

Marx never lived to see the second volume of his epoch-making work published and the first edition in German did not appear until 1885, two years after his death. It was prepared for the press by Engels from a mass of manuscript material representing intensive study of political economy over a period of some fifteen years. The later manuscripts showed increasing signs of Marx's struggle against illness, rendering Engels' task, as he explains in the Preface, extremely difficult. He had to collate and select manuscripts written at different times, principally as working papers in which Marx was working out and eleborating his ideas. As Engels writes:

> The logical sequence is frequently interrupted, and the treatment in places punctuated and especially at the end quite incomplete. And yet what Marx intended to say is said there, in one way or another.[2]

As Engels worked closely with Marx throughout the writing of *Capital* and no doubt provided invaluable assistance, not only from his own high capacity as a theoretician but also from his knowledge of how capitalist business worked, we can accept these assurances. Nevertheless there remain to be published those manuscripts and alternative versions which Engels rejected. A second German edition was brought out in 1893, also by Engels but it was not until 1919 that an English translation was published by Charles H. Kerr of Chicago. This edition, or pirated versions of it, became rare in the English-speaking world and this was in itself a handicap to Marxist studies. In 1957 the Foreign Language Publishing House in Moscow published what was essentially a reprint of this English translation, thus making it available to a much wider readership. The date was not auspicious for a close study of the volume at a time when the crisis following the XXth Congress of the Communist Party of the Soviet Union was the dominant factor in the movement. Today, over two decades later, the eruption of world capitalist crisis on a gigantic scale gives a new urgency to the study of the whole of Marx's *Capital*.

In any case many of those who subsequently acquired the volume probably found it difficult to read and were deterred from giving it the study it deserved. Penguin books have now brought out a new translation in the Pelican Marx library which does something to overcome this difficulty so far as it was a question of style and not of subject matter. Its appearance thus provides the opportunity to summarise the argument of this second volume and to assess its contribution to Marxist theory for the guidance of intending readers. Since the publishers gave the task of introducing this volume, like their edition of Volume I, to the arch-revisionist Ernest Mandel, who uses the opportunity to proclaim his own virtues, it is equally important to expose this gentleman's pretensions to Marxism. This study thus falls into two parts, firstly to introduce the second volume of *Capital* to a wider circle of Marxists and secondly to settle accounts with one of the leaders of the present-day revisionism.

What has been said about the origins of Volume II gives some indication of the problems it presents for the reader. In the manuscripts which compose it Marx was intent on pursuing his own thoughts rather than in conveying them to the eventual reader. Thus few concessions are made in the form of exposition. Marx does not always explain what he is trying to do or provide convenient summaries of the argument or the conclusions of each stage. The reader thus has to dig out the meaning from the text and this imposes a close study of the development of Marx's thought through all its intricacies. Though this is built on the acquisitions already made in Volume I, this may not at first be obvious. The space devoted to concrete examples or to historical applications is small compared with its predecessor or with Volume III. However, the treatment is less abstract than may appear; in fact Marx is tracing out in new fields the working out of the laws of motion of the capitalist mode of production and this required a close attention to the operation of those laws in practice, in the practice, that is to say, of the individual business firm as well as of this mode of production taken as a whole, showing the interconnection between the two in a much fuller and more profound way than does bourgeois economics with its division between micro-economics and macro-economics. This is because in dealing with the individual capitalist Marx places him in the network of class and social relations which make up the capitalist mode of production and provide its specific features.

In this volume, Marx studies not the relation between the capitalist employer and the wage labourer in the process of production (called P) but the circulation of capital in its three forms: 1) the circuit of *money* capital; 2) the circuit of *productive* capital; 3) the circuit of *commodity* capital. The total circulation process requires all three because 'in reality . . . each individual capital is involved in all three at the same time'.[3] A separation is necessary for purposes of exposition; a difference does exist at the individual level but in the movement of capital as a whole they are necessarily combined and 'are continuously executed alongside one another'. It is in Chapter Four that Marx makes this point and it is therefore useful to consult this chapter when studying the first three because it is in the establishment of the unity that the reason for the separation becomes apparent. The abstraction had to be made before the unity could be appreciated. Moreover, it is important to grasp that Marx is not dealing with economic activity as such but with the circuit of *capital*. In short it can be said that capital describes three circuits. As money capital it goes through the circuit from M to M', where M' includes surplus value. As productive capital it goes through the circuit P to P'. As commodity capital it goes through the circuit C to C'. These three forms of circuit are going on continuously and simultaneously to produce the movement of the total capital.

> Each form [writes Marx] both follows and precedes the others, so that the return of one part of the capital to one form is determined by the return of another part to another form. Each part continuously describes its own course, but it is always another part of capital that finds itself in this form, and these particular circuits simply constitute simultaneous and successive moments of the overall process.

Marx goes on to say:

> It is only in the unity of the three circuits that the continuity of the overall process is realised, in place of the interruptions we have just

delineated. The total social capital possesses this continuity, and its process always contains the unity of the three circuits.[4]

It is therefore a dialectical movement, hinging on the relationship between capital and wage-labour where surplus value is extracted from living labour and without which M could not become M' or C, C'.

From this vantage point of the unity of the process to which it will be necessary to return, the significant point made in the previous three chapters can be summarised.

The capitalist begins with money which he uses to buy the commodities needed to carry on production (at this stage Marx is concerned with the industrial capitalist); they then become productive capital — means of production, raw materials, etc., and wage-labour. 'The value that he has advanced in the form of money', Marx writes, 'this now exists in a natural form in which it can be realised as value which breeds surplus value (in the shape of commodities). In other words, it exists in the state or form of *productive capital*, with the ability to function as creator of value and surplus value.' Thus the class relationship between capitalist who owns the means of production and worker who has nothing to sell but his labour power is pre-supposed.

> Money can be spent in this form only because labour-power is found in a state of separation from its means of production (including the means of subsistence as means of production of labour power itself); and because this separation is abolished only through the sale of labour-power to the owner of the means of production, a sale which now signifies that the buyer is now in control of the continuous flow of labour-power, a flow which by no means has to stop when the amount of labour necessary to reproduce the price of labour-power has been performed. The capital relation arises only in the production process because it exists implicitly in the act of circulation, in the basically different economic conditions in which buyer and seller confront one another, in their class relation. It is not the nature of money which gives rise to this relation; it is rather the existence of the relation that can transform a mere function of money into a function of capital.[5]

Thus, in dealing with the circulation of money capital a connection has to be made with the buying and selling of labour-power dealt with in Volume I.

For capitalist production to be fully established, as Marx has shown in Volume I, the separation between the ownership of the means of production and the 'free wage-labourer' must have become general. Labour-power itself becomes a commodity. Workers have to sell their labour-power for money in order to exist. Unless there are such workers whose labour-power can be bought, money cannot be transformed into productive capital. At the same time, 'capitalist production produces not only commodities and surplus value; it reproduces, on an ever extended scale, the class of wage-labourers, and transforms the immense majority of direct producers into wage-labourers'.[6]

Labour-power is the only exchange value that the worker possesses. For the employer who purchaes it, however, it is a use value. 'The use-value of labour-power', as Marx points out, 'can be realised only in the labour process. The capitalist cannot sell the worker again as a commodity, for he is not his slave, and the capitalist has bought nothing more than the utilisation of his labour-power for a certain time.'[7] With labour-power a commodity, commodity-production becomes the general form of production. Workers do not produce for their own needs but sell their labour-power for money with which they have to buy commodities to exist; that is to say, they buy the products of the labour-process of other workers. There is ever greater specialisation between the different branches of production as well as within each branch or each individual production unit. Historically the spread of commodity production had 'a dissolving effect on all earlier forms of production' transforming them into commodity production and then into capitalist production. Capitalist production, based upon the purchasing of labour-power, enables the capitalist to appropriate the additional value, surplus value, created by it in the production process.

Under the capitalist mode of production, labour-power becomes capital (variable capital) in the hands of the purchaser. The means of production become productive capital, 'only from the moment that labour-power, as the personal form of existence of productive capital, can be incorporated with them.'[8] This is what gives the labour-process under capitalism its specific character. As Marx points out:

> The means of production are no more capital by nature than is human labour power. They receive this specific social character only under

certain particular conditions that have historically developed, just as it is only under such conditions that precious metals are stamped with the character of money, or money with that of money-capital.[9]

Under the capitalist production process commodities which issue from it do so as the bearer of capital value, they have been valorised, enriched with surplus value. This surplus value then has to be realised by the sale, i.e. the turning into money of the commodities. The capitalist set out with money capital M, bought means of production and labour-power, used them in the production process P to produce commodities C' which he then sells for M', the commodities he sells having a higher value (because enriched with surplus value) than the commodities he bought. Surplus value thus assumes a commodity form before it can assume a money form; more precisely it first assumes the form of commodity capital while the money for which it is sold is money capital, capital in the money form. The capitalist continues the process by throwing money capital back into the purchase of commodities for the production process where they assume the form of productive capital. Each form of capital performs a specific function. 'Money capital, commodity capital and productive capital', writes Marx, 'thus do not denote independent varieties of capital, whose functions constitute the content of branches of business that are independent and separate from one another. They are simply particular functional forms of industrial capital which takes on all three forms in turn'.[10] Each phase represents the tying up of capital in a particular form and thus contains the seeds of crisis: e.g. the finished commodities may prove to be unsaleable.

In this perpetual dance of capital through its various forms and phases Marx always emphasises that it is industrial capital which they represent, of which they are only different modes of existence. However, the capitalist is intent on money-making, on turning M into M' and 'the production process appears simply as an unavoidable middle term, a necessary evil for the purpose of money-making'.[11] Thus we see many capitalists trying to get rich (and sometimes succeeding) by other means, such as financial speculation and manipulation, which add nothing to production and simply squeeze out surplus value from the industrial sector. Get-rich-quick operators are often disliked by the entrenched industrial capitalists who sometimes are happy to destroy them or to see them destroyed. Marx deals with phenomena like this in Volume III.

The function of the circuit of productive capital is reproduction in which production is a means to an end, the valorisation of capital, i.e. the production of surplus value. If the capitalist consumes the difference between M' and M there will be what is called simple reproduction. That is to say there will be no accumulation of capital; the means of production will be maintained, but not added to and capitalists will spend the additional money accruing to them as surplus value. Of course, the different branches of production will still be interrelated so that there will be production of goods and services corresponding to what the capitalists spend. As a description of capitalist reality simple reproduction is obviously unrealistic, but it provides Marx with a means of demonstrating the circuits of capital without the additional complication of accumulation.[12] For this purpose he takes a number of examples but here only some of the conclusions of the analysis will be noted.

The point that Marx is making is that the different individual capitals are intertwined through the circuits of circulation through money into commodity, commodity into money and so on and thus go through constant metamorphoses as indicated in the title of this part. Any interruption of the process at one point will throw the whole mechanism out of joint and precipitate crisis. Moreover, because the process is spread over time one sector may be doing very well precisely when the conditions for crisis are being prepared. The example Marx gives is the sale of a particular commodity by the industry concerned. But industry sells to wholesale merchants who sell to retailers and stocks may pile up unsold in their hands for a period so that the commodities are not actually being transformed into money. A point is reached where retailers face the consequence of unsold stocks, wholesalers cancel orders to the factories and the reproduction process of capital grinds to a halt. The factories close down, firms go bankrupt and workers are laid off. This could quite well happen, also, if capitalists hoard money from previous sales instead of throwing it back into production. The whole capitalist production process is determined by the valorisation of capital, including the value added by the labour-power employed in the production process. In other words, accumulation, or expanded reproduction, is an integral part of capitalist development. It is 'a necessity for each individual capitalist. The constant enlargement of his capital becomes a condition for its preservation', as Marx had shown in Volume I.

At this point it should be pointed out that Marx abstracts from the existence of credit and assumes that all money is metallic money so that disturbances from the monetary and financial side can be left out of account. The conditions of accumulation can thus be specified, notably that money has to be available from the surplus value already generated but that, for example, technical conditions may prescribe a certain minimum before a capital outlay is made. Further, the growth of capital takes place in a specific way, namely through the growth of constant capital at a faster rate than variable capital. This change in value composition is known as the rising organic composition of capital and it plays a key role, in Volume III, in Marx's analysis of the declining rate of profit.

The investment decisions of the capitalist are thus bounded by certain technical conditions (e.g. a blast furnace has to be of a certain size) and value relations (e.g. production on a given scale permits of a limited number of definite proportions between outlays on means of production and outlays on wages) as well as by competitive market forces (what his rivals are doing or are likely to do.) Such factors as these account for the instability of capitalism, or what Marxists call the anarchy of the market, and Marx has them constantly in mind in following through the circuits of capital in this volume. In order to do this he has to establish the conditions for them to take place where they do so 'normally'. From this standpoint he can reveal the nature of the capitalist process and at the same time expose the errors of classical political economy which wanted, like bourgeois economics today, to present it as though production were its purpose. That was because they confined their analysis to the form of reproduction P-P' (the circuit of productive capital) which disguised the fact that valorisation (the production of surplus value) is the purpose of the process. Even in the circulation of commodity capital C-C' this is not shown up clearly; the nature of the process is more strikingly revealed when it concludes with M', which the valorised surplus value transformed back into money.

In the case of the circulation of commodity capital C-C', C' requires the conversion of C' into the commodities that form the elements of production (i.e. means of production and labour-power). Commodities belonging to others are drawn into the process and changed into productive capital. It thus pre-supposes the production of these elements by other capitals and the existence of free wage-labourers. Marx says that this 'demand to be considered as the *general* form of capital can be considered . . . hence not only as a form of motion common to all individual industrial capitals, but at the same time as the form of motion of the sum of individual capitals, i.e. of the total social capital of the capitalist class, a movement in which the movement of any individual industrial capital simply appears as a partial one, intertwined with the others and conditioned by them.'[13] Of course, any individual capital may appear to move differently from the 'algebraic sum' of all the capitals together (including that part owned by the state). Marx emphasises that 'every capitalistically-produced article is commodity capital, irrespective of whether its use form destines it for productive or individual consumption or for both.'[14] What Marx is showing here is the all-embracing nature of the capitalist process and its continuous motion through the intertwining of the individual capitals and their metamorphoses through the three circuits.

To return to Chapter Four, Marx there makes an important point which helps explain the purpose of his analysis. 'Capital', he writes, 'does not just comprise class relations, a definite social character that depends on the existence of labour as wage-labour. It is a movement, a circulatory process through different stages, which itself in turn includes three different forms of the circulatory process. Hence it can only be grasped as a movement, and not as a static thing.'[15] As well as being an example of Marx's method, he shows the vulnerability of capitalism to crisis.[16] Without explicitly saying so, he means that the working class party must understand how capitalism works to take the revolutionary opportunities given by this vulnerability. Also, the working class has to re-organise the production process so that it is based on a definite social plan and ceases to be a process of the valorisation of capital, i.e. of exploitation. Hence, knowledge of the workings of capitalism is necessary and so is the working of the economy when divested of its capitalist form.

Marx's penetrating eye was able to discern in the competitive and still largely small-scale structure of the Victorian economy the lineaments of twentieth century monopoly capitalism. He saw in the violent fluctuations an accelerator of the process, favouring big capitals over the small. As he foresaw, 'since the scale of each individual production process grows with the progress of capitalist production, and with it the minimum size of the capital to be advanced, this circumstance is added to the other circumstances which increasingly turn the function of industrial capitalist into a monopoly of large-scale money capitalists, either individual or associated.'[17]

Moreover, Marx saw the capitalist mode of production as essentially a world system. The growth of industrial capital made it seek materials from the ends of the earth as well as seeking markets throughout the world. The circuit of industrial capital thus cut across societies of the most diverse kinds and tended to tie them all into a world market while money also necessarily functioned as world money.[18] All preceding forms of production were transformed (or being transformed in Marx's day) into the production of commodities. At the same time 'the intervention of industrial capital everywhere promotes ... with it too the transformation of all immediate producers into wage-labourers.'[19] A few pages later Marx says, referring to the extension of the capitalist mode of production to wider areas of the globe: 'The producer becomes an industrial capitalist to the same extent that labour becomes wage-labour; hence capitalist production (and thus also commodity production) appears in its full extent only when the direct agricultural producer is also a wage-labourer.'[20] At the time of writing only in Britain had this happened and the peasantry had been eliminated; the development of the capitalist mode of production requires the more or less rapid disappearance of the independent class of cultivators and their turning into proletarians. This is going on before our eyes in the so-called 'underdeveloped countries' at the present time.

The circulation of capital is a process spreading over time, as well as over space, and in the remaining two chapters of this part Marx considers some of the consequences. Capital in its various forms moves through the various phases and metamorphoses in the sphere of production and during its circulation. For example, production time includes not only the time during which labour is actually being expended on a product but the whole time in which it is in the sphere of production. Some processes necessarily have to be spread over a certain period. This is obvious in agriculture where seeds are sown and are left to germinate. Wine has to be kept for a certain period in the cellar before it is fit for drinking or wood may have to be seasoned. The flow of production in industry may depend upon the speed at which certain chemical processes take place. During the time when nature is doing its work and the labour process is interrupted neither value nor surplus value will be created. This is why the capitalist is anxious to shorten this period since his costs continue to increase during that time. His object is to reduce the production time as near as possible to the working time; the total production time, however, is the time taken to produce use values as distinct from exchange values.

Note that these points follow from the labour theory of value and from the dual character of the commodity as a repository of use value and exchange value.

During the circulation process, raw materials, finished goods, etc., do not function as productive capital. Capital there exists as commodity capital and money capital; it is being transformed from the commodity form to the money form and from the money form to the commodity form. 'Circulation time and production time', says Marx, 'are mutually exclusive. During its circulation time, capital does not function as productive capital, and therefore produces neither commodities nor surplus value.'[21] Ideally for the capitalist this time should be reduced to zero since it would then enable the whole of the capital to be used for the production of surplus value. There is another important point about circulation. That is, the value added to a commodity *appears* to take place in the sphere of circulation where each capitalist strives to buy cheap and sell dear and thus make a profit. It was this appearance that classical political economy and bourgeois economics take to be the source of profit because otherwise they would have to admit that labour is exploited. They take the negative effects of circulation for a positive, Marx points out. Economics thus 'sticks all the more firmly to this illusion, as it seems to provide it with the proof that capital possesses a mystical source of self-valorisation that is independent of the production process and hence of the exploitation of labour, and derives rather from the sphere of circulation.'[22]

Circulation time covers the transaction period of C-M and M-C, which may mean the movement of commodities through space as well as through time, thus raising the question of the role of transport in the formation of value. First of all it should be noted that agents of circulation (merchants, employees and workers in this branch) are as necessary as those working in industry, but they produce no surplus value. Their role is to assist in its realisation through facilitating the circulation of capital. Capital cannot do without these functions. In fact it might be added, that under modern business conditions they become grotesquely multiplied with the growth of what the economists call 'selling costs', such as product promotion and advertising. Again, commodities are use values as well as exchange values. If they are held too long in the sphere of circulation and 'are not sold within a definite time, thus they get spoiled, and lose, together with their use value, the property of being bearers of exchange value'.[23]

From a consideration of the circulation time, Marx moves on to the question of the costs involved. Marx here considers C-M and M-C as business transactions between different members of the capitalist class as 'personified capital'. In these transactions the different capitalists confront each other as rivals — they want to sell at the highest price and buy at the lowest price that they can; 'a struggle is involved here, in which each side seeks to get the better of the other.'[24] Once again, although for capitalism the labour involved in circulation is necessary it creates no surplus value; and this is the same whether the capitalists do it themselves or pay others to do it for them. In any event, 'the time taken up with buying and selling creates no value.'[25] Under capitalism the reproduction process includes unproductive functions, i.e. which create no value. Workers in distribution are thus part of the overheads as far as their employers are concerned and however hard they work part of the time to cover their own wages and part for the boss they do not produce value. The outlay on their wages is a cost of circulation, necessary for the circulation of capital but adding no new value. It is a necessary cost, so that part of variable capital has to be devoted to this purpose without producing any new products or any additional value.

The same thing with book-keeping. The capitalist has to keep careful accounts otherwise he cannot keep check of his stock, calculate his outgoings and his receipts and thus know whether he is making a profit or not. Accounting is thus as old as commodity production. For the capitalist it represents 'an additional expenditure of labour-time and instruments of labour, which, although necessary, constitutes a deduction both from the time that he can spend productively, and from the instruments of labour that function in the actual production process and enter into the formation of products and value.'[26] Marx also notes that book-keeping becomes 'more necessary in communal production (i.e. socialism) than in capitalist. The costs of book-keeping are however reduced with the concentration of production and in proportion to its increasing transformation into social book-keeping.'[27]

Let us recall again that under capitalism the product takes the form of a commodity, both a use-value and an exchange-value. To pass into use the commodity must assume the money form. Some part of production has therefore to be devoted to producing the money commodities. Marx assumes a metallic circulation but no essential difference is made when paper money becomes the predominant form. The whole activity connected with the production of money, whether it is gold and silver mining or the printing and circulation of bank-notes, while necessary for capitalism is a sacrifice of social wealth, an overhead cost; it is part of what Marx calls 'the *faux frais* of commodity production in general.'[28]

The circulation of capital requires the existence of stocks and thus costs are incurred because some part of capital is 'in the pipeline' and not actually taking part in the reproduction process. The capitalist thus normally tries to hold as small a stock as possible, whether it be raw materials, spare parts or semi-finished goods. However, a basic minimum of stock must be held otherwise the process of circulation and production could be interrupted. Holding stocks requires outlays on buildings and labour; they must be safe-guarded against deterioration and guarded against thieves. Marx sees the costs involved in holding stocks as being different from those already mentioned and says: 'they do enter into the value of commodities to a certain extent and thus make the commodities dearer.'[29] Without the requisite stocks in reserve production could not be carried out. A spare part in stock one day may be a functioning part of a machine the next. A sudden order could not be met unless there were stocks of raw material on hand. Thus, as Marx sees it 'in order for the process to keep flowing . . . there must always be a greater store of raw material, etc. at the place of production than is used up daily or weekly.'[30]

Cheapness of transport and communication plays a great part in minimising the level of stocks which need to be held. There is less need to hold stocks, say of spare parts, if a telephone call to the machine manufacturer will ensure their delivery within a short time.

The growing scale and complexity of capitalist production increases the mass and range of products from the various branches of industry. Thus 'the mass of capital tied up for a shorter or longer time in the form of commodity capital grows, and hence the commodity stock grows as well.'[31] Workers are paid weekly and live from hand to mouth and thus must find their means of subsistence available as a stock, e.g. in the local supermarket. The worker as consumer pays for the cost of stock-holding in the price of the product.

Marx distinguishes between voluntary and involuntary stock formation. The former is what is necessary to carry on the circulation process: 'the commodity stock must have a certain volume in order to satisfy the scale of demand over a given period.'[32] As stocks are called upon they are renewed and the wholesaler or retailer tries to have a stock adequate to meet average demand. Every item is in stock for a greater or lesser period. 'It is only by way of this stock formation that the permanence and continuity of the circulation process is ensured, and hence that of the reproduction process which includes the circulation process.'[33]

The level of stocks (or inventories as they are sometimes called) can be a sensitive indicator of business conditions and if they rise excessively, or involuntarily, they can be the harbinger of a crisis of overproduction in the system as a whole. Stocks then grow because there is an interruption in the circuit C-M; commodities cannot be sold. Production may be going along merrily but the commodities may simply be finding their way into stock until it is suddenly realised that this chain has been broken.[34]

Marx shows that circulation costs involving a change in the form of the commodity do not create new value or surplus value. They simply enable value to be realised or to be changed from one form into another. From the point of view of the capitalist class as a whole, therefore, these costs represent a deduction from their surplus value. A distinction is made for transport. Marx points out that 'the use-value of things is realised only in consumption, and their consumption may make a change of location necessary, and thus also the additional production process of the transport industry. The productive capital invested in this industry thus adds value to the products transported, partly through the value added by the work of transport.'[35]

These chapters evidently required a very close study of business practice and no doubt reflected information supplied by Engels from his own experience, though he is too modest, in this role of editor, to say so. Although this practice has changed in its form over the past one hundred years owing to changes in technology, the immensely greater scale of business organisation and new forms of transport and communication, essentially it has not changed. The capitalist as an individual has largely disappeared from the process of production and capital is personified more often by the giant corporation with its agents. Nevertheless, Marx's analysis remains as exact and penetrating in its main lines as when it was written.

Some account has been given here of what Marx was doing in the first part of *Capital*, Volume II with a view to encouraging readers to study it for themselves. This procedure will be continued in the next chapter which will go on to the second part of the volume.

Notes

[1] *Capital Volume II* by Karl Marx. Introduced by Ernest Mandel. Translated by David Fernbach. Published by Penguin Books in association with New Left Review. Harmondsworth, 1978. Price £2.95. All page references are to this edition.
[2] Preface, p.86.
[3] p.81.
[4] p.111.
[5] p.115.
[6] p.118.
[7] p.118.
[8] p.121.
[9] p.121. 'Whatever the social form of production, workers and means of production always remain its factors. But if they are in a state of mutual separation, they are only potentially factors of production. For any production to take place, they must be connected. The particular form and mode in which this connection is effected is what distinguishes the various economic epochs of the social structure.' *ibid*, p.120.
[10] p.133.

[11] p.137.
[12] As Marx puts it later, if it is assumed that the capitalist consumes all the surplus value: 'This assumption is equivalent to assuming the non-existence of capitalist production and therefore the non-existence of the industrial capitalist himself. For capitalism is already essentially abolished once we assume that it is enjoyment that is the driving motive and not enrichment itself,' p.199.
[13] p.177.
[14] pp.177-178.
[15] p.185.
[16] p.183. 'If $C'-M'$ comes to a halt in the case of one portion, for example, if the commodity is unsaleable, then the circuit of this part is interrupted and its replacement by its means of production is not accomplished; the successive parts that emerge from the production process as C' find their change of function barred by their predecessors. If this continues for some time, production is restricted and the whole process brought to a halt. Every delay in the succession brings the co-existence into disarray, every delay in one stage causes a greater or lesser delay in the entire circuit, not only that of the portion of capital that is delayed, but also that of the entire individual capital.' p.183
[17] p.187.
[18] 'Thus the circulation process of industrial capital is characterised by the many-sided character of its origins, and the existence of the market as a world market', p.190.
[19] p.190.
[20] p.196. Marx here takes a hit at economics: 'It is typical of the bourgeois horizon', he writes, 'where business deals fill the whole of peoples' minds, to see the foundation of the mode of production in the mode of commerce corresponding to it, rather than the other way round.'
[21] p.203.
[22] p.204.
[23] p.206.
[24] p.207.
[25] p.209.
[26] p.211.
[27] p.212.
[28] p.214. As Marx says, these *faux frais*, or overheads or one kind or another grow with the development of capitalist production: 'This is part of the social wealth which has to be sacrificed to the circulation process'. The swollen costs of advertising of competing but virtually identical products trying to convince consumers that they need overpriced, useless, unnecessary or positively harmful things is a striking case.
[29] p.216.
[30] p.219.
[31] p.221. As Marx says 'without the commodity stock, no commodity circulation', p.223.
[32] p.223.
[33] p.224.
[34] 'The rise in the volume of the commodity stock as a result of a stagnation in circulation can thus be mistaken for a symptom of an expansion in the reproduction process, particularly if the real movement is mystified by the development of the credit system', p.225.
[35] p.226-27.

Chapter 12

The unknown 'Capital': Marx's second volume[1] Part 2

Under the capitalist mode of production the commodity becomes the general form of the product; relations between men assume the form of relations between things. The majority of the population becomes transformed into wage-earners who have nothing to sell but their labour-power. Control of production is in the hands of the owners of the means of production which become capital because of the specific social relationship between them and the workers whose labour-power they buy as a commodity. The unpaid labour of the workers, surplus-value, is extracted in the process of production. Labour-power is sold at its value but produces more than its value; this part, or surplus value, is appropriated by the owners of the means of production. These essential relations of capitalism were extracted by Marx through a detailed critique of existing political economy which was unable to perceive and accurately explain the source of surplus-value in unpaid labour time. Instead, the classical political economists saw surplus value, or profit, arising within the sphere of circulation. They did this because they remained at the level of appearances and were unable to penetrate to the essence of capitalist social relations. Later the economists deliberately smothered the reality of capitalist relations in a mass of apologetics and became the hired prize-fighters of the capitalist class.

A major error of the greatest of the classical political economists, Adam Smith and David Ricardo, was their inability to distinguish clearly between *variable* capital (that part of capital laid out in wages) and other parts of *circulating* capital, such as raw materials, fuel, etc. Marx takes up this error in the second part of *Capital*, Volume II and it forms a major theme of that part of his work. To reveal clearly what was distinctive and specific about variable capital and to continue his critique of classical political economy Marx had to go deeper into the matter than he had done in Volume I. He also had to bolt and bar every nook or crevice through which an opposition to the law of value could be developed. With these ends in view Marx had to make a detailed analysis of capital in all its various metamorphoses over periods of time. In short, capital enters onto the scene as money used to buy the instruments of production and labour-power; it then assumes the form of productive capital in the production process where surplus value is extracted; it passes into the form of circulation capital and then back into money as the commodity goes into individual or productive consumption.

Of course, there is no such thing as an individual capital in isolation from other capitals, though in Volume I Marx had begun necessarily with the individual capitalist. The functioning of any one capital presumes the existence of others supplying commodity capital as well as the means to buy the commodities produced. Moreover, time is involved in all the operations of production and circulation and these time spans vary considerably from one field to another. In some cases the capital thrown into production will return after a short interval of time; in others, such as the production of machinery and plant, the interval may be one of months and years. Nature takes a hand in some processes so that, for example, wood cannot be used until it has been seasoned or wine drunk until it has matured. All the various processes of circulation and production must be taking place continuously and simultaneously. They require capital to take on various forms of appearance but always money begins the process and the capitalist is left with a larger sum of money at the end. However, from what has been said, it is clear that different capitals stay in particular forms (say as machines, raw materials, stocks of finished goods) for longer or shorter periods before resuming the money form. The complexity and variety of these forms of appearance thus blur the essential relations. Marx penetrated to the essence; but at the same time he followed all the various forms of appearance as they presented themselves in the day-to-day operations of capitalist business. In fact, he could not have reached the essence without reproducing in thought the movement of matter itself.

Marx's method was to proceed by way of abstraction. Not every aspect could be considered simultaneously; the way to the whole was through an assemblage of the parts; but the parts could only be derived from the whole and could not be grasped in separation from it. In the second part of Volume II he is concerned with specific parts and in doing so he makes certain assumptions so that the particular relationships he wants to examine can be held in focus. In the third part and in Volume III he takes up the movement of the social capital as a whole.

Undoubtedly this method of Marx poses certain problems for the reader who wants to push on to the conclusions and does not always see the point of what may seem to be tedious detail. Even Engels, who edited the manuscripts, was exasperated and intrudes himself to say so. He suggests at one point that Marx could have spared the reader some of the calculations in the text without loss.[2] It does not matter whether Engels was justified or not; Marx clearly wanted to be satisfied in his own mind and required arithmetical and algebraic calculations for that purpose. Perhaps had he lived to see the second and third parts of *Capital* through the press he would have been more indulgent towards the reader.

The turnover time of an individual capital is the time for which the capitalist has to advance his capital for surplus value to be added to it and for him to receive it back in its original state. Its duration comprises circulation time and production time. Different parts of the capital advanced perform different functions and these have to be strictly distinguished and defined. The basic distinction is that between constant capital and variable capital (i.e. the amount advanced for wages). All capital circulates, but it does so over different periods of time. Part of constant capital is fixed capital. This does not mean that it is confined to a particular place; a ship or a locomotive can be fixed capital. It is their form which is fixed by virtue of their function in the labour process. They yield up the value embodied in them over a relatively long period of time, bit by bit. The working life of a machine may be ten years; during that time its value circulates by degrees in the product until at the end of that time it has to be replaced. Other parts of constant capital, such as raw materials, fuel, electricity for lighting, give up their value to the product in a different way have constantly to be renewed. Marx calls them circulating capital. Their value is embodied directly in the product.

Expenditure on raw materials, then, forms part of the circulating capital. As for the part paid out in wages, neither the worker's means of subsistence nor his labour power circulate in the product but only the portion of productive capital spent on it, that is to say, variable capital. Variable capital is part of circulating capital, but classical political economy made a serious mistake in not distinguishing variable capital from the rest of the circulating capital. Not only does labour power transfer its own value to the product, but it constantly adds surplus value, something which none of the other elements of capital are able to do. Apart from this vital point the main distinction between fixed and circulating capital is that the former transfers only part of its value to the product in a given time, while the rest continues to function in the production process, while the latter transfers its whole value to the product and thus has constantly to be replaced.

It was Adam Smith's inability to understand the distinction between circulating and variable capital which made him attribute the formation of profit to something happening in the sphere of circulation. As Marx says, this was 'a crudely empirical conception'; it operated from appearances and accepted 'the everyday idea that, because surplus value is only realised by sale of the product, by its circulation, it therefore arises simply from sale, from circulation.'[3] Again, because variable capital and other parts of circulating capital play a similar role in the turnover of capital, the different roles they play in the formation of surplus-value was, very conveniently, left out. The other parts of circulating capital cannot add more value to the product than they themselves possess. Their distinction from fixed capital lies in the fact that they are completely consumed in the product (even though, of course, they may not pass into it in a physical form, *value* is what counts here).

What Adam Smith left out was the role of variable capital in the production process. It is here that the value laid out on labour power is transformed 'from a definite, constant quantity into a variable one, and the value advanced in capital value, in capital, is thereby transformed for the first time into self-valorising value.

But because it is not the value laid out on labour-power that Smith defines as a fluid component of the productive capital, but rather the value laid out on the worker's means of subsistence, it is impossible for him to understand the distinction between variable and constant capital'.[4] Indeed, his blunder barred the way for his successors coming to such an understanding.

A similar critique is applied to Ricardo who also saw the capital laid out on wages only from the standpoint of circulation. It was thus impossible to see that 'the portion of value that the capital laid out on wages adds to the product is freshly produced (and thus actually reproduced), while the portion of value that the raw material adds to the product is not freshly produced, and not really reproduced, but is simply maintained and conserved in the value of the product, and hence merely re-appears as a component of the product's value'.[5]

Thus Ricardo also obliterates the all-important distinction between variable and constant capital, liquidating it into the distinction between fixed and circulating capital.[6] As a result: 'The basis for the understanding of the real movement of capitalist production and thus of capitalist exploitation, was thus submerged at one blow. All that was involved on this view [which is that of bourgeois economics today] was the reappearance of values advanced'.[7] What is concealed, therefore, is that when an industrial capitalist hires a worker he buys value-creating power which he cannot obtain anywhere else. Surplus value arises from the 'exchange of value for value-creating power, from the conversion of a constant quantity into a variable one'.[8]

Marx makes this clear in an important passage:

> The real material of the capital laid out on wages is labour itself, self-acting, value-creating labour power, living labour, which the capitalist has exchanged for dead objectified labour, and incorporated into his capital, this being the way that the value existing in his hands is first transformed into a self-valorising value. But the capitalist does not sell this power of self-valorisation. It forms throughout simply a component of his commodity capital, like the finished product that he sells, for instance. Within the production process, the means of labour, as components of productive capital, are not distinguished from labour power as fixed capital, any more than the material of labour and ancillaries coincide with it as circulating capital. From the standpoint of the labour process, both of these confront labour-power as the personal

factor, they themselves being the objective factors. From the standpoint of the valorisation process, both are distinct from labour-power, variable capital, as constant capital. Alternatively, if we are to speak of a material difference that affects the circulation process, this is simply that it follows from the nature of value, which is nothing other than objectified labour, and from the nature of self-acting labour-power, which is nothing other than self-objectifying labour, that labour-power constantly creates value and surplus-value as long as it continues to function; that what presents itself on its side as movement, as the creation of value, presents itself on the side of its product in a motionless form, as created value. If the labour-power has performed its function, then the capital no longer consists of labour-power on the one hand and means of production on the other. The capital value that was laid out on labour-power is now value which has been added to the product (together with surplus-value). In order to repeat the process, the product must be sold, and with the money released by this, labour-power has constantly to be bought afresh and incorporated into the productive capital. This then is what gives the portion of capital laid out on labour-power the character of circulating capital in contrast to the capital that remains fixed in the means of labour.[9]

The glossing over of the distinction between constant and variable capital and the lumping together with circulating capital of the latter obscures its specific contribution to the production process, i.e. the production of surplus value. Marx links this up with commodity fetishism previously developed in Volume I. 'What is brought to fulfilment here,' he writes, 'is the fetishism peculiar to bourgeois economics, which transforms the social, economic character that things are stamped with in the process of social production, into a natural character arising from the material nature of these things.'[10] What is involved here is something much more fundamental than whether a definition is correct or not; it is a whole method: bourgeois ideology versus the scientific method of Marxism.

The discussion of variable capital and circulating capital and the exposure of the errors of Smith and Ricardo takes up almost a half of the second part of *Capital* Volume II and is probably the most important section. Marx then goes on to examine the working period, production time and circulation time. The working period is the number of days required to produce a finished product. It can, therefore, vary enormously and thus involve the tying up of capital for different periods of time. Production time is not the same as working time; the latter relates to the labour process but production time includes the natural process involved in the final product. Turnover time also includes circulation time, that is to say the time in which the capital exists in the state of commodity capital, i.e. when it is waiting to be sold. This period may be longer or shorter according to many factors. For example, transport improvements reduce that time while production for more distant markets, with the growth of the world market, tends to increase it. Marx emphasises the fact that capital is constantly passing through the three forms of money capital, productive capital and commodity capital and do so alongside each other. Bourgeois economists forget, he says, the role played by money capital. In going on to establish this he takes a series of examples, making up the most laborious pages of this part for the reader. (Engels' reservations have already been noted.) He then performs a similar operation for the turnover of varialble capital, showing how different durations of the turnover period determine the varying magnitudes of money capital which have to be advanced with the same amount of circulating capital and the same amount of labour.

This is particularly relevant to those forms of production, such as the building of railways, which involve a prolonged turnover period in the course of which neither means of poduction nor means of subsistence are produced. Such outlays under capitalism are a major source of booms, and the cessation of slumps, aggravated by money-market speculation. Under a communist society, Marx points out,

> The matter would be simply reduced to the fact that society must reckon in advance how much labour, means of production and means of subsistence it can spend, without dislocation, on branches of industry which, like the building of railways, for instance, supply neither means of production nor means of subsistence, nor any kind of useful effect, for a long period, a year or more, though they certainly do withdraw labour, means of production and means of subsistence from the total annual product.[11]

In the final chapter of this part Marx deals with what happens to the surplus value. Taken on the basis of the individual capital this may at first take the form of a money hoard, latent money capital put aside until enough is available to make a given outlay, say, on a new factory. This assumes what Marx calls 'expanded reproduction'. Even if the surplus value is consumed unproductively it will still at first assume the form of money, so that some part of surplus value will always have this form. Therefore a part of social production under capitalism must be producing new money, i.e. gold and silver. Some part of this goes towards replacing what has been used up by wear and tear, the rest is necessary if total production of surplus value is increasing. The gold-and silver-producing capitalists realise their surplus value directly in this form of money whether there is simple reproduction or expanded reproduction.

Marx devotes some time to a connected problem. Since surplus value must be realised for money, where does the money come from to realise an increased amount of surplus value? Marx assumes that all third parties must receive their money from the capitalists or the workers. Clearly surplus value cannot be realised by selling it to workers; the primary point of departure must be the capitalist class as a whole who throw money into circulation in the first place. 'The entire capitalist class,' writes Marx, 'cannot extract anything from the circulation sphere that was not put into it already.'[12] He solves this paradox by the nature of the capitalist class: that it must have reserves of money capital adequate to realise the surplus value under conditions of simple reproduction.[13] Under conditions of expanded reproduction the increased supply of money comes from the gold- and silver-producing capitalists. 'If one group of capitalists constantly pump more money out of the circulation sphere than they put into it, the gold-producing group constantly pump more money in than they withdraw from it in means of production.'[14]

What Marx does in this chapter is to bring out the vital role of money in the circulation of capital. This was true historically:

> The capitalist mode of production — since its basis is wage-labour, and therefore also the payment of the worker in money and the general transformation of services in kind into money payments — can develop on a large scale and penetrate deeply only when there is a quantity of money in the country in question sufficient for circulation and for the hoard formation (reserve fund, etc.) conditioned by this circulation. This is a historical pre-condition, even if the situation should not be conceived in such a way that a sufficient hoard has first to be formed before capitalist production can begin. The latter rather develops

simultaneously with the development of its preconditions, and one of these preconditions is a sufficient supply of precious metals.[15]

There is no point, therefore, in lengthy debate about which came first: the development of capitalism or an increased supply of money.

In this part Marx thus links the process of reproduction with the output of the precious metals, leaving aside the credit system and paper money. The breakdown of the monetary system based on the precious metals in the twentieth century, beginning with the outbreak of the First World War, the failure of successive attempts to create it afresh in the interwar period and again in a different form after 1945 have reacted strongly to disrupt and break up the whole system of reproduction and to plunge it into crisis. A full theoretical analysis of this period requires a study and application of the principles established by Marx in this part of his work.

Notes

[1] Karl Marx, *Capital* Volume II. Penguin Books.
[2] Engels writes: 'Despite Marx's firm grasp of algebra, he was never at ease in reckoning with figures, i.e. in commercial calculations, even though there is a thick sheaf of notebooks in which he worked through all the various kinds of commercial calculations in several examples. But knowledge of the proper rules of calculation is not at all the same thing as exercise in the everyday practical calculations of the trader, and in his turnover calculations Marx became confused, with the result that, apart from being incomplete, they contain many errors and contradictions.' p.359.
[3] *Capital*, Volume II, pp. 276-77.
[4] ibid., p.291.
[5] ibid., p.296.
[6] ibid. In criticising Ricardo Marx says of his work that: 'The all important distinction between variable and constant capital is thereby obliterated, and with it the whole secret of surplus-value formation and of capitalist production, namely the circumstances that transform certain values and things in which they are represented into capital', p.296.
[7] ibid., p.297.
[8] ibid., p.298.
[9] ibid., p.298-99.
[10] ibid., p.303.
[11] ibid., p.390.
[12] ibid., p.408.
[13] 'In point of fact,' writes Marx, 'paradoxical as it may seem at the first glance, the capitalist class itself casts into circulation the money that serves towards the realisation of the surplus-value contained in its commodities,' p.409.
[14] ibid., p.411.
[15] ibid., p.418.

Chapter 13

The unknown 'Capital': Marx's second volume[1] Part 3

It can be said that Part Three of *Capital* Volume II is the best known, or least neglected, part of the Volume. For that there is a good reason: it contains notable advances in theory which make up a vital part of Marx's overall critique of political economy. Besides pursuing the consequences of the distinction between variable capital and constant capital made in previous sections and in Volume I, he announces a further discovery, the division of production into its two great branches which he calls Department I and Department II. The first produces means of production, the second means of consumption. Then, on the basis that the determining motive of the capitalist mode of production is the production of surplus value, Marx is able to put these components together to provide the famous schema of reproduction which have subsequently been an unending source of controversy. Indeed, it can be said that they have led not a few would-be interpreters and improvers of Marx's work astray. Within the compass of an expository article it is not possible to deal with these controversies, though more will be said about them in the concluding article dealing with the ineffable Mandel's introduction to the Pelican edition.

The reader should be warned at this point that this book cannot be a substitute for the reading and study of Marx's text. It is intended as a guide, pointing out and explaining some leading themes. It should be remembered that Marx did not live to revise and improve his manuscripts for publication and would perhaps have pruned them down for final publication or emphasised the main conclusions for the reader's benefit. Much of Volume II, including many pages of the Third Part, are a detailed investigation and working out of basic points in the analysis made for the sake of completion and to close all doors to opponents. *Capital* was written as part of an intellectual and theoretical struggle against bourgeois political economy in order to obtain as accurate a picture of the working out of the laws of motion of the capitalist mode of production as was possible. Marx carries on in this volume, and in all his work on political economy, a constant polemic against his bourgeois predecessors who had been unable to explain, or had actually distorted, the process of the reproduction of capital and the production of surplus value. He vigorously opposed those who saw this as a natural, harmonious or even eternal process. At many stages in his analysis he emphasises the potentiality for crisis arising out of the anarchy of capitalist production relations, contrasting the specific features of the labour process under capitalism with what it would be when production was organised by the community as a whole after the socialist revolution.

It should be obvious that in this volume Marx carries forward, assumes and further develops all the scientific concepts already worked out in earlier parts of *Capital*. Naturally, this includes the law of value and the nature and source of surplus value as well as the commodity as a unity of opposites — use-value and value — and the difference between abstract and concrete labour. However, until the third part of Volume II Marx had been mainly concerned with the individual capitalist and his workers; the problem now is the self-expansion of the social capital as a whole. This is what the schemas of production are about, yet it is important to remember that they are abstractions and are not intended as an accurate portrayal of how capitalism works in practice. Marx constructs what Lenin called 'a chemically pure' capitalism in order better to extract the essence of the matter. This is very evident in Chapter 20, the longest chapter in this part, which considers 'Simple Reproduction', that is to say capitalism without accumulation. Of course, accumulation of capital is the very lifeblood of the system. Yet, by means of this abstraction, Marx is able to establish certain definite relationships which hold good under conditions where accumulation is the rule.

The introduction to this part constitutes a watershed between the previous chapters, including Volume I, and the remaining part of this volume and Volume III. Marx points out that he is now concerned with the production process of capital as a whole rather than its individual parts. It was necessary to begin by breaking down the whole into parts — Volume I analyses the movement of an individual capital — but the parts can only be fully grasped in terms of the whole. As he puts it:

> Each individual capital forms only a fraction of the total social capital, a fraction that has acquired independence and been endowed with individual life, so to speak, just as each individual capitalist is no more than an element of the capitalist class. The movement of the social capital is made up of the totality of the movements of these autonomous fractions, the turnovers of the individual capitals. Just as the metamorphosis of the individual commodity is but one term in the series of metamorphoses of the commodity world as a whole, of commodity circulation, so the metamorphosis of the individual capital, is a single term in the circuit of the social capital.[2]

Each individual capitalist is linked with his fellows as a buyer and as a seller to make up the circulation of capital as a whole. He is subject to laws acting coercively upon him from outside. Hitherto it had been assumed by Marx that the individual capitalist found buyers in the market and that he could find the commodity capital needed to continue production as well as a supply of labour power. The emphasis was on 'the purchase and sale of labour power as the basic condition of capitalist production'.[3]

In the first two parts of Volume II, as we have seen, Marx was concerned with the different turnover periods of the various components of capital, the different forms of appearance it assumed in the course of circulation and in the production process where new value is created. In particular he was able to show the specific role assumed by money capital in enabling the whole process to function. The capitalist began with a given sum of money with which he bought the elements of constant capital and variable capital (the purchase of labour power) and ended up with a larger sum of money, augmented by the surplus value added by living labour. Something more was required for, as Marx puts it, 'the circuits of individual capital are interlinked, they presuppose one another and condition one another, and it is precisely by being interlinked in this way that they constitute the movement of the total social capital'.[4] To consider the circulation process of the total social capital was to take the reproduction process of capital as a whole.

Money capital has to be considered as an integral part of the total social capital. Each individual capital begins its career as money capital; commodities are constantly being exchanged for money and money for commodities. All the calculations required in the course of these metamorphoses are made in money terms. The total social output must be realised for money in the same way as the output of the individual capitalists. According to the different turnover periods, money is being paid out or received. For instance, the capitalist who provides elements of fixed capital, or the capitalist who uses up fixed capital over a period, comes into possession of a sum of money. In the latter case, it will be equal to the value transferred to the product. On the other hand, he does not have to buy that amount of fixed capital from the supplier. No seller of a commodity is obliged to use the money so received to buy another commodity; hence the possibility of crisis is present from the start, at many stages in the circulation process of capital.

The advances of money capital required will depend upon the scale of production and the length of the turnover period. Large-scale projects of the kind inseparable from advanced capitalism, such as railways in Marx's day, demand larger amounts of money capital than can be provided by the individual capitalist and lead to formation of joint stock companies and resort to credit. Marx points out: 'Disturbances in the money market therefore bring such business to a halt while those same businesses, for their part, induce disturbances in the money market.'[5] He goes on to point out that 'on the basis of social production', it would be necessary to determine how labour-power and means of production could be withdrawn without producing a dearth of goods in the short period while at the same time supplying means of subsistence for those employed in such projects. This problem would be solved by planning and without the use of money.

> With collective production [writes Marx] money capital is completely dispensed with. The society distributes labour-power and means of production between the various branches of industry. There is no reason why the producers should not receive paper tokens permitting them to withdraw an amount corresponding to their labour time from

the social consumption stock. But these tokens are not money; they do not circulate.⁶

In other words, workers would receive a share of the total social output according to their contribution or according to needs (in the higher stage of socialism, communism). The paper tokens could not be saved up so that some men could employ others and get rich at their expense.

Marx only refers to such differences between capitalism and socialism in passing. His main concern is how reproduction takes place under the capitalist system.⁷ As he says, 'the immediate form in which the problem presents itself is this. How is the *capital* consumed in production replaced in its value out of the annual product, and how is the movement of this replacement intertwined with the consumption of surplus-value by the capitalists and of wages by the workers?'⁸

As already mentioned, Marx handles this problem by an assumption, namely he takes simple reproduction — quite unrealistic as far as the real world of capitalism is concerned — because this enables him to get to the essence of the problem in a more direct way. The classical political economists were unable to provide a correct solution to the problem of reproduction because, like their descendants (or more properly their epigones) today, they were trapped in the tripartite formula of three 'factors of production' and three 'sources of revenue'. Thus the price of a commodity was supposed to be 'made up' of profits, rent and wages; or, according to neo-classical theory, each 'factor' receives its 'marginal product'. This theory completely obliterates the real social relations of the capitalist mode of production and is particularly unable to explain profits. Marx traced the weakness of Adam Smith's explanation specifically to the failure to distinguish between *variable* capital (paid out to purchase labour power) and other forms of *circulating* capital (like raw material) and to see the latter as only part of *constant* capital.

The distinction between constant capital and variable capital had already been made in Volume I, but it is here that it comes into its own. This is because Marx was now able to couple it with another great discovery, the breakdown of society's total production into two departments: Department I produces means of production; Department II produces means of consumption. The use-values produced by Department II enter directly into the consumption of workers and capitalists. Those produced by Department I, steel ingots, machines or locomotives, can only be consumed productively and cannot enter into individual consumption. Quite different types of concrete labour are involved in making steel ingots, machines or locomotives than are needed to produce loaves, shoes or ballpoint pens.

In each department, as for the individual capitalist, capital has two components: variable capital (paid for labour power) and constant capital — all the means of production employed, so far as they are used up or worn out and their value is transferred to the product. Constant capital already exists as the product of past (dead) labour; it cannot create *new* value. This is the specific contribution of *living* labour, which both reproduces the value of labour power paid for by the capitalists and creates new value, surplus-value, appropriated by the owners of the means of production. The annual value of each department thus breaks down into $c + v + s$ (where c = constant capital, v = variable capital and s = surplus value).

Having established the concepts necessary to solve the problem, Marx then proceeds to apply them in a detailed working out of the manifold interconnections between the two departments. The basis of these interconnections lies in the fact that Department I has to provide the means of production for Department II as well as for its own production. Since Department I produces no means of consumption, both workers and capitalists have to purchase them from Department II; definite relationships are thus established between the c, v and s in the two departments. These relationships are brought about through the circulation of money (and would not otherwise be possible) and Marx traces them out in considerable detail and in a way which readers may find tedious or difficult to follow. However, this is a necessary scientific enterprise if the laws of motion of the capitalist mode of production are to be reproduced in thought.

In the course of his analysis Marx develops a number of propositions concerning the relationships between the two departments under conditions of simple reproduction, i.e. where surplus value passes into individual consumption. A few examples of his conclusions may be given. Thus, Department I has to sell its product to Department II;[9] for this to happen its v + s must equal the means of production used up in Department II, i.e. its c. Department II must produce necessities for workers and capitalists, as well as the luxury goods on which the latter spend much of their surplus value (on the assumption of simple reproduction, that there is no accumulation). In this connection Marx makes one of his most emphatic statements against underconsumptionism as a cause of crises.

> It is pure tautology [he writes] to say that crises are provoked by a lack of effective demand or effective consumption. The capitalist system does not recognise any forms of consumer other than those who can pay, if we exclude the consumption of paupers and swindlers. The fact that commodities are unsaleable means no more than that no effective buyers have been found for them, i.e., no consumers (no matter whether the commodities are ultimately sold to meet the needs of productive or individual consumption). If the attempt is made to give this tautology the semblance of greater profundity, by the statement that the working class receives too small a proportion of its own product, and that the evil would be remedied if it received a bigger share, i.e. if its wage rose, we need only note that crises are always prepared by a period in which wages generally rise, and the working class actually does receive a greater share in the part of the annual product destined for consumption.[10]

Against all the shame-faced underconsumptionists and Keynesians of the late boom, the world crisis of capitalism magnificently confirms Marx's position and exposes the revisionist theories of 'neo-capitalism' and 'permanent war economy'.

Of course, the money paid out by the capitalists as wages (i.e. variable capital from the latters' point of view) flows back to them in payment for commodities and makes up a considerable portion of the monetary circulation. But the sale of goods to the working class is not the source of enrichment of the capitalist class as a whole: that always comes from the surplus value extracted in the process of production. The circulation process helps to distribute this surplus, accruing first of all to the industrial capitalists, to other capitalists. In this volume Marx does not deal with the other recipients of surplus value since he assumes a society consisting only of capitalists and workers and this aspect is not taken up until Volume III. Within this assumption, however, it is clear that it is the capitalists who must throw into circulation the money needed to realise this surplus value.

Department I, producing means of production, thus provides its own constant capital. But this department is made up of various branches of production and many firms so that products in their natural form change their places and go through many transformations without leaving this department in a process of mutual exchange.

Assuming simple reproduction, the total value produced by labour within the course of a year must be equal to the total value of the means of consumption produced because there is no accumulation of capital. The value of the means of production has been maintained and the value equivalent of the new production added to that of the means of consumption. But this could not have taken place if means of production did not already exist, so that the transfer of value does not necessarily correspond with the material constituents transferred. Marx is dealing with an ongoing process and the schemas of production, so to speak, break into this and examine its working in the course of one (or several) years. In dealing with the two great departments Marx considers not the individual firm but the 'collective capitalist'. 'The total capital,' as he says, 'appears as the share capital of all individual capitalists together.'[11] It is only in this way that some capitals can be used exclusively for producing means of production and others for producing means of consumption.

Marx claims that the value of the total product, on his assumptions, will be greater than the value added by labour in the current year. 'The *value product* of the current year,' he writes, 'the value newly created during the year in the commodity form, is smaller than the *value of the product*, the total value of the mass of commodities produced during the year.'[12] This follows from the fact that value that existed beforehand, embodied in constant capital, is transferred to the product to a greater or lesser extent. It is a characteristic of capitalist society that it spends a large proportion of current income on the production of means of production that can only function as capital. Marx then examines the circumstances under which capital for one person becomes revenue for another, taking c, v and s in the two Departments and assuming the 'collective capitalist' and the 'collective worker' in each of them.

The clearest example is that of variable capital which exists first as *money capital* in the hands of the capitalist employer, is used to buy labour power and then becomes revenue (wages) in the hands of the wage-labourer. He must convert this money into means of subsistence, producing and reproducing labour-power. Whether employed in Department I or Department II he can only do this by purchasing commodities produced by the latter. The money only acts as *capital* in the hands of the buyer of labour power. The worker simply buys means of consumption sold by capitalists in Department II who are thus enabled to buy means of production, c, from Department I. These capitalists are not enriched by these transactions which merely enable them to realise part of the surplus value already created by the collective worker. The workers in Department I also buy means of consumption but no means of production, the product of their Department. The collective capitalist here sells means of production to the capitalists in Department II, getting back the variable portion of its capital in money form to continue the process. However, the capitalist who receives money in payment does not have to buy anything with it. Nor does constant capital used up have to be replaced at once. He may simply hoard the money, thus interrupting the process.

At the heart of these interconnections stands the relationship between the owners of the means of production and the wage-labourers. Variable capital plays the decisive role because it alone creates new value (as well as preserving and transferring to the product already existing value embodied in constant capital). This variable capital assumes different forms: money capital, an element of productive capital, a value component of the commodity and once again money when the commodity is sold.[13] Moreover, the employer only pays out the worker after he already has the replacement value that labour-power creates for itself in the production process as well as the surplus value.

The various elements of constant capital are used up at different rates in the course of production. Some have to be replaced forthwith. As regards fixed capital, with a lengthy turnover period, its value is transferred to the product by degrees as it slowly wears out, having eventually to be replaced completely by new plant or machinery. The value transferred to the product is recouped in money as it is sold and may be held by the capitalist as a hoard until the time comes to transform it back into the elements of fixed capital. Or, indeed, the capitalist may decide to do something else with the money; a seller does not have to buy. In any case the flows within or between the two Departments are not simply an exchange of products. 'Money plays a specific role in it, one which is expressed in the very manner in which the fixed capital value is reproduced,' Marx writes.[14] The various commodities produced in the two Departments contain differing proportions of constant capital, requiring to be replaced at different intervals of time over the year. As far as fixed capital is concerned its life may be ten years or more at the end of which it has to be entirely replaced, as already shown.

Depreciation has to be accounted for by the allocation of successive sums of money which have then to be reconverted into the material elements of fixed capital supplied by Department I. If this does not take place on the requisite scale then there will be over-production in Department I. As Marx points out, 'in this way the whole basis of the schema would be destroyed, i.e. reproduction on the same scale, which presupposes complete proportionality between the various systems of production'.[15] Disproportions between the two Departments or the different branches of industry of which they are composed can be a potent source of crisis, though not the main one as some Marxists have claimed.

These proportions (or, for that matter, other causes of crisis) cannot be got round by having some 'third parties' come onto the scene to make good the shortfall by buying commodities which would otherwise be unsold.[16] These 'third parties', such as landlords or receivers of interest, could not have a separate source of income where capitalist relations of production prevailed. Their revenues derive from the surplus value originating in Department I or Department II and could not, therefore act as a *deus ex machina* precisely to realise surplus value as some of the classical political economists such as Malthus claimed. Nor is it any good to suggest that merchants can play such a role since they would fare no better in disposing of excess production arising in one or both departments. After dealing with these cases Marx sums up as follows:

We see here how, apart from our specific purpose of considering the reproduction process in its fundamental form — setting aside all obscuring circumstances that intervene — it is necessary throughout to do away with the false subterfuges that provide a semblance of 'scientific' explanation, if the process of social reproduction in its intricate concrete form is to become the subject of our analysis.[17]

In the course of this chapter on Simple Reproduction Marx considers various conditions under which the schema of reproduction might operate. It is clear from a reading of these sections that no credence can be given to the view that Marx saw reproduction as a harmonious process. On the contrary, he is at pains to show how unlikely this was if only because of the difficulty in maintaining the necessary proportions between the different branches of production. For example, there will be a crisis of production if more fixed capital than usual or less fixed capital than usual has to be replaced in a given year. For instance, in the latter case there will be a surplus of production in Department I leading to its contraction with losses for the capitalists, plant closures and unemployment. Difficulties of a different kind would result from the inability of Department I to meet an exceptional need for fixed capital. Ups and downs arising from such causes are unavoidable under capitalism. On the other hand 'once we dispense with the capitalist form of reproduction' and assume a socialist plan in which society takes charge of the objective means of its own reproduction, such problems become manageable and no longer result in crisis. It is the 'anarchic element' in capitalism that produces disproportions.[18]

Marx then returns to the role of money, assuming first that it consists of gold. The production of gold thus forms part of Deparment I and the producers exchange their gold directly for commodities. Capitalism requires an increasing supply of the money material. Indeed, the existence of available money is a condition for the reproduction process to continue since the entire output has to be converted into money. Indeed, the process begins with the throwing of money into circulation for the purchase of constant and variable capital. A new business will require the supply of money to tide it over the period before the product is realised, including the surplus value it contains. A great part of the money required goes on the purchase of variable capital, i.e. is paid out as wages. 'To the degree that the wage system develops,' writes

Marx, 'all products are transformed into commodities and all — with few exceptions — must therefore jointly undergo the transformation into money as a phase of their development.'[19] The spontaneous flux and reflux of money gave rise to the development of paper money and the credit system. Marx would develop this question more fully in Volume III.[20]

The final chapter of Volume II is entitled 'Accumulation and Reproduction on an Expanded Scale'. The unrealistic assumption of simple reproduction, which served its purpose in enabling certain relationships between the components of the two departments to be established, is now removed. Expanded reproduction means that part of the surplus value is accumulated, used to buy fresh means of production so that what is nowadays called 'economic growth' can take place. The schemas of reproduction with expanded reproduction could vary indefinitely according to the assumptions built into them. Marx takes a few examples to illustrate the points he wants to make, namely that the nature of the reproduction process under capitalism drives inevitably towards crisis, not for any one reason but for many. As he puts it:

> The continuous supply of labour-power on the part of the working class in Department I, the transformation of one part of Department I's commodity capital back into the money form of variable capital, the replacement of part of Department II's commodity capital by natural elements of constant capital — these necessary pre-conditions all mutually require one another, but they are mediated by a very complicated process which involves three processes of circulation that proceed independently, even if they are intertwined with one another. *The very complexity of the process provides many occasions for it to take an abnormal course.* [Emphasis added][21]

For expanded reproduction to take place and to be analysed theoretically it must already have been going on. All that means is that the existence of the capitalist mode of production is assumed (because it could not exist without expanded reproduction). We are not therefore concerned with how it came into being: this was dealt with by Marx in Volume I and can be taken for granted.

The principal conclusions derived from the study of simple reproduction still apply; the new factor to be explained is accumulation and the demands it makes on Department I and the relations between the different components of both departments.

At any moment the various firms and branches of production in Department I will be transforming surplus value into potential money capital and money capital into productive capital, new means of production. Assuming now that the credit system exists, it is not necessary for each capitalist to constitute a money hoard. He can bank money as it is received and the banks make it available to other capitalists; it is disposable capital on which the banks can draw an interest (i.e. a share of the surplus value) when it is lent out. Thus some capitalists can cast money into circulation which they have borrowed and this provides another possibility of sales and purchases not balancing. Marx shows that in the entire process money plays a vital role, giving rise 'to certain conditions for normal exchange that are peculiar to this mode of production, i.e. conditions for the normal course of reproduction, whether simple or on an expanded scale, which turn into an equal number of conditions for an abnormal course, possibilities of crisis, since, on the spontaneous pattern of this production, this balance is itself an accident.'[22]

Accumulation in the two departments has to be distinguished, bearing in mind that it originates in surplus value (unpaid labour time) which does not cost the capitalist anything. Expanded reproduction must mean that Department I tends to expand faster than Department II in value terms. This means that the surplus labour of Department I is spent directly on new means of production for that department. But since it produces means of production only it must sooner or later find an outlet in selling them to Department II. In turn, Department II's demand for means of production will depend upon its ability to realise the product and the surplus value by sale. Thus the possibilities of expanded reproduction following 'an abnormal course' are manifold. Adequate supplies of money must be available; in practice this may be achieved through the credit system itself, the source of other possible shocks and things going wrong. Marx says that it can always be assumed that supplies of labour-power will be available; but there are times when certain kinds of labour power are scarce and in a boom this may be relatively true of labour power as a whole (e.g. so-called 'overfull employment' witnessed in some countries in the 1960s by way of exception).

The main thing about these schemas of expanded reproduction

is that capitalists, in pursuit of surplus value, are constantly tempted to overshoot the mark, either provoking disproportions (as already seen) or a general crisis of overproduction. This is the sense of the examples worked out arithmetically by Marx in this part of the book as in others, and the reader can study them for himself. There is no general conclusion offered by Marx at this stage. The manuscripts selected and arranged by Engels simply break off, a witness to the unfinished state of the volume. As Engels put it in the Preface:

> The brilliant investigations of this Volume 2 and its entirely new results in areas that up to now have been almost untrodden, are simply premises for the material of Volume 3, in which the final results of Marx's presentation of the processs of social reproduction on the capitalist basis are developed.[23]

Notes

[1] See previous chapters and Chapter 14.
[2] *Capital*, Volume II, pp.427-8.
[3] *ibid.*, p.429.
[4] *ibid.*, p.429.
[5] *ibid.*, pp.433-434.
[6] *ibid.*, p.434.
[7] In that sense, too, he abstracts from the class struggle, or rather its outward forms, dealing only with its origins in the basic relations between capitalists and workers in the production process. It should be noted, also, that the schemas make various other assumptions, such as a constant rate of surplus value, no changes in productivity, no foreign trade and so on.
[8] *ibid.*
[9] Always excluding what it needs for its own use.
[10] *Capital*, Volume II, p.486.
[11] *ibid.*
[12] *ibid.*, p.521. But as he writes earlier, 'On the premise of simple reproduction, therefore, the total value of the means of consumption annually produced is equal to the annual value product, i.e. equal to the total value produced by the labour of the society in the course of the year, and the reason why this must be so is that with simple reproduction this entire value is consumed,' p.501 There does not seem any reason why the value product should not be *greater* than the value of the product if the means of production are used up and not replaced. The statement on p.501 would presumably accord with an equilibrium position.
[13] At the same time, with his wages the worker has to maintain and reproduce his labour power and the only commodity he has for sale. Thus, 'just as the money advanced by the capitalist on the purchase of labour power returns to him, so the labour-power, too returns to the labour market as a commodity exchangeable for this money,' p.522. The worker constantly recreates the social relations under which he is exploited.
[14] *Capital*, Volume II, p.527.
[15] *ibid.*, p.530.

THE UNKNOWN CAPITAL

[16] See p.497 and more particularly p.532: 'If the part of the surplus value in commodities that the industrial capitalist has to deduct as ground rent or interest for other persons with a claim on the surplus-value cannot be realised in the long run by the sale of the commodities themselves, there is then an end to the payment of rent and interest, and the landlords or the recipients or interest cannot serve as *dei ex machina* for the arbitrary realisation of certain portions of annual reproduction. It is just the same with the expenditure of all so-called unproductive workers, state officials, doctors, lawyers, etc., and others who, in the form of the "general public", perform "services" for the political economists by explaining what they leave unexplained.'

[17] *ibid.*, pp.532-3.

[18] Thus, speaking of what is obviously a socialist planned economy, and a situation where more is produced in one year than is needed in that year he writes: 'Overproduction of this kind is equivalent to control by the society over the objective means of its own reproduction. Within capitalist society, however, it is an anarchic element,' pp.544-545.

[19] *ibid.*, p.554.

[20] *ibid*, p.555-556 and later, in dealing with expanded reproduction, Marx deals with the role of money, see pp. 570-571. Thus Marx is against any view that sees money as 'neutral' — or thinks that the schemas of reproduction assume proportionality or equilibrium.

[21] *ibid.*, p.571. The older translation has 'This process is so complicated that it offers ever so many occasions for running abnormally,' p.495 in the Lawrence and Wishart edition.

[22] *ibid.*, p.570-571.

[23] Preface by Engels, p.102 in the Pelican edition.

Chapter 14
Mandel or Marx?

The revisionist 'economist' Ernest Mandel must have been an inevitable choice to write the Introductions when New Left Books, in cooperation with Penguin Books, conceived the project of a new translation of Marx's *Capital*.[1] In itself the project was laudable. The existing translations are in places defective and a rendering into a more modern English could, at the same time, obviate some of the difficulties of comprehending Marx's meaning and make the work as a whole accessible to a wider circle of readers. The publishers saw fit, however, to provide for these readers' benefit, lengthy introductions by the said Mandel, in case Marx's meaning might escape them.

Mandel's credentials for the job consisted of a prolific mass of pseudo-Marxist writing, most notably a textbook-style exposition entitled *Marxist Economic Theory*, and a university thesis with the strange title *Late Capitalism*. From the point of view of the now ageing New Left gyrating around Euro-Stalinism and hostile to genuine Marxist revolutionaries, Mandel could be counted upon to provide the right mixture of pretentious erudition and skilful evasion of the real lessons of *Capital*.

What we have in the Introductions to the first two volumes so far published fully lives up to expectations. Mandel shows his customary ability to pay respects to the form of Marxism while emptying it of real revolutionary content. Subtly, Mandel washes the face of the old Marx and dresses him up in a way acceptable to a society of professional economists and assorted seekers after truth. Amid much of what appears to be formally correct explanation or commentary, Mandel betrays Marx in true revisionist style. He turns these introductions into a vindication of his own position for which he fraudulently claims Marx's posthumous endorsement.

The first point is: who is Mandel writing for? It is evident that he is not primarily addressing workers and students who are new to *Capital* or want to begin a serious study of the work. Such a mundane task would not permit him to display his knowledge of the literature, Marxist and non-Marxist, concerned with *Capital*. Nor would it enable him to enhance his reputation as an authentic expositor of 'Marxist economics' with the international economic fraternity in the various universities where Mandel has been an honoured guest. Thus he will willingly spend a page or two refuting some silly theory which has appeared in the *American Economic Review*, the leading US journal of the academic economists, while passing over in a sentence, 'commodity fetishism', the corner-stone of Marx's theoretical contribution.[2] Mandel's task is to try to make Marxism respectable while, as befits his *alter ego* as a leader of the revisionist 'Unified Secretariat of the Fourth International', appearing to be very revolutionary at the same time. Such a double game is not beyond Mandel's talents; indeed, it might be said that he thrives on it.

For instance, Mandel assures us that he is all for dialectical materialism and spends several pages of his Introduction to Volume I discussing it. He never explains how Marx came to begin his work with the *commodity*, and passes over the first chapter, the crucial one in the entire work, with no special comment. No amount of repetition of the point that capital is a social relation can substitute for a grasp of fetishism, the key to Marx's analysis of value and of the labour-process under capitalism. Yet Mandel mentions fetishism only in passing and in the introduction to Volume II does not bring it up at all. For Marx, on the contrary, it is the key to understanding both the nature of capital and the ideological basis of bourgeois economics.

Thus, in criticising a contemporary American economist Marx writes:

> The capital values advanced to production in the shape of means of production and means of subsistence here both equally reappear in the value of the product. The capitalist production process is thus successfully transformed into a complete mystery, and the origin of the surplus-value present in the product completely withdrawn from view.

What is also brought to fulfilment here is the fetishism peculiar to bourgeois economics, which transforms the social, economic character that things are stamped with in the process of social production into a natural character arising from the material nature of these things.

And Marx goes on to refer to the section on the labour-process in Volume I and emphasises that 'means of labour are fixed capital only where the production process is in fact a capitalist production process and the means of production are thus actually capital, i.e., possess the economic determination, the social character, of capital . . .'[3]

Mandel no doubt would claim that he knows all that and has said it. Why then does he not take up the question of fetishism? The answer is that he is happy to remain at the level of appearances, just as he does in his economic commentaries. But not only that; he does not want to take on bourgeois economists in a real battle to expose their apologetic character as hired prize-fighters of the ruling class. No, he prefers a friendly debate, an abstruse discussion around technical issues and a polite agreement to peacefully co-exist. And for that matter his attitude is no different towards those economists who defend the material interests of the Stalinist bureaucracies of the Soviet Union and Eastern Europe.

In the course of the intellectual games that Mr Mandel plays he degrades Marx by making him just another, although superior, economist. This is most evident in that section of the Introduction to Volume II dealing with the reproduction schemes, where we have formulations like the following: 'Marx's giant step forward in economic analysis may be gauged by the fact that, until this very day, most academic economists have still not fully grasped this basic innovation of his schemas of reproduction' — that is to say, the role of the 'reserve army of labour' in the process of expanded reproduction.[4] This avoids the conclusion that Marx's aims were quite different, as well as his methods; and Mandel implies that there are *some* academic economists who have fully grasped this point and its revolutionary social consequences.

Pandering to fashionable economic theories, this time what is known as input-output analysis, Mandel makes out that 'Volume 2 may be seen in a very real sense as the predecessor and initiator of modern aggregation techniques which were sometimes even directly inspired by the book'.[5] But this was because for a long time bourgeois economics was dominated by 'partial equilibrium analysis', and was hardly ever able to describe, let alone explain, the working of the economy as a whole. As the imperialist state was forced to intervene to prop up the economy in its death agony, so bankrupt bourgeois economic thought had to take some lessons from Marx in a formal — and futile — attempt to come to grips with reality.

In a similar vein, Mandel later speaks with evident approval of one Michio Morishima 'who has devoted much effort and ingenuity to rehabilitating Marx in the eyes of academic economists as one of the principal forerunners of aggregation techniques'.[6] His own role has not been dissimilar; in these Introductions he continues to try to make Marx out to be a respectable precursor of modern academic economics in some of its branches. Not excluding Keynes, it would appear, because later on we read that in connection with the role of money in the trade cycle, 'Marx fundamentally anticipates the Keynesian problematic of money-hoarding, that is, withdrawal of money from the process of productive circulation'.[7] The use of the term 'fundamentally' is itself a gem.

What is involved here is once again, the long-time adherence of bourgeois economists to the famous Say's law, that supply creates its own demand and that there can thus be no general overproduction. Surprising as it may seem, it was not until the 1930s, under the impact of the World Economic Depression as much as the influence of the famous British economist and man-about-town J.M. Keynes, that this fatuous theory was finally abandoned. To speak of Marx as some kind of precursor in this direction (he had, needless to say, exposed Say's law in Volume I of *Capital*) is an insult. Mandel emits no criticism of Keynes and his like, ignorant of Marxism and hostile to the working class as they were, because he wants to be accepted by the latter-day Keynesians and other tendencies to be found among academic economists. This was not Marx's way, as any reader of *Capital* knows: always he was seeking to penetrate the ideological cover of his opponents. The question, then, is not that 'Keynes was correct when he discarded the assumption of more or less permanent unemployment of manpower and capital' but why, as a representative of capitalism, he did so only belatedly and under strong objective pressures (the crisis) and the conclusions, political as well as economic, which he drew as a staunch defender of capitalism and an enemy of socialism.[8] To say, in this connection, that Marx's 'understanding of the fundamental mechanisms of the capitalist mode of production proved more profound than that of Keynes' amounts to another insult.[9]

Mandel panders to fashion in bourgeois economics and lets off the Stalinist economists just as lightly. The first thing to ask here is why the important controversies generated by the second and third volumes of *Capital* among Marxists in the period of the Second International before 1914 and in the early years of the Communist International were never followed up for a whole historical period, corresponding with the rise and dominance of the Stalinist bureaucracy in the Soviet Union and subsequently in Eastern Europe, as well as in the Communist Parties of the capitalist countries. Mandel gingerly avoids this question and simply takes up points made by Stalinist economists on their merits, as it were. What, after all, is Mandel's position on Stalinism? The almost complete absence of any mention of it gives the answer. It is one of compromise, as benefits an advocate of the theory of the self reform of the bureaucracy. As a matter of fact, Stalinism does get a mention in the Introduction to Volume I and the dictator who ordered the extermination of the Left Opposition and all critics and opponents (including not a few brilliant economists, Preobrazhensky, Vosnessensky and others) appears in the guise of economist in the Introduction to Volume II.

In the first case Mandel says that as a result of the failure of the revolution to spread to other countries after 1917, 'the victorious Russian revolution itself became isolated, and the international working class movement went through *the dark interlude of Stalinism, from which it only slowly began to emerge in the nineteen-fifties*'.[10] So, for him, Stalinism is not the theory and practice of 'socialism in one country', expressing the material interests of the Soviet bureaucracy, it is a 'dark interlude' now in the past. That means it is now possible to build bridges, to see Soviet and other Stalinist economists as erring theoreticians and not the sycophantic ideologists of a parasitic caste. One only has to go back to the literature generated by Stalin's notorious excursion into economics near the close of his life, the article called *Economic Problems of*

Socialism in the USSR. Not a bleep of criticism was to be heard from eminent 'Marxist' economists like Maurice Dobb or Robert Meek in this country, let alone from the Soviet Union or Eastern Europe, where only three years later statues of the defunct dictator were being torn from their foundations.

As Mandel mentions, Maurice Dobb continued to take part in the so-called 'great debate' about the 'law of the priority development of the means of production' under socialism which continued after Stalin's death and in the period which saw the production of a new textbook of political economy. But he can only criticise Dobb in the most polite fashion for a misunderstanding of Marx's reproduction schemas which enabled him to excuse what Mandel himself describes as 'a policy which sacrifices the consumption of four generations of workers and their families merely to increase the rate of growth of that consumption starting with the fifth generation.'[11] In any case that was only half of the problem. If nothing but a sacrifice of consumption had been involved something might be said for this policy if the fifth generation *did* show benefits. It was not the consumption of the bureaucracy which was sacrificed, on the contrary. Nor was it only a matter of consumer goods shortages; it was above all the murderous policies of Stalinism which Mandel, for the sake of good feeling, passes over in silence. Obviously no one would accuse Mandel of ignorance in this respect. When he wants to engage in debate with the Stalinists about the schemas of reproduction he simply keeps quiet about it.

The same Mandel, as a leader of the United Secretariat, covers up for the agents of the Stalinist GPU inside the Trotskyist movement in the United States who opened the way for Trotsky's murder. He has resolutely oposed the enquiry called for by the International Committee of the Fourth International. He prefers to prepare the way for a reconciliation with the Euro-Stalinists in some new and still more treacherous Popular Front.

Throughout these Introductions, and most strikingly in that to Volume II, runs a strain of self-justification. A characteristic of Mandel's long career as an economic commentator is that he has never admitted that he has been wrong; on the contrary, he points proudly to the many occasions on which he claims to have been right. Some of these claims have been dealt with in a previous chapter; now they come up in a more subtle way.[12] Mandel chooses his antagonists carefully and avoids confronting his most serious critics. Instead we have references without names or sources to 'dogmatic pseudo-Marxists' (we wonder who they are?).[13] And later he asks petulantly: 'What lies behind the frenetic accusations of "under-consumptionism", referred to as grave "deviation" or shameful disease, and levelled by some of Marx's followers against others?'[14]

Although he does not openly defend the right to be an under-consumptionist, and goes out of his way to distance himself from 'pure' under-consumptionists — note the distinction — he does not even tell us who the 'under-consumptionists' are. In fact, as a whole number of 'Marxists', succumbing to the pressure of Keynesianism, or sometimes drawing on the weak sides of Rosa Luxemburg, took up such a position. Paul Sweezy provides such an example and he was followed by others lesser known in the period after 1945.[15] The 'permanent war economy' theory put forward by the school of revisionists now going by the name of the Socialist Workers' Party in Britain was a form of under-consumptionism. Most of all, Mandel himself, from a different point of view, in his exposition of what he called 'neo-colonialism' in the 1960s was tarred with the same brush. Hence the manner in which he deals with the question while hastening, in the light of the enormous world crisis which has developed since, to re-establish his reputation for orthodoxy, hoping that no one will look up his previous writings. The point at issue was a neglect of the law of the tendency of the rate of profit to fall and an attempt, by selective quotations, to provide some sanction from Marx for an under-consumptionist approach.

Mandel knows when to make an adaptation and makes it in these Introductions. There is no word about 'neo-capitalism' here but much about crisis and collapse and a general assertion that Marx has been proved right (leading the unwary reader to assume that Mandel, too, has been right all along). Presumably Mandel is going to write at length about Marx's theory of crises in the Introduction he is preparing for Volume III, for it must be said that in the already published Introductions his treatment remains at his most superficial level.

At the end of the Introduction to Volume I he remains non-committal on the hard theoretical questions. He writes:

> The concrete mechanics [!] of the economic breakdown of capitalist economy may be open to conjecture. The interrelationship of the downturn of value production (decline of the total number of labour hours produced as a result of semi-automation), of the increasing difficulty of realising surplus-value, of increasing output of waste not entering into the reproduction process, of increasing depletion of national resources [does he mean 'natural'? — *T.K.*] and, above all, of long term decline of the rate of profit, is still far from clear.[16]

There is something for everybody here: the ecologists, the Baran-Sweezy waste-merchants and even the underconsumptionists — while 'the long term decline of the rate of profit' is brought in for effect, but properly distorting Marx's exposition of the law of the *tendency* for the rate of profit to decline. Mandel writes as though it does always decline: Marx is referring to an inevitable tendency which does not necessarily manifest itself, on the surface, as an actual decline in the rate of profit.

In the peroration which concludes the Introduction to Volume II we hear about a 'spiralling movements of growth' and 'the contradictions of production for its own sake (which) . . . must lead to periodic discharge in huge social and economic convulsions'.[17] We also hear that 'Capitalist growth cannot but be uneven, disproportionate and unharmonious. Expanded reproduction necessarily gives rise to over-production. The search for the philosopher's stone which would enable market economy (i.e. private property, i.e. competition) to coincide with balanced growth, and mass consumption to develop apace with productive capacity (despite the capitalists' drive to force up the rate of exploitation) — this search will go on as long as the system survives.'[18]

All this may sound very correct, even a truism as far as Marxists are concerned; in fact, it contains great dangers. Once again it leaves out the declining rate of profit and has an undertone — yes — of underconsumptionism. And who are these people searching for the philosopher's stone 'which would enable market economy . . . to coincide with balanced growth, and mass consumption to develop apace with productive capacity'? Perhaps this would apply to some latter-day Keynesians and sundry reformist social democrats who still have some faith in capitalism, but it does not apply to the capitalists themselves or to their ideologists as a whole. Anyway, capitalism is not historically doomed because of it failure to secure balanced growth or to develop mass consumption in line with productive capacity, but basically because productive forces come into inexorable conflict with the social relations of production (phrases which are presumably too vulgar for Mandel to use). Most important, however, is in fact that Mandel again does not refer in this section on 'Growth and Crisis' at any point to the tendency for the rate of profit to fall; this is not one, or even the most important, but the crucial factor driving capitalism to crisis and collapse.[19]

Failure to see this was the error made by all those Marxists, like Rosa Luxumburg, who wanted to erect a crisis theory exclusively, or principally, on the schemas of reproduction in Volume II. Mandel himself is happy to dilate at length on the reproduction schema and even to propose some improvements of his own.[20] This has long been a happy hunting ground for 'Marxist economists' — along with 'the transformation problem' and the difference between productive and unproductive labour — and one on which a meeting with certain bourgeois economists was possible. Hence a large and technical literature has grown up around these theoretical questions. While not without interest or importance for Marxists such discussions have to be seen in proportion and not severed from the rest of Marx's thinking.

Mandel's treatment of the reproduction schemas is typical of his whole approach to *Capital*. He says 'there is nothing extraordinary or magical in this two-department schema': as if anyone had suggested that there was. He refers to them a page later 'not as a simple conceptual or analytical tool but a *model*' (emphasis added). His discussions, where he compares them with attempts by bourgeois economists to depict the working of capitalism as a whole, makes clear that he regards them as a superior model, but a model just the same. For Marx, it was not a question of improving on his predecessors in the art of model-building, now so much in vogue amongst economists. For him the schema, like *Capital* as a whole, represented not something final, but a stage in the movement of cognition in the understanding of this mode of production, penetrating from appearance to essence. He was thus able to move towards the understanding of its movement in a dialectical way, revealing its necessity and its contradictions rooted in the commodity (use value-exchange value), through commodity-money, to the whole process of the metamorphoses of capital dealt with in Volume II. Such a process of self movement, through the unity and identity of opposites, is not at all the same as model-building which, by its formal nature, excludes contradictions and is inherently biased towards smooth and harmonious working after the fashion of a machine, excluding living men, class conflict, exploitation, and, above all, revolution as the only way out of the contradictions. Everything in Mandel's approach, for all his parading of dialectics, smacks of formalism and rationalism, not of Marxism at all.

Most of Mandel's Introduction to Volume II is concerned with the reproduction schemas and the controversies to which they have given rise. As we have seen, Marx regarded his division of production into two great departments, Department I producing means of production and Department II producing means of consumption, as an advance of crucial importance for understanding the working of the capitalist mode of production. It enabled him, not to show that balanced growth was possible or was the norm but rather, that, by means of the schema which assumed such balance, the sources of crisis — of interrupted reproduction — could be found. The various assumptions and qualifications surrounding his exposition made it clear that he never regarded the schemas as representing directly the real world of capitalism. They were an abstraction necessary in order to approach more closely to the concrete. Marx dealt with the turnover of capitals, and their intertwining and metamorphoses, in terms of value. The schemas were a dialectical working out in theory of the real movement of capitals in this abstract form. Having established certain relationships and the necessity for certain proportions to be maintained if simple, or expanded, reproduction was to take place, while emphasising that the schemas contained the germs of crises, he moved on to another phase of his analysis. The results of this — still unfinished — formed the manuscripts collected by Engels in Volume III. They concerned, notably, the formation of an average rate of profit and the law of the tendency for the rate of profit to decline which formed no part of the analysis of the schemas of reproduction in Volume II.

Mandel's treatment of the reproduction schemas, like others

before him, isolate them from the subsequent analysis in Volume III. Marx well knew the limited applicability of the schemas, otherwise we could have expected that he would have devoted much more attention to their development and to variants on them. This wa to be left to various 'disciples', mostly in the period of the Second International and among the Stalinists who tried to turn the reproduction schema into a model for planning, leading to the Byzantine discussions leniently dealt with by Mandel. Both approaches led to distortions of Marx's intentions. While rejecting, politely, the Stalinist misuse of the schema, Mandel is happy to play the game of improving on them.

The problem is that to bring the schemas closer to reality they would have to be modified both by lifting the restrictive assumptions built into them — like a constant rate of surplus value or commodities being sold at their value — and by incorporating the subjects dealt with in Volume III. For instance, they would have to be made more complicated in order to show how technical advance raised the organic composition of capital and brought about a tendency for the rate of profit to fall. But this in turn brings about structural changes, such as the growth of monopoly and finance capital, imperialist expansion and expenditure on armaments, which could only be brought within the scope of the schema by an enormous as well as futile intellectual effort. We can say that a precise and accurate theoretical model of the workings of the capitalist mode of production is impossible if only because the system is itself anarchic. A 'model', however complicated, can never represent living reality, with its contradictions and movement. This is why the reproduction schemas were used by some to 'prove' that a harmonious expansion of capitalism was possible (or, in Rosa Luxemburg's case, would only be possible if it could find new consumers outside the system).

Instead of approaching the problem in this way, Mandel wants to improve the reproduction schemas along the lines of orthodox economics. Why not, for example, break down each department and make a number of further separate departments and then see how they can be quantitatively related in the economy as a whole? Or, again, why not separate out arms production and call it Department III to see whether, on that basis, an explanation can be found for the apparent boost which arms expenditure gave to the capitalist economy in the decades after World War II? We do not propose to follow Mandel into such a field of discussion. What seems necessary to say, however, is that as far as capitalism is concerned there is no qualitative difference between armaments and other forms of production, as commodities, comparable with the distinction drawn by Marx between means of production and means of consumption, and therefore no theoretical grounds for placing them in a separate Department III. The use values in which value is embodied are of no concern to the capitalists; they produce commodities, not products. Tanks and jet-fighters can just as well be seen as means of consumption as the bandages and coffins needed for the victims of war. At the same time, armaments are bought by governments and have been one of the most inflationary forms of expenditure in recent history with consequences for the monetary system which Mandel does not even mention.

In writing these Introductions, Mandel is not slow to recommend his own writings and does so as regards the articles which have now appeared in book form as *The Second Slump* and presumably held up as a model. Mandel's position on the crisis has already been dealt with in a previous chapter. However, he has recently ventured forth with some new predictions in an article entitled 'Outlook for the World Economy in 1979-80'.[21] Here we see at work the method expounded in Mandel's Introductions.

Instead of seeing the world crisis of capitalism as a whole, Mandel's method is to take it piece by piece. He begins not with the overall picture (or any accounting of his previous predictions) but with the situation in the United States. According to Mandel, following day-to-day market trends, the years 1976-78 had witnessed an 'up turn', while the first signs were now visible of a downturn, reinforced by President Carter's measures to defend the dollar taken in November, 1978. His main point is that the Carter administration 'wants to provoke a moderate recession in 1979, which could be limited in its depth and duration'. He sees upturns and downturns in different capitalist countries feeding on or counteracting each other. He analyses the weakness of the dollar in very undramatic terms as a result of the loss by the United States of its position as leading exporter of manufactured goods. It is not clear how a stronger dollar could improve that position, but that does not prove that dollar devaluation has been determined by a desperate attempt to boost exports. What is involved is the whole world position of US imperialism as an exporter of capital, as the home of most of the multinational corporations and the financial and military spearhead of the so-called 'Western Alliance' aimed at the Soviet Union and Eastern Europe. The fact that the US is also forced into trade war with its 'allies' is only one of the contradictions in a situation where what is at stake is the future of the world capitalist system as a whole.

As always, Mandel lives off surface impressions and writes a commentary differing only in emphasis from those produced by banks and research institutes all over the capitalist world. He depicts trends, produces figures and quotes from the financial press, but there is no application of the Marxist theory in which he is supposed to be such an expert. What is the relevance of *Capital*, which he is busy editing? He does not tell us and it is not visible in what he writes about the economic outlook.

As usual, Mandel hedges his bets with a vague overall statement which could be right — whatever happens! He says:

> Hence the decade ahead of us will be a long period of slow growth, or even stagnation, interspersed with grave recessions and hesitant upturns. There will be a succession of economic, social, political and military crises, over all of which will hang the threat of a financial panic and a collapse of the international system of credit.[22]

It would not be difficult to find equally, if not more pessimistic appraisals of the prospects of capitalism from many of its devoted supporters. But Mandel's most dangerous claim is that defeats for the working class are now impossible 'in the context of the present relationship of forces'. While paving the way for an alliance with counter-revolutionary Euro-Stalinism, Mandel's recipes disarm the working class and open the way for the very defeats he claims are impossible.

Mandel's commentaries on the economic situation are of a piece with his Introductions to *Capital*. He comments on surface phenomena, follows the to and fro movement of business conditions and adds on a few formulae to show how revolutionary he is. As regards an analsysis of the actual course of the world crisis of capitalism and its causes, that is conspicuously lacking. Whether he is 'waiting for the upturn' or predicting more depression he retains the impressionist method that enabled him to develop the theory of so-called 'neo-capitalism' in the 1960s and to hastily dropped when signs of the crisis began to appear. The revisionists like Mandel have been stripped bare by the depth and intensity of the crisis and their Marxist pretensions have been exposed. Behind the erudition of these Introductions is a complete rejection of the method and the content of Marx's great work.

While Mandel and his colleagues, the bourgeois and Stalinist economists, study the capitalist mode of production as a going concern, its actual contradictions, laid bare by Marx, are driving it towards slump, war and the socialist revolution.

Notes

[1] *Capital*, Volume I, Pelican Marx Library, translated by Ben Fowles, 1976; *Capital* Volume II, translated by David Fernback.
[2] This is the theory Mandel refuted: since the different 'co-operating units' in production all tend to shirk, whoever checks the shirking should receive the 'residual' when all other factors have been paid. On the other hand, Mandel polished off commodity fetishism in one sentence in his Introduction to Volume I, p.74. See, 'Commodity Fetishism in Marx's *Capital*' Chapter 2.
[3] *Capital* Volume II, p.22.
[4] Mandel's Introduction, Volume II, p.22.
[5] *ibid.*, p.38. [6] *ibid.* [7] *ibid.*, p.74. [8] *ibid.*, p.76. [9] *ibid.*
[10] Mandel's Introduction to Volume I, p.85.
[11] Mandel's Introduction to Volume II, p.33.
[12] See 'Revisionism in Crisis', Chapter 10.
[13] Mandel's Introduction to Volume II, p.14; he says of these unnamed people that their 'understanding of Marx is based more on second-hand vulgarisations than on the genuine article'. We can be sure that whoever they are they have at some time dared to criticise Mr Mandel and contested his claim to purvey 'the genuine article'.
[14] *ibid.*, p.71.
[15] See his *Theory of Capitalist Development* where he claimed that Marx 'was giving advance notice of a line of reasoning, which, if he had lived to complete his work, would have been of primary importance in the overall picture of the capitalist economy' and would have been resolutely under-consumptionist. See p.178 of Sweezy's book.
[16] Mandel's Introduction to Volume I, p.86. Mandel says : 'a very strong case can be made for the thesis that there are definite limits to the adaptability of capitalist relations of production, and that these limits are being progressively attained in one field after another'. This would have been a good moment for Mandel to explain how he invented the theory of 'neo-capitalism' precisely to explain its adaptability.
[17] Mandel's Introduction to Volume II, p.78.
[18] *ibid.*, p.79.
[19] On this see 'Marx on the Declining Rate of profit', Chapter 7.
[20] Thus, on p.28 he suggests that gold production could become Department III of the reproduction schema. Marx, however says quite firmly, 'The production of gold belongs, along with metal production in general, to department I, the category which comprises the production of means of production', *Capital*, Volume II, p.546.
[21] *Intercontinental Press*, January 22, 1979.   [22] *ibid.*, p.41.

Index

Accumulation, 57-69, 70-73, 88, 94, 101, 105, 106, 148, 149, 168, 173, 174, 178
— primitive, 116, 121, 126
Adorno, T., 15
Althusser, 7, 41
Anderson, James 121
Aristotle, 48

Banks, 26, 64, 95, 103, 104
Baran, 189
Bernstein, E., 129

Capital, *passim*
— circulating, 144-157, 158, 169, 170, 172
— constant, 67, 72, 75, 78, 88, 89, 90
— fictitious, 28
— finance, 25
— variable, 67, 72, 75, 78, 88, 89, 90, 94, 106, 120, 158
Classical political economy, 9, 13, 149, 152, 158, 171
Commodity, 10, 12, 17, 30, 33, 54, 1, 83, 100, 191
Competition, 63, 6, 73, 75, 87, 90, 91, 118, 125
Contradiction, 9, 10, 12, 27, 30, 40, 48, 57, 59, 60, 79, 96, 97, 101, 107-9, 112, 125, 129, 190, 195
Corey, Lewis, 111, 114
Cost price, 75, 76, 79, 81, 89
Credit, 25, 26, 102-104, 149
Crisis, 10, 11, 99-114
Critique of Political Economy, 6, 11, 12, 16, 46
Critique of the Gotha Programme, 33, 42, 51
Cutler 8, 29-42

Dialectics, dialectical materialism, 3, 7-11, 17, 21, 23, 32, 34, 35, 40, 41, 44, 49, 73-74, 79, 80, 82, 27, 94-97, 145, 183, 190
Division of labour, 38
Dobb, Maurice, 5, 6, 43, 138, 187

Economic and Philosophical Manuscripts, 7, 24, 46
Engels, Frederick, 8, 35, 42, 51, 56, 71, 74, 85, 94, 142, 156, 160, 164, 166

Fabians, 41, 115
Fetishism, 15-27, 44, 48, 55, 66, 71, 74, 78, 109, 163, 183, 195
Feudalism, 20, 21
Feuerbach, Ludwig, 15, 21

George, Henry, 115
German Ideology, The, 46
Grundrisse, 6-14, 16, 24, 32, 38, 39, 42, 44, 46, 71, 72, 85, 87, 89, 94, 98, 113

Hegel, G.W.F., 2, 7, 9, 10, 14, 44, 71, 74, 77, 78, 85
Hilferding, R., 25, 129, 132
Hindess, 8, 29-42
Hurst, 8, 29-42
Hussain, 8, 29-42

Imperialism, 125, 126, 132, 192, 194
Industrial reserve army, 103
Interest, 24-26, 64, 93, 115, 176, 179, 181

Keynes, J.M., 5, 43, 44, 46, 60, 66, 96, 109, 110, 111, 129, 136, 141, 173, 185, 186, 189
Kondratiev, 133-141

Labour, 17, 18, 21, 23, 43-56
– abstract, 11, 30, 31, 47-50, 55, 57
– concrete, 11, 30, 47, 48, 50, 172
Labour-power, 18, 20, 22, 32, 36, 37, 45, 53, 55, 72, 105, 145, 146
Lenin, V.I., 7, 10, 14, 67, 77, 81, 96, 98, 132, 168
Loria, 35
Luxemburg, Rosa, 96, 106, 188, 190, 192

Machinery, 37, 39
Mandel, E., 3, 14, 15, 43, 128, 141, 143, 156, 167, 182-195
Marcuse, H., 15
Marginal utility, 59
Materialism, see dialectics, dialectical materialism
Means of production, 21, 23, 61, 66, 71, 104, 145, 146, 158, 163, 167, 170, 172, 173, 174, 179, 187, 193
Meek, Ronald, 5, 9, 14, 43, 187
Money, 10 18, 19, 24, 25, 27, 32, 33, 45, 61, 62, 100, 101, 102, 104, 105, 106, 112, 145, 147, 149, 164, 175, 177, 179, 191
Monopoly, 24, 80, 90, 95, 117, 119, 120, 122, 125, 126, 127, 151, 192
Morishima, M., 185

Nature, 20, 22, 42, 51, 52, 56, 63, 119, 120, 121, 125, 127, 146, 152, 159
'Neo-capitalism', 128-141, 188, 195
Nicolaus, Martin, 12, 14
Notes on Wagner, 6

Organic composition of capital, 66, 70-98, 112, 118, 123, 138, 149, 192
Overproduction, 60, 107, 108, 112-114, 130, 141, 155, 176, 180

Physiocrats, 121, 127
Preobrazhensky, E.A., 186
Price of production, 32, 83
Productive forces, 13, 16, 20, 60, 90, 108, 124, 125, 190

Rate of profit, 31, 32, 42, 65, 67, 70-98, 111, 118, 126, 138, 149, 189-91
Realisation problem, 96, 97, 107
Religion, 19, 21
Rent, 64, 88, 115-127, 181
– absolute, 122, 123, 127
– differential, 120, 122, 123, 127
Reproduction, 153-155, 166-168, 171, 184, 190
– simple, 105, 107, 148, 165, 174-177
– expanded, 105, 108, 149, 164, 178, 179, 184, 189
Ricardo, David, 2, 21, 30, 43, 58, 60, 87, 88, 95, 96, 101, 102, 108, 113, 115, 117, 122, 127, 158, 162, 163, 166
Robinson Crusoe, 19
Rodbertus, 117
Rosdolsky, Roman, 2, 8, 11, 13, 14, 34, 35, 42
Rubin, 2, 16, 22, 23, 42, 47, 48, 55

Say's Law, 185
Schumpeter, 98, 134
Shaw, Bernard, 41, 115,
Smith, Adam, 36, 87, 88, 95, 115, 117, 158, 161, 162, 163, 171
Social relations of production, 11, 13, 16-18, 22, 25, 38, 45, 49, 62, 64, 66, 71, 74, 109, 180, 190
Socialism, 20, 26, 54, 154, 171, 177, 181, 186
Socialist revolution, 124, 168, 195
Sowell, 9
Stalin, Stalinism, Euro-communism, 5, 7, 14, 16, 82, 130, 133, 182, 184, 186, 187, 192, 194
State, 95, 135, 185
Strachey, John, 111, 114
Surplus value, 22-26, 31, 37, 50, 54, 61, 63, 65, 71, 73, 76, 78, 84, 87, 92, 94, 96, 98, 104, 110, 116, 119, 126, 145, 147
– relative, 92
– absolute, 92
Sweezy, Paul, 5, 6, 43, 188, 189, 195

Theories of Surplus Value, 1, 6, 7, 16, 24, 28, 68, 86, 98, 113, 114, 121
Trotsky, L.D., 9, 135, 140
Turnover, 160, 161, 164, 166, 169, 179, 191

Underconsumptionism 109-111, 114, 172, 188, 189

Value, 12, 21, 22, 25, 29-41, 45, 48, 54, 64, 77, 101, 152
– exchange 11, 12, 47, 49, 53, 64, 146
– use, 11, 12, 27, 33, 47-50, 53, 64, 101, 118, 146, 152, 156

Vulgar economics, economists, 8, 24-26, 59, 109, 168, 184

Wage-Labour and Capitel, 61
Wilson, Harold, 137